The GENERAL

LUKE HODGE

HODGE

The GENERAL

with **SCOTT GULLAN**

MICHAEL JOSEPH
an imprint of
PENGUIN BOOKS

MICHAEL JOSEPH

UK | USA | Canada | Ireland | Australia
India | New Zealand | South Africa | China

Penguin Books is part of the Penguin Random House group of companies
whose addresses can be found at global.penguinrandomhouse.com.

First published by Penguin Random House Australia Pty Ltd, 2017

10 9 8 7 6 5 4 3 2 1

Cover design by Alex Ross © Penguin Random House Australia Pty Ltd
Text design by Samantha Jayaweera © Penguin Random House Australia Pty Ltd
Cover photograph by Lachlan Cunningham/AFL Media
Back cover photograph by Michael Dodge/Getty Images
Endpapers (front) by Daniel Carson/AFL Media and (back) by Adam Trafford/AFL Media
Photo used on case by Scott Barbour/AFL Media
Typeset in Sabon by Midland Typesetters, Australia
Colour separation by Splitting Image Colour Studio, Clayton, Victoria
Printed and bound in Australia by Griffin Press, an accredited ISO AS/NZS
14001 Environmental Management Systems printer.

National Library of Australia
Cataloguing-in-Publication data:

Hodge, Luke, author.
The general / by Luke Hodge with Scott Gullan.
9780143797098 (hardback)
Subjects: Hodge, Luke.
Hawthorn Football Club.
Australian football players—Victoria—Hawthorn—Biography.
Australian football teams—Victoria—Hawthorn.
Australian football—Victoria—Hawthorn.

Other Creators/Contributors:
Gullan, Scott, author.

penguin.com.au

CONTENTS

Introduction

SEALED WITH A KISS

I don't know why I did it. I didn't want to hit Buddy and I knew he didn't want to hit me. We'd been through a lot together and the respect was mutual. But I had to do something. So I leaned over and kissed him.

From the moment my lips left his cheek, I knew it was a mistake. Not because of how my former teammate Buddy Franklin would react. I was more worried about the reaction of the guy sitting on the second level in the coach's box.

Maybe I'd got away with it. The ball had left the area so maybe no one was looking. Maybe. Maybe. Maybe . . . Talk about extreme optimism.

With 99 000 inside the Melbourne Cricket Ground for the 2014 Grand Final and hundreds of cameras around the ground, the odds of no one noticing a player kissing another were zero.

Then I heard it. The crowd was going nuts.

There was nothing happening up the field – it was just another stoppage – so I turned around and looked up at the scoreboard. And there I was, kissing Buddy.

I was dead, I thought. There was no way Alastair Clarkson hadn't seen that. Buddy and I looked at each other. He smirked and wandered off.

Even though there was a very positive aspect to that scoreboard, which was the actual score at that moment – Hawthorn 16.11 (107) to Sydney 7.4 (46) – my thoughts were already drifting ahead to the three-quarter-time huddle. In my mind, there I was having a drink of water, with Clarko charging towards me, whacking the bottle out of my hands and launching into one of his trademark sprays with a lot of expletives around the word 'arrogant', which was on repeat.

But that never happened. I'd got away with it. I'm not sure if I was more excited about that or the fact that we were about to start the last quarter of a Grand Final with an unassailable lead of 54 points.

The day had been perfect from the start. It was my 250th game, which meant I got to run through the banner with my two kids, six-year-old Cooper and almost-two-year-old Chase. That was special – as was the way we'd played in the opening three quarters.

It had been an emotional build-up and Clarko had played off that. There were two main factors: the hurt of losing the 2012 Grand Final to Sydney and the fact that Buddy had left and was trying to take a premiership off us. The words from Clarko at the final team meeting still rang in our ears. 'Yeah, you love him as a mate but tomorrow he's the enemy.'

It's a rare delight to be able to enjoy the final 15 minutes of a Grand Final, safe in the knowledge that you've won the premiership. When the siren finally sounded, I was alone in the centre square and simply raised both arms in the air. Initially there was no one around to celebrate with, but soon the cavalry arrived and the mayhem began.

It's impossible to describe what happens after you win a Grand Final. There's the pure joy of achieving something with your mates, going through all the ups and downs, and then delivering an extraordinary performance when it matters most.

Everyone had written us off. No team had been able to win back-to-back premierships in more than a decade. All these emotions were bubbling as the presentations began and I realised a speech was required. Public speaking was my least favourite part of being captain, and my mind was ticking over about that when an AFL official approached me.

'Make sure you thank your teammates, family and sponsors, and remember – don't swear,' he said.

I'd been in this situation the previous year and had managed to come through unscathed, so I didn't worry too much. But then I heard my name read out and I was momentarily confused. This was a bit early, I thought.

North Melbourne champion Glenn Archer was standing on the stage and had just read out my name as the Norm Smith Medallist. I was shocked. I'd thought the AFL official had been briefing me about my captain's acceptance speech, not about the Norm Smith. I knew I'd had a bit of the ball, but we'd had so many good players who could have been voted best-on-ground, like Jordan Lewis or Sam Mitchell, or Jarryd Roughead, who'd kicked five goals.

It was weird to feel dread as I walked up to receive such a great honour but I was really nervous. I managed to thank Sydney, the

AFL and our sponsors – even though I couldn't remember them by name – before signing off with, 'Thanks very much for a super year. Cheers.'

As I walked off the stage, I knew I needed to be better prepared for my next effort in a few minutes. Thankfully I'd been given some good advice a number of years earlier to have a card ready with a few dot points to help ease the nervousness.

The captain is always called out last for the premiership-medal presentations, which in recent years had been handed over by a fleet of primary-school-aged Auskick kids. When I bent down so my Auskicker could loop the medal around my neck, he said quietly, 'You're my hero.'

As I stood back on the dais and waited for Clarko to come up and receive his medal, the little kid's words stayed with me.

I'd been just like him. When I was his age, I was a mad Richmond supporter and my heroes were Wayne Campbell and Matthew Richardson. I've never forgotten one particular game back in 1995. I'd come up from Colac with my father and grandpa to the MCG to watch Richmond play North Melbourne. Wayne Carey was North's star, but on this night the Tigers were on fire and I couldn't believe how loud the crowd was. The noise as Richmond surged to a ten-goal lead in the third quarter was deafening.

I was ten years old. I already loved footy, but at that moment I fell in love with the MCG. That was where I wanted to play.

My daydreaming was interrupted by the master of ceremonies, Craig Willis. Clarko was finished. I was up again.

I

THE SANCTUARY

I hated it. The teams would be picked and I'd be left out. No one wanted the fat kid.

Often it was because we'd played footy earlier and, given I was bigger than the rest, I'd easily beaten them or I might have roughed them up. So to get back at me they wouldn't pick me the next time. They called me fat, so I called them a sook if they started crying. It was a two-way street.

The problem was that, by age 11, I'd already learnt to fight above my weight. Even though my uncles and cousins were all older and bigger than me, I spent every moment I could competing against them – whether it be in football, cricket or basketball. I refused to give up. They'd knock me down all the time but I'd just keep coming back for more.

That's what made it so hard when I was left hanging, standing there clinging to the hope that I'd get the nod. I hated that feeling. I hated being told I wasn't part of the game. 'Bad luck, fat boy,' they'd say.

I didn't know why I was bigger than everyone else – I liked food, but I figured everyone else did too. My father, Bryson, was big, tall . . . and sometimes scary. I'm tipping he never experienced anything like this.

I'd been given the nickname Pumbaa, after the warthog from *The Lion King* movie, and it was one of those that stuck and lingered for a long time.

My fallback plan to getting snubbed would be to try and play with the Grade 6 kids, who were more my size. That worked sometimes, but not all the time.

The teasing would get worse on the school bus. I normally tried to give back as good as I got, but sometimes my brave face would break and I'd come home in tears. Mum was the only one who would see them.

The way I dealt with this was the way I dealt with everything – I grabbed my footy. I'd been known to sleep with it. Every day after school I'd park myself in the front yard and harass any neighbour who showed their face to kick the ball with me. It was a waiting game. I had to ensure that when Dad got home from work he didn't make it into the house without a diversion.

We lived at the back of the Western Oval, which was the home ground of one of the local football clubs, the Colac Imperials. Dad worked at a tyre outlet, and the second I saw his ute come around the Jennings Street corner I was on high alert.

I'd heard stories that he had been a good footballer at Imps and Warrion in the Colac and District Football League. I never saw him play – by the time I came along he'd moved into the umpiring ranks. He was certainly good at controlling proceedings and being the man in white out in the middle. He wasn't one to take any shit.

He certainly didn't take any from his son.

One of Dad's many theories when it came to football was that good players needed to be able to kick on both feet. I was a natural left-footer and would spend most of my time at the Western Oval practising snaps and torpedoes. Dad would make me kick on my right. He'd want ten on the right foot and they all had to hit the target. Being the sort of kid I was, I would try to get away with doing all my kicking on my left. Things would inevitably turn sour when it was time to leave. 'There's your footy – go and kick it by yourself. I'm going home,' he'd say.

Some nights I'd chase after him, kicking the ball with my right foot; on others I'd crack it and sit in the middle of the oval in tears. There was a stubbornness about the Hodges. It started at the top and had worked its way down.

Playing sport was all I was interested in – there was nothing else. Our house was set up accordingly, with the yard effectively a mini sports field.

Luckily my mother, Leanne, and older sister, Bianca, were also into sport. It seemed like that was pretty much the way for most families in Colac. It was the only world I saw, anyway. On weekends in the winter the boys played footy and the girls played netball; in summer it was cricket and tennis for everyone.

We had a large block. The driveway was about 20 metres long and at the end of it was the basketball court. The ring and backboard were attached to the shed, and in a giveaway about my lack of handyman skills, the ring was around the wrong way. The little square that is supposed to be closest to the bottom part of the ring . . . wasn't. And the Nike sticker that I thought added some Michael Jordan coolness to the set-up was around the wrong way as well.

In the backyard there was a three-quarter-length cricket pitch that was immaculately mowed in summer to keep it up to scratch. We used a golf net that I'd been given to smash golf balls into, but I wasn't much of a golfer so the net became a key part of our cricket games. It did a very good job as the automatic wicketkeeper, as it covered leg slip and around as far as third slip.

We always used a taped tennis ball. There were none of these regulation balls – we wanted the ball to be flying all over the place, and that can happen with the right tape job. If you hit it over the fence into next door, then that was six and out. We introduced another rule when an extension was put on the house. That was pretty exciting, but not as exciting as another development – the introduction of a backyard pool. After that, any shot landing in the pool was also out.

I was a right-hand batsman and our set-up meant I had to pre-dominantly play on-side shots. There weren't many runs to be had on the off side, as thick bush started about 3 metres from the edge of the pitch, but there was plenty of space for leg-side shots. That ended up being a bit of trap, because when I played club cricket on the weekends I'd continually look to play the same shots that I played in the backyard.

Sometimes in summer we'd build a tennis court using deckchairs with brooms across them as the net. And while most of our footy was played at the nearby oval, we sometimes put up makeshift goalposts in the yard.

The extension proved a winner for my indoor sporting endeavours. The house had been relatively small previously, but when it became four bedrooms with two large living areas it was a whole new world. My bedroom was at the back, and the new space meant a lot of goal-kicking practice, with some particularly impressive banana kicks being executed in between the living areas with a soft football. Then there was the basketball ring on the back of the door, where I'd practise my jump shots and do spectacular slam dunks using a foam ball.

I'd try to drag Bianca into my games, but that often backfired. She was very competitive and we'd invariably end up in a fight. I never seemed to win – she was a hard nut and a lot like Dad in many ways. If she gave you an angry stare, it was time to get out of there.

The beauty about living in Colac was that you were only a bike ride away from an oval, basketball court, tennis court or mate's house. There was always something to do and mischief to get into.

I had something serious to focus on in my last year at Sacred Heart Primary School. It had nothing to do with reading or writing, which I wasn't very enthusiastic about. An opportunity to try out for the Victorian primary school football team came up, and given that I was a lot bigger than most kids, Dad and I went up to Melbourne for a look.

We travelled to Windy Hill, home of the Essendon Football Club, for the trial. There were hundreds of kids there and we ended up having to go back several Sundays in a row. I wasn't the only one from down our way to make the final 40 – there was a guy called Jake Carmody who went to school at St Joseph's, which was just a 15-minute drive from Colac.

Fortunately, I made the final cut. Not bad for a fat kid. Getting a Big V jumper was pretty cool, and I was surprised Carmo wasn't getting one as well, as from what I saw he was a good player.

Playing teams from other states was certainly an eye-opening experience. I thought I was big, but I swear there was a kid playing for the Northern Territory who already had a moustache and could kick it a country mile.

There were a few players in our team who stood out, including a kid from Melbourne named Luke Ball, and twins from Bendigo, the Selwood brothers. We won our first game, against New South Wales, but lost the next one, against South Australia. I played all over the place – across half-back, in the midfield and also up forward. Next to me in the forward pocket was a little kid from Geelong called Gary Ablett. That was a bit weird – I had a poster of his dad on my bedroom wall.

I'd do any job to be involved in sport. Being the water boy for Imps seniors was a responsibility I cherished, even though it provided me with my scariest moment so far on a football field.

One day I was doing my job when the play suddenly came directly at me and I froze like a rabbit in the headlights. One of our players, Timmy Hassett, a solid little unit, bowled me over. I picked myself up and bolted for the sanctuary of the boundary line with my head down, too scared to look up and catch anyone's eye. I've never been more embarrassed.

On Saturday mornings I'd also boundary-umpire for the under 17s. My hard work would be rewarded with a can of Coke, a pie and a hot dog, which may have contributed in some way to my size issues.

I had to wait until Sunday mornings to get the chance to play footy in the youth club competition. The teams were matched with AFL teams, so there were the Cats, the Bulldogs, the Magpies and my team, the Tigers, who wore the yellow and black jumper of Richmond.

It wasn't until Grade 6, when I was 11 years old turning 12, that I progressed to the big time, which was the Imps under 17s. Playing with the big kids was something I'd craved, and I loved every minute of it.

I was also pretty excited about some news Mum and Dad had for us – I was going to be a big brother. Another partner in crime sounded like a good idea, even though there would be an 12-year age gap.

The arrival of Dylan meant Mum had her hands full. She was already amazing in the way she worked two jobs to ensure there were never any issues about Bianca and me pursuing our dreams. I was a typical teenage boy who took his mother for granted. I took it for granted that even though she was working night shift my sports clothes would always be ready, school lunch would always be made and dinner would always be organised, whether she made it in advance or made it at work and then brought it home for us on her break.

Mum had been a jill-of-all-trades – working in a bank, an accountant's office, the local supermarket and a Chinese restaurant – before taking on a full-time role at Colanda, a residential service for disabled people. Dad always worked multiple jobs, one of which was driving trucks up and down to Melbourne every day.

The Hodge house was always busy, particularly on school mornings. Dad would be gone early and Mum would get us ready before she headed off. Our grandma Maureen was responsible for taking us to primary school.

Sometimes we caught the bus, and when we moved to secondary school – Trinity College, which was closer to home than our primary school – we always rode our bikes. Getting up to go to school, getting to school and attending school were never issues for me. What I was supposed to do when I was at school was a different discussion.

It was obvious to everyone early on that school wasn't my thing. I was one of those kids who didn't have the attention span to finish a book. In primary school, one teacher actually started bringing in the *Herald Sun* newspaper for me because he thought I'd at least read the sports section. I didn't – I just looked at the pictures.

Secondary school was fun purely for social reasons. I got to hang out with my mates and kick the footy at recess and lunchtime. I wasn't a disruptive student in the classroom, but as Dad always used to say, I spent most of my time looking out the window watching the grass grow.

Life was good. Life was fun. Life was normal.

Sport was my sanctuary. If anything bad happened or I was having a bad day, my default position was to play sport. It's what came naturally to me – and it was what I relied on to get me through when my life was turned upside down by the separation of my parents.

I was 14 and in Year 8 when Mum and Dad decided to live apart. We'd just bought a new house around the corner from the old one. Instead of everyone moving into the new house together, Mum and Dad lived in separate houses. Initially, Bianca and I went with Dad, and Dylan, who was only three, stayed with Mum.

It wasn't something we'd seen coming. Sure, they had arguments, but I thought everyone's parents had arguments. They'd got together when they were young, with Mum having Bianca when she was 17, on 4 February 1982, and I came along a couple of years later, on 15 June 1984. The strain obviously became too much for them.

It was an awkward situation when they separated and I found the best way to deal with it was to play sport. If I had the option to go home or go to cricket or basketball training, I would always go to training. If something isn't normal, often your first instinct is to try to avoid it as much as possible. My mindset was to go and play sport with my mates.

The break-up was harder on Bianca, who was going into VCE at school. She had to run Dad's house and took on Mum's role in many respects, organising meals and leaving notes outlining chores for me to do, such as unpacking the dishwasher or preparing vegetables. None of my chores would get done.

Before long we were alternating between houses, spending a few nights at each. While this might not have been normal for some kids, it worked for us. What helped the situation was that there was no anger between Mum and Dad – or if there was, it was well hidden. They were both as dedicated to their kids as they had been when we were all under the same roof.

Dad was my driver on most weekends as I started to be selected more often for representative teams, including the Victorian under-15 Schoolboys football team. We played in the national carnival in Canberra and I managed to earn All Australian selection.

I dodged a bullet in the lead-up to my Big V heroics. I was keen to play footy and didn't care where or when, even if it was against the grown-ups in the reserves. But Dad was dead against this – he wanted me to focus on the Schoolboys carnival instead. I figured I could do both. One day the Imps reserves were short a couple of players, which happens a lot in country footy. After finishing the under-17 game, I put my hand up to have another run around.

My enthusiasm had a lot to do with being pretty sure Dad wasn't at the ground.

It's fair to say my reserves debut didn't go according to plan: I was cleaned up and rolled my ankle. To add salt to my wounds, as I was feeling sorry for myself on the bench, Dad appeared. 'You stupid little prick. I told you,' he sneered. Lesson learnt. Luckily my injury was only minor as it could have been a lot worse.

After the success of the national carnival, I was selected in the Geelong Falcons under-16 squad. This development squad was the first step on the path to the main Falcons team, which played in the under-18 TAC Cup, the competition that was seen as a big stepping stone to being drafted to an AFL club.

Not that I'd given that much thought. In fact, I'd thought more about playing cricket for Australia.

I was already playing senior A grade cricket for Colac West, where I was an erratic right-arm fast bowler. I made the Dowling Shield, which was for the best under-16 players in Geelong and surrounding areas, along with a familiar face, Micah Buchanan, who'd also attended Sacred Heart Primary School. The captain of the team was a gun from Geelong named Jimmy Bartel.

When I had the ball in my hand, my first instinct was to try to scare someone. I had that fast bowler's mentality even though I had no idea where the ball was going to land. I just charged in and tried to bowl as fast as I could.

At some stage I was going to have to choose between footy and cricket, but at the age of 15 I figured I could keep doing everything. 'The more sport, the better,' I said.

For the 2000 footy season, it was decided that I should move from the Imperials to the Colac Tigers Football Club. They played in the Hampden league, which was a step up in standard from the Colac and District league. The Hampden league was one of the strongest competitions in Victoria. It stretched from Colac to Warrnambool and as far as Port Fairy, a good two-hour bus trip.

Before Imps would sign off on my clearance, though, they wanted me to play a senior game. If I happened to get drafted to an AFL club down the track, then my original team would get some money from the AFL (or something like that). Imps didn't want to miss out, given I'd been in their junior system since I was 11 years old.

I started the season in the Colac under 18s and then, when they had a bye, I was granted a one-match clearance to make my senior debut for Imps against Irrewarra-Beeac. It was certainly a memorable experience. First of all, I got sent off for swearing. I miskicked and sent the ball out on the full, which resulted in an angrily released expletive. There had been a recent crackdown on swearing in the league, and if you were loud enough to be heard beyond the boundary, you got a yellow card, which meant 15 minutes on the sidelines. My F-bomb was certainly loud enough. After my freshen-up on the bench, I managed to keep my mouth shut and kicked six goals as Imps won easily.

I didn't have to wait long to get a taste of the seniors at Colac, but my call-up in Round 5 had a lot of cloak-and-dagger about it. On the Thursday night, I got home from training and Dad met me at the door.

'Come in here,' he said, ushering me into the living room. 'Forssy wants you to play seniors this week, but your mother's not keen. She says you're too young.'

'Forssy' was Darren Forssman, who'd played 45 games for Geelong in the early 1990s and was now coach of Colac.

I was more than up for it and agreed to keep the news on the down-low for as long as we could until Mum found out. 'We'll go across there early for the under-18 game so she thinks you're doing that, and then you can line up in the seniors instead,' Dad said about our ambitious plan. He figured playing against men was ideal for me at this point of my development, and I didn't have to be asked twice about such a challenge.

While Mum found out early and voiced her disapproval, I still got the green light for my senior debut at our home ground, the Central Reserve, against South Warrnambool.

Growing up, I'd always competed against older people. My uncle Jason had boarded with us when he got his first job in Colac (Mum's family lived out on a farm at Irrewillipe), and he didn't mind giving it to his little nephew. I was also always around at my cousin Pete's house. He had a few years on me as well as size and strength, and would school me in one-on-one basketball. 'You're too small – you can't do it,' he'd tell me. That only made my blood boil, and all I could think about was showing him what I could do. I was stubborn and, while it didn't work most of the time, I kept coming back at Pete and his mates.

It was this attitude that I channelled in my first senior game, and I managed to kick three goals. I loved it.

The following week was a game changer in a lot of ways. We had an away game against Cobden under lights. I lined up at centre half-forward and had a night out, getting on the end of a few cheapies over the top in the goal square to finish with six goals.

My third game in the seniors was against South Warrnambool again, and even before the opening bounce I knew things had changed – I had a target on my head. The South players went out of their way to try to intimidate me physically. Thankfully I had a lot of good teammates around me who weren't going to have a bar of blokes trying to rough up a 15-year-old kid. Despite the attention, I managed to kick three goals.

On the Monday, I received a call that ended my senior career at Colac. Michael Turner, a former Geelong captain who was the regional manager for the Falcons, had heard about what happened against South Warrnambool and phoned to say he wanted me to come and play in the TAC Cup instead. He was worried that I'd get targeted every week, so to avoid that happening he wanted to get me involved in the Falcons set-up full-time.

Things had started to move fast. My dream was getting closer.

2

THE SACRIFICE

'What the hell are you doing?'

I'd seen my father angry before, but nothing like this. He grabbed me and pinned me against the wall.

I managed to say, 'I got home a bit late.'

'Why didn't you call? You have a phone, use it.'

I'd been to the Colac Tech School ball and had told Dad I'd be home at midnight. I was playing for the Geelong Falcons the next day in Tasmania. The problem was that it was now past 2 a.m.

And an even bigger problem was about to rear its head. 'Did you drink?'

Dad had been adamant that I wasn't to touch a drop of alcohol the night before a game of football. I remember I'd waved to him as I walked out the door, offering, 'No problems.'

There were problems now – big problems.

We'd all met at Mum's house to get dressed and then we'd caught a stretch limousine to the ball. Champagne went around in the limo and I had a couple of glasses, plus a beer or two. When I got home I wasn't drunk by any stretch, but neither was I in any position to argue my way out of this, particularly given the steam coming out of my father's ears.

'I had a couple,' I said. It was getting more and more uncomfortable.

'If I say you're not going to drink, you don't drink!' he yelled. 'If you drink the day before a game again, you won't play.' With that, he let go.

I was in shock, which soon turned to anger. Why had he done that to me? If it was to teach me a lesson, then it certainly worked, but the way he'd done it had left me shaken. There was no way I was ever going to have a drink the night before a game of football again.

Technically I was still two years away from the legal drinking age. I'd only turned 16 about six weeks earlier, but part of the culture of growing up in a country town like Colac was playing as much sport as you could and spending every other minute hanging out with your mates. On weekends there might be a few beers floating around. We just wanted to do what our heroes did – the guys we looked up to at the football club who would enjoy a beer after games. At school parties you'd find someone's older brother to buy you some cans and then you'd hide them in a bush nearby and sneak a few in.

When Mum moved to a house just behind the Central Reserve, I'd get a handful of mates around and we'd have a few beers and order pizza. Most of the time Mum would be at work, but all the parents knew what we were doing and were on board as long as we didn't do anything stupid.

My tastebuds had certainly come a long way since my first experiences with alcohol. I remember an incident in Year 7 when I'd spent a full day working with Dad on his truck. We'd been up at 5 a.m. and had driven to Melbourne, getting back to Colac at about 4 p.m. It had been a long day, and I asked Dad, 'Can I have a beer with you?'

He looked at me with a smirk and said, 'You want to have a drink, do you? You reckon you've earnt it after a day's work? All right then – pick whatever you want.'

I'd already tasted beer and didn't like it, so I decided to try something else and picked out a passionfruit UDL can, which I knew was a vodka mix. That brought an even bigger smile to Dad's face – he obviously knew it tasted like crap. The Friday-night football was on and I settled into the chair next to him and cracked the can. It was horrible, but I knew he was staring at me so I pretended to enjoy it. I got up shortly after and snuck back into the kitchen, and as I grabbed the fridge door to put the UDL back in there, he yelled out, 'What are you doing?'

'Ahhhhh . . . I'll have it later.' I didn't.

Dad had taught me a lesson there about how alcohol wasn't as exciting as it may seem to a teenager, and he'd handed out another lesson when I'd come home late that night. While I resented him for how he'd reacted and hung on to that for a while, as time went by I started to get an understanding of why he'd done it. He wanted me to realise I had an opportunity that my mates didn't have. I was playing in the TAC Cup, which was the first step towards getting drafted. I wanted to play AFL and the message Dad was sending was simple: don't blow it.

*

There had been a definite shift with my football, with talk already about my chances in the following year's draft. I tried not to pay much attention to it. A lot of it had come about after the Under-16 National Championships in Tasmania. I was Victoria's vice-captain and managed to have a pretty good carnival – good enough to be rewarded with All Australian honours. As a result, I'd also been selected for an Australian Institute of Sport (AIS) scholarship, which meant I got to attend a few camps at the AIS facility in Canberra, where former Footscray coach Terry Wheeler was in charge. And there was an opportunity to represent Australia in a test series against Ireland the following year.

The Falcons were also going well and were finals bound. I'd come a long way in a short period since that phone call from Micky Turner. I was a different athlete – or should I say I was now becoming an athlete. Training three times a week and being introduced to a weights room had resulted in a steep rise in my fitness level and the shedding of some weight. The fat kid was getting slimmer.

The Falcons had players spread throughout western Victoria, so each area had a training base. Twice a week we'd train in Colac, and then everyone would come together on a Wednesday night in Geelong. I enjoyed the weekly trips up the highway. Usually I'd get a lift with a couple of the older Colac lads, Andrew Siegert and Amon Buchanan (older brother of my mate Micah).

The other country players took the bus back to their homes. Sometimes Andrew, Amon and I would make it our thing to torment them. A regular prank was to go to the McDonald's drive-through, purchase some small ice-cream cones and then pitch them at our teammates on the bus. One night we stepped it up, with eggs our missiles of choice.

The camaraderie was the best bit. I loved the fact that I was a 16-year-old who got to hang out with 18-year-olds. That was a big reason why football was winning the battle over cricket for my affection. To play cricket for Australia, you had to be very, very special, and very few got that opportunity, which was another reason why I was leaning towards taking the better odds of AFL.

The fork-in-the-road moment came when I was selected in the Victorian under-17 cricket squad but it clashed with training for the AIS International Series. I couldn't do both, and footy won out.

Cricket had, however, been responsible for fulfilling one of my dreams – playing on the MCG. It had only been Kanga Cricket, with dozens of other kids during the lunch break at a senior match, but just walking on the hallowed turf had been a memorable experience.

I got to do it properly in the TAC Cup semifinal in 2000, which was played as a curtain-raiser to the North Melbourne v Hawthorn semifinal. We touched up the Sandringham Dragons, and Amon certainly enjoyed himself by kicking ten goals. The following week I managed to get onto a few and kicked three goals as we defeated the Dandenong Stingrays to book a spot in the grand final.

There isn't a more beautiful place in the world than the MCG on Grand Final Day. The all-conquering Essendon were playing Melbourne in the big one, and we were running around a few hours earlier. We played the Eastern Ranges and managed to get the ascendancy in the second quarter, with Amon and I kicking two goals each. It helped that Eastern's best player, Sam Mitchell, had been sent off. This was the first time I'd come across him. Amon had actually taken a dive in the incident that was more of a heavy spoil, but the umpire hadn't been impressed.

The result was a 22-point win, with Amon kicking five goals to take best-on-ground honours. It was an exciting day, and even though I was a bottom-age player compared to most of my team-mates, I was front and square for the celebrations. Unfortunately the bouncers at the Eureka Hotel, Geelong's main nightspot, didn't share my enthusiasm for the victory. They weren't keen on a 16-year-old getting in, so I went around the corner to a small bar where a few beers were snuck my way.

By midnight I was gone, totally exhausted from the day. It was one hell of a way to celebrate a premiership – and possibly a snap-shot of the future, given that I clearly already had the mindset of working hard on the field and playing just as hard off it.

But my season wasn't over yet. I'd qualified for the finals with the Colac under 18s, and because of the Sydney Olympics the AFL had brought its season – and also the TAC Cup – forward to clear September for the biggest show on the planet. The country leagues hadn't followed suit, which meant I was available for the Tigers' preliminary final. I wasn't too sure about going back after not playing with them for most of the season. If I was picked, it meant a player who'd played all year would miss out. But my close mates convinced me to do it and we got through to the grand final.

Then things got harder. One of my best mates, Dave McVeigh, was the one who was dropped. We'd played cricket together and footy at Colac Imperials before he followed me over to Colac. I wasn't going to take his spot – it was non-negotiable, I told the coaches. But Dave wasn't having a bar of it. 'Look, mate, go and play. We're more of a chance if you play,' he said. It didn't feel right, but he was adamant. We were playing South Warrnambool, who hadn't lost a game all season.

The night before the game I was hanging out with Micah and

another mate, Andrew Walters, and to pass the time we decided to dye our hair peroxide blond. It was a strange idea and not without drama – it actually burnt our scalps, forcing us to make a mercy dash to the hairdresser.

But the new look seemed to work. We pushed South Warrnambool all the way, with the match going down to the wire in the final quarter. There were only a couple of minutes left when I marked at centre half-forward and, with a bit of breeze behind me, unloaded from 50 metres. Fortunately it sailed through to give us the lead, and we managed to hold on for a magical win.

It was like the whole town of Colac was there, such were the celebrations after the siren. The medal presentations happened out on the ground, but as we were walking back into the rooms something didn't feel right to me. I handed my medal to one of the coaches, Jason Cuolahan, and said, 'Give this to Davo.'

'What are you going to give up?'

My father was seated across from me at the kitchen table and I knew he was deadly serious.

'What do you mean?'

I'd just turned 17 but wasn't playing football because I'd been diagnosed with osteitis pubis, which is a fancy term for a very sore groin, and basically couldn't run. It had started as a dull pain over the summer but I'd just pushed through it, which probably wasn't the smartest thing as it's an overuse injury. Apparently my running style hadn't helped – I tended to thrust my right foot out, which then sent all the shock through the groin area.

I'd played a full season of cricket and was also training with the Falcons and the AIS squad for the 2001 test series against

Ireland. The series involved a hybrid game that is a cross between Australian Rules and Gaelic football. A round ball replaces the Sherrin and there is a soccer net as well as goalposts like those in rugby league, so you can score overs and unders. It seems confusing but is actually a lot of fun, and we managed to pick it up quickly.

The first test was on a Thursday night at the MCG as the curtain-raiser for the Round 3 Carlton v Essendon game, with more than 70 000 fans watching. We won it easily, 125 to 35, and progressed to Easter Monday, where we got to play before the Melbourne v Geelong game. The third test was over in Perth.

The Irish boys were pretty willing and there were a few scraps during the series, but our superior skill saw us win all three games. I was fortunate enough to receive the Ron Barassi Medal for best player. Barassi was a legendary figure in the game, having played for Melbourne and Carlton and coached Melbourne, Carlton, North Melbourne and Sydney, so it was an honour to win something named after him.

I only managed to play the first three games of the 2001 season with the Falcons before we decided to pull the pin due to my injury. I was slightly anxious as it wasn't ideal to miss a big chunk of the season leading up to the draft. But Mick Turner assured me it wasn't an issue. In fact, he wasn't concerned about me not playing – he was more concerned about my lifestyle when I wasn't playing. He'd given me a few pep talks over the previous 12 months, often pulling me into the property room at the Falcons and giving me a spray.

This time he was more fired up than normal. 'Mate, you have to pull your head in,' he said. 'I have had so many recruiters ask about you, but they are hearing that you're drinking and going out.' Mick was concerned that I'd be throwing away a golden opportunity if

I didn't improve my attitude, and that I was vulnerable to slipping off track if I had to sit around on my arse for three months.

He was right. And that's why my father was staring at me across the table now, searching for a way to keep me engaged in the big picture. 'What commitment are you going to make to show that you really want this?' he asked.

'Commitment? What – you want me to go to bed early? Is that what you're talking about?'

Dad leaned further forward. 'You think you're a young man already. You love football and you want to play it for the next ten years, don't you?'

I nodded. I had no idea where he was going with this.

'Why don't you prove that to me right now? From now until the end of the Falcons season, promise me you won't have a drink.'

Wow. I hadn't expected that. He made it sound like I was an alcoholic, but I knew what he meant. It was about breaking the cycle.

The norm was to have a few beers after playing footy, whether at Colac or with the Falcons. A couple of quiet beers would turn into a few more, with a party on the agenda almost every weekend at someone's house when their parents were away. Throw in a pizza or other fast food and it wasn't a good mix for someone like me, who had a propensity for putting on a few kilos quickly, particularly if I wasn't playing.

Dad added, 'I'll pay you $500 if you do it.'

Bingo. We had a deal. I got up and we shook on it. Three months without a drink – I could do that.

The draft speculation had gone to another level. It was no longer chatter – we were now receiving letters almost every day from player managers and clubs. The thought of having a manager was bizarre. It was hard to get my head around it given that I was a Year 11 student in Colac. Why did I need a manager? But it was the way of the world, and Mick had explained to us at the Falcons how it worked and why it was necessary. It certainly got Mum and Dad a few free feeds, with potential managers on the charm offensive when they arrived, trying to work every angle to impress us.

The letters from the clubs basically said they were following my career and would be considering me as a potential recruit in November's draft. I would have a quick read but not pay too much attention. Mum kept all of the letters in a drawer that was quickly filling up.

After 14 weeks on the sidelines, I eventually got the all-clear to play in the Falcons' final home-and-away game of the season. I never wanted to see a Swiss ball again – most of my rehab had been spent doing strengthening exercises on one, which was mind-numbing stuff but critical to my recovery.

We had a gun team, with Bartel, Ablett, Matt Maguire, Brent Moloney and Nick Maxwell some of the more prominent players. A couple of my old mates, Jake Carmody and Micah Buchanan, were also on the 2001 Falcons' list.

In the elimination final against Oakleigh, I kicked four goals and enjoyed every second of being back. However, a hip injury the following week meant I only played one quarter against the Murray Bushrangers.

We had the team to go back-to-back but never even made it to the final two, losing to Calder in the preliminary final. That match was played before the Essendon v Hawthorn preliminary final, which we all stayed to watch before heading back to Geelong and having a family meal at Buckley's, the highlight of which was my first alcoholic beverage in three months. I had a few more – in fact, several more – and finished the night asleep under the pool table at Maxwell's house.

Alcohol would be a topic of conversation a couple of weeks later at the draft camp. Recruiters and coaches from every club converged on Canberra for the camp, which was at the AIS facility and was part of the lead-up to the national draft. The AFL invited the top 80 prospects to attend and we were put through a range of tests, including vertical jumps, sprints and time trials. All things I knew I wouldn't excel at. I wasn't athletic. It was simply the way I'd been born, and given I'd hardly played or trained in the previous six months, it's fair to say I wasn't exactly in the shape of my life. It was a weird feeling, because with every step I knew I was being watched.

Another part of the camp was having meetings with the clubs, supposedly for them to get an insight into your personality. Some were pretty laid back but others were full-on, with some curly questions. I had one of those thrown at me by West Coast. 'What would you give up to play AFL?'

I nearly burst out laughing, because I knew my answer was going to raise eyebrows. 'Well, I had a bet with my dad back in June that if I didn't touch a drop of alcohol for the rest of the year, he'd give me $500.'

Their faces fell, considering I'd only turned 17 a few months earlier. I certainly got the reaction I'd expected. (I failed to mention that Dad was still to pay up.)

'Which player do you model your game on?' was another regular question, and I liked to give as my answer another left-footer, Collingwood's Chris Tarrant, as he was a medium tall who could play both ends of the ground. His strength was versatility, and the recruiters already seemed to find that quality attractive about me.

The draft was an interesting scenario. I tried not to pay too much attention to it because I didn't care which number I was drafted at or to which club. It seriously didn't bother me. I just wanted to play AFL football.

Hawthorn, who'd been a bit unlucky not to win the 2001 preliminary final against Essendon, rocketed into the picture when they sensationally traded star defender Trent Croad to Fremantle in return for the No.1 draft pick. There were a couple of other picks involved and another Hawk, Luke McPharlin, also went to the Dockers. But Croad was the cornerstone of the deal, which surprised many.

The top three places in the 2001 draft were all priority selections, with Fremantle, St Kilda and West Coast receiving an extra pick at the start of the process. Priority picks were given to the poorest-performing teams in a bid to help them improve their on-field performance. So there was Hawthorn at No.1, St Kilda at No.2, West Coast at No.3 and then Fremantle.

I was clearly in the mix, given that after the draft camp, the coaches from all of those clubs made the trek down to Colac for a chat. These visits would send Mum into a panic – she was always worried about having cake or biscuits ready to have with their cups of tea. I never really understood what the clubs were trying to find out and often spent the meetings cringing at the behaviour of my parents – but I knew they were both exciting and daunting for Mum and Dad.

Hawthorn's recruiting manager, John Turnbull, had been in regular contact and coach Peter Schwab came down for a visit.

St Kilda's recruiting boss, John Beveridge, was a dinner guest while new Fremantle coach Chris Connolly also called in.

The West Coast contingent hadn't been deterred by my revelation about the drinking bet, with Eagles coach John Worsfold particularly keen to discover what he could about me. Clearly the issue for Worsfold was whether I could commit to moving to the other side of the country. It had been an issue with players in the past, but they didn't need to worry about that with me. 'I'll pack my bags now, if you want,' was my response to his question about it.

Worsfold stood up, shook my hand and said, 'That's the answer I was after.'

Hawthorn got me to come up to Melbourne several times for medical tests to make sure the osteitis pubis wasn't a long-term issue. I had every scan available – an MRI, a CT and bone scans – to make sure they wouldn't be buying a crook if they went with me. On one occasion Turnbull got one of his offsiders, Greg Boxall, to take me home. I don't think Bocca realised that Colac was a couple of hours away. By halfway, the sun was really annoying him and he asked if I would have a go behind the wheel. I had my learner's permit and Mum had let me have a couple of drives of her car, so I was confident enough. The problem was that while I was concentrating on driving, Bocca got to focus on his love of Roy Orbison. He made me listen to the Big O all the way home.

He did start to freak out about my driving when we arrived in Colac and a police car began to follow us. I quickly put his mind at ease. 'Don't worry, I know 'em,' I said. I knew them because of Dad, who was one of those people who knew everyone. He'd been with the State Emergency Service for 16 years and had worked alongside the police at major incidents in the area.

That was another great thing about living in a country town –
everyone knew each other, and you had the sense that people
always had your back. This community feel was evident even
though Colac wasn't exactly a dot on the map, having a popula-
tion of more than 10 000 with three secondary schools and four
pubs. The biggest industry in town was the Bulla ice-cream
factory, while the local abattoir was another of the larger
employers in the area.

My only venture into the workforce at this stage had been as
a paper boy for Tanis's Milk Bar, a couple of blocks from where
we lived. I only worked on Sundays and made $10, which I spent
on a chocolate Big M and lollies. There were plenty of times when
the papers were too heavy for my bike, making it fall over, or the
straps weren't tight enough to carry my load. A couple of times
I cracked it and just walked home, but Dad would march me back
there to plead for my job back. The lesson was that you don't quit
just because it's hard work.

Other times I would stay in bed when the alarm went off,
because I knew Mum would drive me around in our old orange ute.
I'd sit in the back and throw the papers into the front yards, always
making sure Mum and Dad got a paper even though they weren't
on my list. I'd deliberately miss a house nearby, and it was easy for
me to make it up later on after the people informed my boss their
paper hadn't arrived.

The paper round and, later, basketball refereeing were my
streams of income when I was at school. I'd get $4.50 for umpir-
ing a junior game and figured I was better off doing three games of
basketball two nights a week than sitting at home doing nothing.

But my income was about to get a whole lot bigger.

*

There seemed to be a good deal of confusion about the draft rankings with four of us in the mix. From what I'd seen, I thought a West Australian named Graham Polak was the best player. Everyone thought he'd go at No.1, but when Fremantle traded that pick everything changed.

Chris Judd was being talked about, but I didn't really know him, and he'd missed the national championships because of shoulder issues. Luke Ball, with whom I'd played cricket and football in many squads over our junior careers, was highly regarded and very professional even at such a young age.

At the draft camp they'd also done a skinfold test. I'd already figured out that this test, which measures your body fat in millimetres, was going to haunt me throughout my career. The results were a little alarming. My stomach came in at 34, bigger than Ball's entire body, which came in at just under 33. I didn't know if that said more about him or about me.

There was another major difference between us – he was going to defer his first year in the AFL so he could finish his schooling. That was never a consideration for me. In fact, in my eyes it was complete madness.

What Bally and I did share was the same manager. We'd received dozens of letters and phone calls from various managers, but it was a chance lunch date that saw me introduced to Paul Connors.

As part of the AIS scholarship we got to spend a week at an AFL club, and Jimmy Bartel and I were allocated Geelong. Jimmy had already signed with Connors and had lunch plans with him and a few other Geelong players who were his clients. He said I should tag along. It was a big crew, including Cameron Ling, Matthew Scarlett, Darren Milburn and Jason Snell. Connors shouted everyone the meal and I figured it wasn't a bad set-up. Who would have thought he already knew the way to my heart was via a good feed? He also invited the family up to a Geelong v Richmond game during the year and took us down into the rooms. That certainly helped get him in the good books.

There were many phone calls to Paul as the days ticked down. The unknown had everyone on edge.

I was pretty calm about everything until the countdown got to the final week and the nerves started to kick in. Hawthorn had told us they were having a draft summit with all the key stakeholders at the club, and from that they'd make the decision about who to take as No.1. The draft was on Sunday 25 November 2001 at Rod Laver Arena in Melbourne. Turnbull said we'd get a call at 4 p.m. on the Friday – Hawthorn wanted to make their decision early and then, as a courtesy, tell Judd, Ball and myself their intentions so we wouldn't be caught out on the day.

Clockwatching is not my favourite pastime but at least I had a distraction – getting ready for a school graduation dinner that I was attending with my girlfriend, Lauren Kirkman. Lauren was a year older than me and had just finished Year 12. A couple of links had brought us together. She played netball at Imps with Bianca, who had also coached her in juniors, and I had played at Imps with her brothers, Tom and Ben, in juniors. We'd had a bit of a rocky start when I'd stood her up on our second date – by mistake, of course – but I'd managed to smooth it over.

Our timing had been perfect, given we'd both just broken up from long-term relationships. Lauren had gone to Colac High School. This turned out to be a bonus because it gave me something to do at lunchtime.

There were three secondary schools in town: Trinity College,

Colac High School and Colac Tech. In Year 12, students could switch schools to do subjects that weren't available at their own campus, and to facilitate this, there was a shared campus bus that travelled between the three schools.

It meant I could hop on the bus and head over at lunchtime to see my girlfriend. It was a win-win situation as I got to hang out with her and also miss the odd class if I made the terrible mistake of getting the bus schedule mixed up.

Lauren had a part-time job at the Woolworths supermarket. Her boss was Bianca, which sometimes got us in trouble. Often Bianca would ring up looking for Lauren to do a shift, and Lauren would say she was too busy with homework. My sister soon cottoned on that this was code for 'I'm with Luke.'

We didn't do a very good job of hiding it. Bianca would get home from work a couple of hours later and find us snuggled on the couch watching a movie.

But there was no snuggling on the couch now. I was at Mum's pretending to be cool, calm and collected as I waited for the phone to ring. Then it happened.

'Luke, it's John Turnbull. Welcome to Hawthorn.'

Wow. I managed to get out a thank you. He explained that I needed to keep it a secret because if it got out, there would be media all over our front doorstep in the morning.

I handed the phone to Mum. She was quite emotional and we had a hug. The fact that I would be staying in Victoria was the bit that had her the most excited. That part had never really worried me, but Hawthorn had been a very successful club in recent times and certainly appealed as an exciting destination.

Turnbull said he also wanted to ring Dad and convey the news, given that they'd had a lot to do with each other over the past few months. But the second we hung up, Dad rang. 'What's going on?' he asked. 'Have you heard anything?'

'Get off the phone,' I said. 'They're ringing you now.'

It felt bizarre knowing this big thing that I wasn't allowed to tell anyone, but the news certainly made the dinner a lot more enjoyable.

I had a few mates around on draft eve and we watched a movie, *The Replacements*, to help pass the time. There were still plenty of nerves even though I knew the result, and my attempts to sleep weren't helped when one of my Falcons teammates texted me at 2.15 a.m. to wish me luck.

We arrived at the draft nice and early. There were a few players there and I sat next to my Falcons teammate Jimmy Bartel. He'd won our best and fairest award and was a certainty to go in the top ten.

The formalities seemed to drag on before Turnbull was instructed to read out Hawthorn's pick. I think I pulled off the surprise smile, and I shook hands with Jimmy as the cameras zoomed in. While I had known what was going to happen, a massive wave of relief swept over me when I actually heard the words.

In the end, St Kilda went with Ball at No.2, Judd went to the Eagles at No.3, and Polak went to Fremantle at No.4. Jimmy didn't have to wait too long – he was snapped up by Geelong at No.8 – and my Falcons teammate Luke Molan went next, to Melbourne. We already knew Ablett was going to Geelong via the father–son rule, but there were a few more Falcons who had their names read out, including Matt Maguire (St Kilda), Tom Davidson (Collingwood) and Joel Reynolds (Essendon).

My one instruction to Mum had been not to cry, but that was wishful thinking. In the very first interview she couldn't help it and the tears came. After numerous interviews and pictures, Hawthorn chief executive Michael Brown invited us out to the club's headquarters at Glenferrie Oval for a barbecue lunch and to meet some key people. There was one problem – Mum and Dad had no idea where it was.

In the end, Brown got into our car and drove us there. We had lunch in the Peter Crimmins Room, which was pretty impressive with all the premiership cups displayed throughout.

Hawthorn had taken four others in the draft, including a couple of Bendigo lads, Rick Ladson and Daniel Elstone, as well as Campbell Brown and Sam Mitchell. They were all commencing training the following day, but the club allowed me a few days to get sorted and I didn't start my new life as an AFL footballer until the Wednesday.

This was a very good thing, given the party I walked into at the Colac Imperials club rooms that night. My family and friends had been going hard at it since my name was read out at No.1. The rooms were decked out in Hawthorn colours, with brown and gold streamers and balloons everywhere. It was a big night that continued back in the shed at Mum's, where my uncles, cousins and friends kept the party rolling.

It was some sort of celebration, and when I finally showed my head the next day to start helping with the clean-up, the party was reignited. A few mates rocked up with a couple of slabs, pointing out that you don't get drafted at No.1 every day of the week. I found it hard to argue against their theory. Mum was at work, and, to step it up a level, we started a game of NBA Jam on Super Nintendo, which involved doing shots. Things soon got out of control, and a couple of times I had to remind myself that I was now an AFL player.

I wasn't behaving like one, but I was sure that would come . . . in time.

3

THE ROOKIE MISTAKE

Riding a bike. Over and over and over again.

Talk about boring – but it was my welcome to the AFL.

It wasn't how I'd envisaged the start of my career, but thanks to the osteitis pubis flaring again at the draft camp, I was effectively chained to a stationary bike and wasn't allowed to set foot on the training track.

The first thing you want to do as a draftee is impress your new teammates and coaches. There was a bit more to it than that for me, given I was the No.1 draft pick. I'm sure they all wanted to see what the fuss was about – not to mention that the club had traded away one of their mates and one of the stars of the side, Trent Croad, to get me in the door.

I did get to know John Barker and Jonathan Hay quite well – they were next to me on the bikes as part of their recovery from post-season surgery.

The club set me up in a home in Glen Waverley with Pat and Rob Benham, who'd looked after a number of recruits over the years, including Shane Crawford and Ben Dixon. This time they had three boarders: Daniel Elstone and Rick 'Laddo' Ladson, who'd played together for the Bendigo Pioneers in the TAC Cup, were also staying there.

I knew nothing about Melbourne or about looking after myself. Things like cooking, cleaning and laundry were completely foreign to this 17-year-old from the bush! The Benhams were my saviours.

I'd met Dan at the draft camp and we seemed to have a similar outlook on life. He was also a boy from the bush who liked to have a drink and a good time. It was obvious we were a match made in heaven, with the added bonus that he was already 18, which meant he was our designated driver and purchaser of alcohol. We were soon inseparable. The bright lights of the city attracted us and we embraced the fact that there were bars open every night of the week.

Dan was a small nugget who'd been a ball magnet in the TAC Cup. He was physically ready for the AFL from the start, which is why he got picked for the opening pre-season game.

I eventually managed to get off the bike, but I was a long way behind and nowhere near ready by the time the 2002 season arrived. Despite this I'd still learnt a lot of things over the summer on the training track, including that my teammate Ben Dixon was a man of his word.

This became apparent when I lined up on him in a match simulation drill. He was at half-forward and I was the defender assigned to him. As he went to lead I was holding onto him and after the second time he turned and said, 'If you do that again, I'll hit ya.'

I figured he was trying to bluff the new kid, plus I wasn't going to give him a free ride to the ball, so when he went to lead again I scragged his jumper. Dicko turned around and planted one on my chin.

The punch wasn't that hard but it had caught me by surprise and I went down. Peter Schwab came running over. 'What the hell are you doing?'

Brett Johnson also came over and had a go at Dicko for picking on the young kid. Once things cooled down we resumed the drill and there was no way I was going to be intimidated by what had happened. When Dicko went to lead I did exactly what I'd done the previous three occasions. This time it got a very different reaction.

'I think we will get along just fine,' he said with a smile.

I'd passed that test and managed to get through a few more, because after a couple of games at Box Hill – the VFL team affiliated to Hawthorn where you played if you didn't make the seniors – I made my way onto the emergency list for Round 4. Laddo also made it, and on the Friday night the three of us headed up the road to the Village Green Hotel for a counter meal.

It was supposed to be a quiet night, but we met a couple of friends up there and things got slightly out of control. It was after 2 a.m. by the time we got home and we had to be at the MCG at midday in case there were any late injury issues. We were playing Collingwood and I was the third designated emergency, so I figured I was pretty safe. Nathan Lonie was the first one up, with Laddo second.

I was still feeling the effects of the night before when we arrived. Panic set in, particularly for Laddo, when we got word that a couple of players were in doubt. They ended up playing and we dodged a bullet – although the team didn't. Hawthorn didn't have a great day against the Magpies, and it wasn't the best start to the year with three losses in the opening four games. The heat was on and opportunities were opening up. On the Tuesday leading into Round 5, Laddo was told he would be making his senior debut the following Saturday against Richmond at the MCG.

They say 24 hours is a long time in football – well, try one hour.

Laddo found out he was in before training. Then, in the final couple of minutes of the training session, he seriously injured his knee. It was devastating, and certainly put a dampener on the news I received from Schwabby that night that I was replacing Laddo in the senior team. There were going to be three debutants against the Tigers, with Sam Mitchell and ruckman Robert Campbell also getting a call-up.

When the news broke about my selection on the Thursday night, it was hysteria in the Hodge household. Mum and Dad were flooded with requests for tickets, as half of Colac wanted to be there on the Saturday. I tried to stay away from all that, and left it to the club to liaise with them.

Unlike the previous Friday night, there was no Village Green activity as I got ready to fulfil my childhood dream. Ever since I'd been to the MCG for the first time, for that Richmond v North Melbourne game, my answer to the question of what I wanted to do when I grew up had always been the same. I didn't want to be a fireman or a policeman – I wanted to play footy. So each time I would say, 'I am going to play football on the MCG at 2.30 p.m. on a Saturday afternoon.'

It was actually on the MCG at 2.10 p.m. on Saturday 27 April 2002.

*

It had to be on my right foot. I could sense my father's smile up in the stands when my first touch in AFL football was a kick using my non-preferred foot. All those nights when I'd whinged at the Western Oval were worth it – it was the first skill I had to execute in my senior career.

Unfortunately I kicked it out on the full.

I'd started the game on the half-forward flank and it took a little while for me to get the hang of things. One of my first acts was to try to tackle Richmond defender Darren Gaspar. He just brushed me off like a rag doll, which wasn't a good look.

After my clanger kick, I managed to redeem myself by getting a handball off to our captain, Shane Crawford, who ran to 40 metres out and kicked a goal. His reaction took me by surprise. I thought he was coming to tell me off but he was very excited about the goal and delivered me a double high-five with an aggressive 'C'mon!' He was pumped up and so was I after my first influential act as an AFL footballer. My opponent, Mark Chaffey, had been right on me, and I'd actually had to run at full speed and then slide onto the ball and deliver the handball off in the one motion.

The other highlight, if you can call it that, was managing to get into a fight with the biggest person on the field: Brad Ottens, Richmond's ruckman. He wrapped his massive hands around me after I started a scrap with him. I quickly realised that wasn't the best idea I'd ever had.

Everyone talks about the pace of the game and how it's a significant step up from anything you've experienced before. That was definitely right, but I felt okay out there. I managed to collect 12 possessions on my debut, and, more importantly, we had a good win, taking down the Tigers by 42 points.

The most awkward moment of the day came in the rooms afterwards, when we all linked arms to sing the Hawthorn theme song. I wasn't 100 per cent sure how it went (though I could have sung Richmond's word for word), but I think I managed to get through.

That wasn't the case in my second match a week later, when I tweaked my Achilles early and had to sit out the rest of the game. My stats were one kick, one goal. I'd actually hurt the Achilles moments before I took the mark 30 metres out from goal, but there was no way I was going to give up my first opportunity to kick a goal on the MCG.

I missed the next four matches and used the time wisely . . . to end my brief university career.

Before I was drafted, Hawthorn had offered me the chance to do what Luke Ball was doing and finish Year 12. There was an option of taking up a scholarship at Caulfield Grammar, which would mean I'd play footy there and train at Hawthorn when it was convenient.

'I'm not doing that,' I declared. 'I'm here to play football.'

I sensed Hawthorn were happy with my decision to want to play straight away. It had been an important point of difference before the draft when they were weighing up all the factors. But the compromise was that I'd do my Year 12 studies two nights a week at Swinburne University of Technology's Prahran campus. From 6 to 9 p.m. every Wednesday and Thursday night I was required to attend Swinburne, which was at least not too far away.

In my first class we were all asked why we were there. I explained how I'd finished Year 11 the previous year and moved down to Melbourne to play football. I wanted to tick off my VCE, although I admitted it wasn't my main priority.

The others in the class then told their stories. There was a guy who had quit school a few years earlier to work on his car and then realised he couldn't get a job, and a girl who'd had a baby at 16 and wanted to come back and finish her schooling.

I lasted a term. One of the main reasons was simply that I was stuffed by the time I got there most nights. When you're a 17-year-old trying to adapt to a full-time training load, it takes a lot out of you. Doing the main session for the week and then going off to school was a recipe for disaster, and I often found myself falling asleep in class. Something had to give, and it wasn't going to be football.

There had been a common theme throughout my schooling: I would try to do the work, but if I couldn't, I'd quit. It was the complete opposite of my attitude towards footy, which was, 'If I can't do it, I'll find a way to prove you wrong.'

Rather than just stop showing up at Swinburne, I knew I had to be honest with the club. Schwab and David Parkin, the former Hawthorn premiership coach who was back at the club as director of coaching, were very strong on players furthering themselves outside of football. Simon Lloyd, the player development manager, had set it all up, and I had spent a lot of time on the couch in his office discussing my studies. He was the perfect person for his role – he was a great listener and the boys would queue up to see him.

During one of the couch sessions, I dropped the bombshell. 'Look, mate, it's not for me,' I said.

He tried to talk me around, urging me to stick at it, but I just wanted to play football. I explained my theory that it was actually hindering my sleep and energy levels for training.

The club eventually gave in – I think they were learning quickly that I was a pretty hard man to shift when I'd made up my mind.

Some would call it pig-headedness, but I'd been that way as a kid and wasn't about to change now.

If I had my time again I would definitely stick at it and complete my VCE, as not having it became an issue down the track. But I was a raw, immature kid who was still learning the ropes, not just of football but of life.

When I returned to the seniors in Round 11, Schwabby played me across half-back. I enjoyed the freedom this gave me. Because of my injury-interrupted pre-season and the fact that I'd hardly played the previous year, I didn't have the same engine as the other players. Playing at half-forward was tough because you had a defender chasing you all the time and had to work hard to get into positions to get the ball. At half-back, I could use my smarts and judgement to get to where the ball was going and, to a degree, control the physical output.

I managed to get a few kicks – and my first Brownlow Medal votes – in Round 15 on a Friday night against the Western Bulldogs at Docklands Stadium. My performance was enough to get me the round's nomination for the NAB AFL Rising Star Award, which was for first-year players, or second-year players who hadn't played more than ten games in their debut season. It was a prestigious award, with the winner receiving a $20 000 bank account. The weekly nomination also meant a day of media interviews, which normally wouldn't bother me, but I wasn't looking my best courtesy of an incident on the Saturday night.

I'd been out in the city with a group of 12, including Lauren, celebrating my mate Leon Kopp's 19th birthday. There were a few couples in the group and we were walking along the street when a car came tearing past, tooting its horn and nearly knocking down Koppy and his girlfriend, who were a bit behind the rest of us. They yelled at the car and it stopped and turned around. Two guys got out armed with steering-wheel locks and started charging at us. Lauren tried to cool them down but was shoved out of the way, and I instantly saw red. I can't tell you what happened in the next 60 seconds, but I soon realised that Koppy had been whacked in the head when I saw blood streaming down his face.

I didn't realise until the two guys had taken off that I'd also suffered a cut, smack bang in the middle of my forehead. It all happened so quickly. The police arrived and it didn't take them long to track down the offenders, who were well known to them. I had to go to hospital to get a few stitches, which meant I looked a bit battered and bruised for my Rising Star media commitments. Plus I had to wear a big bandaid for the next match, which wasn't my best look.

We finished the season in tenth with 11 wins, missing the finals on percentage. I'd managed 15 games in my debut season and placed sixth in the best and fairest count behind Crawford, which I was quite proud of given how far behind I'd been at the start.

I was physically exhausted and needed to put my feet up and relax. That was my rookie mistake.

It was a ceremony along the same lines as the one in test cricket where a batsman raises his bat to celebrate making 100. I'd dreamt about doing that plenty of times, but I'd never heard of raising the calipers to celebrate making a ton.

On day one of pre-season training, there was clear excitement among the other players, who clapped and cheered when they found out about my skinfold reading. 'C'mon – raise the calipers!' they screamed.

I found myself in this bizarre celebration because I'd returned from the end-of-season break with a skinfold reading of 104. I took some solace in Rick Ladson's being 109 (although he was recovering from a knee injury). To put the 104 in context, most players got around with 'skinnies' of between 50 and 60.

What was even more disturbing was the weight gain I'd achieved in my two months off: 7 kilos. It hadn't been a deliberate campaign to pile on the weight; I'd just been back in Colac hanging out with my mates, where, it must be said, takeaway food and beers were a constant.

I was also just following the lead of the senior players, who saw the off-season as a time to let their hair down. 'Pre-season is to run off all the weight you've put on' had been Mark Graham's advice. I may have taken it a bit too far, but that was the culture. I fitted in perfectly.

The real issue was that I was a kid who only heard what he wanted to hear. Guys would talk about going out and enjoying themselves in the off-season, drinking beer and relaxing, and that's all that sank in. The part about being sensible at the same time and doing the work to keep yourself in decent shape didn't register. The older guys had been around long enough to understand that you had to do both.

The problem for me was that my increased weight had probably played a role in my latest injury setback – a foot stress fracture. So once again, for the start of pre-season training, I was on a stationary bike and nowhere near a football ground. The injury also slowed my weight-loss program, and the 'fat boy' tag from my primary school days was well and truly back. My teammates took great delight in pointing out the size of my girth.

My eating habits were already borderline, and it's fair to say there wasn't a lot of optimism about them improving if I moved out of the Benhams' place. But Dan and I felt it was time to spread our wings. The Benhams had been great for us and we'd certainly left an impression on them – they declared that we'd easily enjoyed ourselves more than any of their previous boarders.

During that summer, Friday nights were always big at the Benhams'. Pat and Rob would go round to a friend's house to play cards and Scrabble, leaving us to our own devices. When they returned, we'd do our best to hide the brown bottles, but overflowing bins are hard to disguise.

One of my great achievements during my time with Pat and Rob was getting my driver's licence. Rob was actually a driving instructor, which came in handy when I failed my test at the first attempt. The driving side of it wasn't an issue but I bombed in the written. Thankfully, Rob was able to pull some strings and got me a re-test the following day, which I managed to scrape through.

Despite having lived in Melbourne for 12 months, my understanding of it was limited. I'd never seen many parts of the city, so when Dan and I started thinking about where to live, we were guided by other people. My uncle Matt lived in Doncaster and I'd been to his place a few times for dinner. It turned out he was moving interstate with his partner, and he said Dan and I could take over his lease.

It was a two-bedroom flat with a little area out the back that was perfect for backyard cricket and table tennis. As it turned out, Liam Buchanan, older brother of Amon and Micah, lived just around the corner. He was a state-level cricketer who had a contract with the Victorian Bushrangers. Liam was a couple of years older than we were, and had often been our go-to guy back in Colac when we required under-age refreshments. He lived with another cricketer, Andrew Kent, who played with the Melbourne Cricket Club, so we had a bit of competition in our backyard cricket matches.

My hatred of losing saw the end of our table tennis competition. I controlled the match-ups with Dan, but when he beat me for the first time I lost it and smashed the table, which wasn't the smartest thing to do. Dan immediately claimed the title as reigning champion and has run with it ever since – we weren't able to play again.

In an attempt to get us on track, the club sent its dietitian to go shopping with us. She took us to the supermarket, where we filled up a couple of trolleys with beautiful fresh food. We were given some meal plans and advice on how to cook.

The trip cost us around $400, but we may as well have flushed the money down the toilet. The fruit and vegetables sat in the fridge for a couple of weeks and then had to be thrown out.

We had Nando's down the road, which we thought was a respectable option. The chicken wrap was healthy but we failed to count the chips and soft drink that always accompanied it. Subway was advertised as being a healthy alternative, so we figured their chicken schnitzels got the tick of approval. I'm not sure their choc chip cookies did, though.

Mum would bring food up to us and clean the apartment when she was able to get to Melbourne. All those things I'd taken for granted as a kid – well, now I understood how important they were. Her visits were cause for celebration.

While you couldn't say we hadn't got out and about when we were living at the Benhams', the lid was certainly off once we were free of anyone observing our after-dark affairs. We went out every weekend and occasionally during the week. It was the life of a university student without going to uni.

We soon worked out that a lot of the senior players received drink cards from venues, so we started tapping into that resource and used their cards when they weren't going out. The Spy Lounge in the city got a regular workout, while the Mountain View and Village Green were other regular haunts.

We didn't put a lot of thought into the timing of our nights out. Often we'd hit the town the night before our main training session for the week. What would start out as a low-key couple of beers would escalate to 4 a.m. and trouble the next day. The senior players always had our back, whether that was a good or a bad thing. I remember on one occasion I was doing weights with Daniel Harford, who took one whiff of me and said, 'Mate, your breath smells like piss. Why don't you go and have a banana and a Gatorade to try and cover your breath?'

Dan and I were often struck down by 'Mondayitis', where both of us would call in sick to the club. This mostly happened during the pre-season (of the 21 sick days I registered that year, 15 of them fell on a Monday) and sometimes the club doctor, Bernie Crimmins, would come around because he lived in our area. I'd be in position on the couch trying my best to look like I was at death's door when he arrived, but, naturally, we'd failed to clean up properly from the night before and he'd notice empty beer bottles throughout the lounge room.

'Ahhhh, good old Grandpa's cough medicine,' he'd say.

The truth was we were both struggling by mid-season. Dan didn't see eye-to-eye with the Box Hill coach, Donald McDonald, and even got dropped to the VFL reserves. I felt like I was always playing catch-up after not getting onto the training track until January. Then I tore my ankle ligaments in Round 3, which forced me to the sidelines for a few more weeks. When I got back, I proceeded to break my thumb.

I'd also struggled with a change in my role. While I'd played half-forward as a junior, I found it a lot harder in the AFL.

The previous year I'd had the freedom to read the play across half-back, which helped to hide the fact that I wasn't physically fit enough. As a forward, I was exposed.

Dan and I started a ritual where I'd text him after each game and ask him how he'd gone. It would be the same response every week. 'Shit. Terrible. Didn't get a kick. I fucking hate football.'

I'd go down to the bottle shop and make sure the fridge was stocked by the time he got home. We'd sit there for hours, just chatting. That was a throwback to my Colac days where you'd always have a beer after footy. The easiest way to forget about whether you'd played well or badly was to have a beer with a mate.

It was as much a release for me as it was for Dan – I was also searching for a way to take my mind off football. At every opportunity I headed home to Colac on the weekend. There was a comfort in being with my childhood mates, who didn't care if the No.1 draft pick wasn't getting a kick. There was no scrutiny down there. It was the only place where I could be myself.

I'd heard the talk about second-year blues, and it wasn't a myth. I was certainly experiencing it. It didn't help that as a team we were inconsistent. While we managed to win the last four games of the season, it wasn't enough to play finals.

The Round 20 clash with the Kangaroos was the most memorable game of the season, but not in a good way. It was the first time I was genuinely scared on a football field. There had been a bit going on during the game, and I found myself in a tussle in the goal square with one of the Kangaroo boys. He grabbed me from behind, and when I turned around and saw who it was, my heart sank. Glenn Archer was universally regarded as the toughest player in the AFL, and here I was going toe-to-toe with him.

The first thing I thought was, 'Don't let go.' I knew if I let go he was likely to jumper-punch me one more time and probably knock me out. The other reason why I hung on for dear life was to save myself from embarrassment. I knew my dad and uncle would abuse me for being a weak little prick. So I hung in there, trying desperately not to show Archer how scared I was, counting down the seconds before my teammates came to the rescue.

The end of the season couldn't come quickly enough.

I wanted to get away and had the perfect place to go: Cairns. Lauren's parents had moved up there and she'd lived there on and off over the past two years. She was thinking about coming back to Melbourne permanently and we came up with the idea of doing a road trip. I was smart enough to fly up to Cairns and put my car on a truck. When it finally arrived, we packed up all Lauren's stuff and took our time driving back down the east coast to Victoria.

We'd purchased tents, swags and a blow-up mattress as we thought camping would be the way to go. It wasn't.

We stayed at a roadhouse in Rockhampton and that was an interesting experience. There were lots of funny noises throughout the night and the place had an eerie feel about it. All of Lauren's belongings were in the car and that was playing on her mind – it didn't feel like the safest place.

We moved on to Airlie Beach, where my lack of practical skills was exposed and Lauren proved to be more adept than me at putting up the tent. What she wasn't adept at was shutting the flywire – I woke up in the morning covered in mosquito bites. The little bastards had always loved me for some reason, but this was insane.

I declared to my girlfriend that our camping days were over. It was hotels for the rest of the way home.

Before I'd left for the break I'd had a meeting with Schwabby. Every Monday during the year we'd caught up to talk through my game and have a chat about whatever was happening in my personal life. If there was anything on my mind, I could raise it with my coach – his relaxed nature certainly appealed to me. This end-of-season meeting ended with the suggestion that this time round I lead a 'healthier' existence during my time off. I wasn't going to make the same mistakes again and spent a lot of time in the off-season riding a bike to keep my skinnies under control and avoid any foot issues flaring up.

It's funny how footy clubs move on so quickly. When I fronted up to pre-season training the following year, my world was completely different from what it had been just two months earlier. Dan had been delisted, the Doncaster bachelor pad was no longer, and I now lived with my girlfriend just a couple of minutes away from Glenferrie Oval.

4

THE JUDD EFFECT

'Don't worry about what other people are doing. You've just got to get over your injury.'

I was sitting in Simon Lloyd's office looking down at the moon boot on my left foot. At least I had the complete set now – my right foot had given me trouble the previous year.

After playing the opening three games of the 2004 season, I started to feel pain in my foot. I played against the Western Bulldogs in Round 4 with a painkilling injection, but afterwards I was in all sorts and only got home with the aid of crutches. A scan revealed that I had a stress fracture in the left metatarsal, which, the doctor told me, meant at least six weeks on the sidelines.

Lloyd was doing his best to calm my frustration. It was my third season, I'd managed to do more training over the summer than the previous two seasons, and now this had happened. Adding to the whole scenario was what Chris Judd was doing at West Coast. He'd finished second in the Eagles' best and fairest in 2003 and was the talk of the competition.

'It's bullshit how Judd is going,' I said. I didn't like knowing that almost every Hawthorn supporter was questioning my worth. Even my teammates would throw in a few gags about it. I knew they were joking, but I've always believed that in every joke there is an element of truth.

I knew that when my body gave me the chance to have a consistent run at things, I'd be more than able to hold my own in the AFL. But the pressure was getting to me. The weight of expectation had been there from the moment my name was read out at No.1. I thought I'd be able to handle it, but the continued run of injuries and Judd's impressive start to his AFL career were hard to take. Lloyd was the only person I opened up to, and that was a big thing for me, because showing weakness wasn't something I usually did. If the subject of Judd was raised by anyone else, I'd just act cool and say, 'It's fine.'

It was anything but fine. My way of dealing with it was to retreat, to get away from the football club as much as I could. Rather than train harder or work on improving my game, I'd get in the car and head to Colac to be with my mates. There was no talk of footy with them – we'd just hang out and go to a movie or have a hit of golf.

I needed that mental release because the Judd comparisons were everywhere. Every newspaper article that talked about his brilliant season would mention me. It was hard to avoid, and I didn't know how to deal with it. Lloyd did his best to help, telling me, 'It doesn't matter what people say on the outside – it's what people inside these four walls say that matters.'

At least the club's second-favourite son, Trent Croad (no one was ahead of Shane Crawford at Hawthorn), was back in brown and gold after two years at Fremantle. Hawthorn had given up its No.10 pick in the 2003 draft to get him back from the Dockers.

The problem was that the more I sat on the sidelines, the more the evidence mounted against me. I knew Peter Schwab was already being asked if the club had made a mistake by not taking Judd at No.1. And John Turnbull, the man who'd gone out on a limb and selected me, had left the club. The rumour mill said he'd been under extreme pressure for not picking Judd.

The coaching staff had more important things to worry about than the Hodge v Judd debate: our season was in freefall. We were on the bottom of the ladder with just two wins when I returned in Round 11 against Essendon.

What a game to come back in. There had been rising tensions between the two clubs because of what Hawthorn perceived as the Bombers standing over our team physically, which people liked to call 'good old-fashioned footy'. Over the years there had been some epic battles, but Essendon had enjoyed the upper hand in recent years and been dominant since their 2000 premiership victory.

Just before half-time in the Round 11 game, Essendon's Mark Johnson slammed our young ruckman, Robbie Campbell, into the turf. When we got into the rooms Schwabby was fuming. He made it clear that he didn't want Johnson to walk off the ground without requiring assistance. A number of club greats, including Dermott Brereton, were going around having quiet words in the ears of a few players. Their message was clear: it was time to draw a line in the sand.

And that's what Richie Vandenberg did. He went at Johnson early in the third quarter, and shortly afterwards a few brawls broke out. I floated around the edges, doing a bit of pushing and shoving. The atmosphere was electric, with almost every contest ending in a scuffle. We were certainly standing up to them physically, even if it was going to cost a few of us holidays. The weirdest clash was between Simon Beaumont and Justin Murphy, who'd been teammates at Carlton but now played for Hawthorn and Essendon respectively. They were actually good mates and their partners were sitting next to each other in the stands, but they went at it toe-to-toe. Apparently they were supposed to go out to dinner together that night – I'm not sure if that eventuated.

While we made a statement physically, Essendon kicked away in the second half and ended up winning by 12 goals. The fallout at the tribunal was significant for us, with Vandenberg suspended for six weeks, Campbell Brown and Lance Picioane getting four weeks each, and Beaumont out for one. There were plenty of melee fines handed out, too, but I managed to save my money.

Unfortunately the passion we showed against the Bombers wasn't sustainable, and we lost our next five games. This had Schwabby under siege. During the pre-season he'd been quoted in the media as saying Hawthorn could win the premiership in 2004. Now those words were coming back to haunt him, given that we were last on the ladder after 16 rounds. He decided to announce that he would step down at the end of the season.

However, after the Kangaroos pumped us by 80 points the following week, my first AFL coach decided to walk and

Donald McDonald was installed as interim coach. It was sad to see Schwabby go – he'd been like a father figure to me in many ways and we'd catch up every Monday to talk about life – but for some reason things hadn't clicked that year for us as a team.

McDonald's first act was to organise an old-fashioned Monday bonding session, which involved a trip to a quiet pub in the country. I certainly liked the idea but unfortunately it didn't work, with Melbourne beating us by seven goals the next week.

We did manage to win a couple of games before the final home-and-away match of the season, which was in Geelong. I had a stroke of genius and arranged for a bus to take us to the game and back. Normally we'd drive our own cars down there, but because it was the end of the year I thought it would be a perfect way to let us drown our sorrows after a tough season. The emergencies for the game were asked to make sure the eskies were full of ice and beers for the trip home.

Everything was looking good until McDonald got wind of my idea. In response, he got the club to hire another bus and made it compulsory for all players to travel in it. There would be no alcohol on the way home. 'And if you guys are serious about your football, you also won't drink at the function back at the social club,' McDonald said.

The social club was always a good starting point for a night out, but the hierarchy clearly had their noses out of joint after our disappointing season, so we stayed on the soft drinks. Ironically, McDonald was on the beers. He clearly had a few too many, as the next day, in the review of our final game, all he served up were replays of Geelong's goals. It was a comical end to a season that we all wanted to forget.

I managed to earn myself a new contract, signing a three-year extension. The extra cash assisted in my first real-estate purchase, a house in Glen Iris.

One other thing: Chris Judd won the Brownlow Medal.

'Who the hell is he?'

Peter 'Spida' Everitt was summing up the feelings of the boys as we digested the news of the appointment of our new coach, Alastair Clarkson.

Spida had come across from St Kilda the previous season and was our best player in 2004; his tap work as a ruckman was first class. He was also very much a lad who enjoyed a laugh and a beer, and I'd gravitated to him.

'Mate, he was one of your assistants at St Kilda,' one of the boys told Spida, which had us all in stitches.

Clarkson was certainly a left-field candidate; he hadn't been mentioned in the weeks after Schwabby's departure. He'd been an assistant coach at Port Adelaide, who'd just won the flag, and had played for North Melbourne and Melbourne, although I didn't remember his work. Dad reminded me that Clarkson had addressed the Victorian under-12 primary school team, but my memory of that was also hazy.

The off-season had involved a footy trip to Bali and then I'd planned to accompany Spida and another teammate, Danny Jacobs, to Amsterdam and on to the Oktoberfest in Germany. We never made it.

Danny fell asleep for several hours lying by the pool in Bali and got severely sunburnt, which forced him to abandon the rest of the trip and head home. Spida and I made it to Amsterdam, but after a few days we ran out of steam and headed home early. It was probably a good idea, because with a new coach coming in there was a need to impress. The overseas trip had added a few points to my skinnies, but at least I was injury-free when the new regime arrived.

Clarkson – or Clarko, as he became known – was a small unit. The mail was that he'd been a tough scrapper as a player, and you could instantly see that; he had that annoying back-pocket look about him. From early on, it was obvious he had a certain way of doing things and wouldn't deviate from it. He brought with him from Port a fitness coach, Andrew Russell, who, like the coach, didn't mince his words. Their aim was specific: to change the culture of the football club.

Russell's early observations were that in terms of preparation we were the most unprofessional team he'd come across. That wasn't going to change overnight, but there was certainly an edge to how we approached training over the summer. I actually didn't mind it – the one thing I loved doing was training. I'd always been that way, and given that I'd been limited in what I could do over the previous couple of years, I enjoyed the new hardline approach. The off-the-field preparation was a completely different story.

Clarko's first major statement was the appointment of Vandenberg as captain. Crawford had been in the job for the previous six years. He was our best player and had won the Brownlow Medal in 1999 (his first year as captain) and was also a four-time best-and-fairest winner. Crawf was someone who led by example on the field and was an unbelievable trainer, who prepared himself better than anyone I'd ever seen. If we were doing eight sprints in a session, Crawf would do ten. He would do extra every time because his mindset was that he needed to be ahead of everyone else. He was an 'actions more than words' man and expected us to have the same level of professionalism as he did. Clearly most of us didn't.

To enforce change you need a bulldog, and Vanders was Clarko's bulldog. The new coach was all about discipline, and he needed a like-minded leader enforcing his message to the players. Vanders was the perfect man for the job. He was by nature a very disciplined person and wasn't afraid to challenge people or shoot from the hip. If you were out of line, Vanders wouldn't hold back letting you know about it.

There were several other changes to the leadership group. A number of young players were promoted to the group, including me, Sam Mitchell and Tim Clarke. Joel Smith was Vanders' vice-captain, and Crawf remained in the leadership group with Spida and Chance Bateman.

The appointment forced me to become engaged in the day-to-day running of the football club, when previously all I'd thought about was turning up to training, playing on the weekend and going out for a few beers after the game. I'd never looked into why we did certain things or how training was structured. As part of the leadership group, we dealt with this sort of stuff on a daily basis, and it started to open my eyes.

But if you're talking about eye-opening experiences, nothing comes close to Clarko's choice of pre-season camp: the famous Kokoda Track. Most of us knew nothing about it when it was first mentioned. Our preparation involved reading a book about what had happened there in World War II, and, three times a week, going for two-hour marches around Melbourne wearing a full backpack. That part I was able to tick off, but the book was more of a struggle.

However, nothing could have prepared us for the enormity of what we experienced. It was physically demanding. For five days, we hiked for 12 hours a day in 33-degree heat and 95 per cent humidity. The amount of sweat that came out of our bodies was exceptional – guys were drinking up to 12 litres of water on the hike without requiring a toilet stop as the water just evaporated in sweat. We were allocated basic rations, which included nuts, instant soup, pasta, noodles, canned fruit and protein bars.

The mental side was also very challenging. The lack of sleep and lack of food combined with the obstacles placed in our way really tested us.

Each day we would be faced with different challenges on top of just navigating the steep trail, which was hard enough in itself. We had to carry logs and stretchers with 60-kilo sandbags on them to replicate the weight the soldiers had carried 60 years earlier.

For Clarko, the challenge was to see who would fold, who would be selfish and who would help their teammates.

A brilliant example of the latter was produced by Trent Croad. Some of the steps we had to navigate were three-quarters of a metre high and we were all carrying a 20-kilo backpack and a 20-kilo sandbag. Harry Miller was a small indigenous kid and he was almost falling backwards as he tried to get up the steps. Croady intervened, took Harry's sandbag off him, connected it to his own and then helped push his teammate up the steps.

That was exactly the type of leadership Clarko wanted to see.

Some of the stories of what the Australian soldiers did on the trail just to save their mates and fight for the freedom of our country were extraordinary. Significant moments for us included singing the Australian national anthem at Mission Ridge, where 72 Australians had died, and a visit to the Port Moresby War Cemetery, where there were 3776 graves, many unmarked.

In terms of a bonding exercise, it was Clarko's first stroke of genius. We went into the trip as a loose collection of new and old players with a new coach; we returned different people.

There are four signs or pillars along the track commemorating the brotherhood of the Australian soldiers and the Papua New Guinea military, who came together to fight off the Japanese. The signs say 'courage', 'endurance', 'mateship' and 'sacrifice'. The soldiers lived by those principles, and the new coach wanted us to follow suit.

The Kokoda experience was a key part of Clarko's messaging for the season. He was forever bringing up the four pillars. If someone stepped out of line, the group was punished.

On one occasion, early in his reign, Clarko called for a 6 a.m. swim in Port Phillip Bay because someone had been late for training. Young defender Zac Dawson rocked up late to the beach. Nothing was said initially as we waded through the icy water, but when we finished, Clarko calmly said, 'Righto, boys. Zac was late so we're down here again tomorrow – this time at 5 a.m.'

It was his way of teaching us that if you behave like an individual and just look after yourself, you're going to hurt everyone. It was one in, all in, and there was nothing like having to go for a swim at the crack of dawn to ram that point home.

There was certainly a new look and feel to the Hawthorn of 2005. We'd managed to have three picks in the top seven at the draft and had acquired three pretty impressive types. Jarryd Roughead was a tall, red-haired country boy from Gippsland who we got at No.2, and at No.5 we selected a kid from Perth named Lance Franklin. The mail was that 'Buddy' was a special talent, and he certainly showed a few tricks on the training track. The other interesting draftee, at No.7, was Jordan Lewis, a hard nut from Warrnambool.

After a couple of losses to start the season, we renewed acquaintances with Essendon in Round 3. It was the first time we'd crossed paths since the infamous 'line in the sand' game, and it's fair to say there was a bit of spring in our new captain's step. The combination of what had happened the previous year, the impact of Clarko and our new players meant we weren't overawed by the Bombers this time, and we showed that in the second half. By half-time we'd only kicked one goal and were down by 30 points, but a six-goal third quarter got us back to within a kick.

It was some of the best football we'd played, and I found myself in the middle of it almost by accident. I floated across half-back until the second quarter, when Mitch went down injured. I was his replacement in the midfield. I'd been bugging the coaches to give me a go on the ball, but in previous years I hadn't been physically ready. This year I'd put the kilometres in the legs, which at least gave me a chance to put my hand up.

I loved every minute of it. Being constantly around the ball gave me a new sense of freedom, and when I started to get a hold of it a few times, something clicked inside. Unfortunately we got beaten by two points, but it wasn't just the dynamics of the Essendon–Hawthorn rivalry that changed that day: I became a different player. I finished with 25 possessions, which was a personal best – I'd had 20 or more possessions only five times in the previous three seasons.

Three weeks later I had 32 disposals against Carlton, which was the start of a five-game stretch where I had more than 30 possessions each week. This midfield caper was a bit of fun, and it's amazing what confidence can do in football.

The only drawback to the new life I was leading was that we only managed to win three games in the first half of the season. We needed a circuit-breaker, and I was more than happy to provide it in the form of my 21st-birthday celebrations. The draw was kind to me – we played Port Adelaide in Adelaide on the Friday night two days after my birthday – which meant the rest of the weekend was free to indulge ourselves – and then we didn't have a game the following weekend because of the mid-season break. So I hired out a bar in Lygon Street, Carlton, for the party on the Saturday night.

I figured I should do the right thing and run it past the coach, and went with the understatement of the year, saying there might be some beers involved. 'Of course. No dramas with any of that,' Clarko said. 'My only stipulation is that you present on Monday morning.'

The party was big, as expected. A number of speeches were made, including one by Dan Elstone, who came over from Adelaide where he was now playing footy. There was a late change, with Spida not able to come and arranging for John Barker to do his speech instead. While I obviously got on well with Barks, he hadn't been given a lot of notice and he actually told Lauren he had nothing good to offer in his speech and asked whether he could make something up. He eventually produced a story about a footy trip to Thailand.

I wasn't offering much the following morning, but I'd organised a Sunday session at a pub in Hawthorn. Spida was particularly keen and saw it as his way of making up for being a no-show at the main event. I could have done without it but I had a few mates from Colac staying in the city for it, so I pulled myself together and made an appearance. I was clearly just topping up from the night before and was home by 7 p.m., where the beers still flowed and

Spida and my uncles had settled in for the evening. I barely got through one before passing out.

The next thing I remembered was Richie Vandenberg's face looking down at me. For a few seconds I didn't realise where I was. Next to me on the bed was my niece, who was watching *The Simpsons* on TV. It was very bright in the room, which gave me a bad feeling.

'What are you doing?' Vanders asked.

I was trying to adjust my eyes. 'What do you mean?'

'We had weights at 9 a.m. It's nearly 11.'

My heart sank. I'd seen Clarko go off a couple of times, and he could be a very angry little man. The only thing he'd asked of me was to make sure I turned up on Monday morning. A spray was definitely coming my way.

As I bolted from the bed, Vanders explained that if I made it to the next skills session, which started shortly, then I would have a chance to atone a little bit.

I was trying to figure out what had happened. There was no sign of Spida – just some of Lauren's family, who I rushed past as I headed to the door. Many thoughts ran through my head as I tried to sneak into the club without being noticed. I was very sheepish and my mood didn't improve when Andrew 'Jack' Russell called everyone into the locker room.

'Hodgey, you're a bloody disgrace,' was his opening line.

I knew Jack had been concerned about my approach since he'd arrived at the football club, and it had been a constant issue between us.

'What the hell are you doing? Who do you think you are? You're the most unprofessional footballer I've ever seen. You're lazy, you don't train hard enough, and your body is never going to get right if you continue down this path.'

I sat there and stared at him, a bit in shock, but I knew nothing would be gained by snapping back. While the message was about me, I knew a part of it was aimed at the whole group.

'Do you want to have the respect of this group?' Jack continued. 'Because right now I don't respect the way you go about it, and these blokes don't either.'

It was a good spray. I felt like I'd done ten rounds in the ring with Mike Tyson by the time Clarko called me in.

There was one bonus in the meeting with Clarko: I had a companion. Campbell Brown had got himself into trouble at a 7-Eleven after the party by abusing the staff because the store's ATM didn't work. They'd called the police and Browny had found himself in the back of a divvy van.

Clarko actually seemed calm when we sat down in front of him. 'Look, boys, you're both going back to Box Hill,' he said. 'Hodgey, the punishment doesn't fit the crime, but you made a mistake and we're trying to set a standard at this club now – a standard for what we are about and where we want to go as a club. You're going to have to cop it.'

I was pissed off, but it was hard to argue with the coach. He gave both of us the option of actually not playing in the VFL if we didn't want to – the punishment was more about missing out on an AFL game than having to serve our penance in the VFL.

'My shoulder's a bit sore,' Browny said, but I was happy to go down there and do my time. I said, 'I'll play.'

That provoked a dirty look from Browny – but it was nothing like the one Clarko gave both of us in the rooms at Docklands Stadium two weeks later.

Geelong had touched us up to the tune of 55 points. Browny and I had actually watched it in the coach's box but had escaped before the final siren to avoid Clarko. We were planning an early exit from the rooms when Clarko trapped us. He had an evil eye that was seriously scary and rendered you powerless. You were virtually frozen to the spot, because if you responded in any way, he'd jump down your throat. When he was like that, the one thing you didn't want to do was engage in any sort of conversation. He was making sure that a tough lesson had been learnt. Things were starting to click on the field – maybe it was time for the penny to drop off it.

I'd discovered by chance a way to limit my social activities: playing in the midfield. I was legitimately stuffed after every game, and the energy that had been there in my first couple of years, pushing me through to 4 or 5 a.m. on a Sunday morning, just wasn't there any more. The couch was as far as I got, and if I did catch up with friends, midnight was the absolute latest I'd stay up. The midfield gig was having an impact.

We lost seven in a row midway through the season, which was as much about our lack of experience as anything. Clarko had stripped back the list and moved on a lot of senior players, so we were starting from scratch and it was going to be a bumpy ride for a while.

A good high came in Round 20 against our arch rival, Essendon. Things again got heated, and Browny was reported twice for striking Bombers full-forward Matthew Lloyd. They'd slipped down the ladder, with their dynasty on the wane, and we took great delight in beating them to register our fifth win of the season. We almost beat Richmond the following week, going down by just four points, but then Sydney, who were third on the ladder, got hold of us in the final round and won by nine goals.

*

The off-season started with something new: invitations. My presence was required at the All Australian dinner and the Brownlow Medal count. There had been a bit of talk about the Brownlow, and earlier in the season a few of my Colac mates had invested in me winning at 500/1, so they were pumping up my chances. I didn't share their optimism – there were plenty of players who'd had an amazing season, particularly over at West Coast, who had dominated all year.

I also wasn't expecting much at the All Australian function, so I was pleasantly surprised when my name was read out on the half-back flank. As I made my way to the front, my stats for the season were read out, including having the second-most disposals in the whole competition. Next to me on stage was my Hawthorn teammate Trent Croad, and we were soon joined by Spida Everitt, who'd been named in the forward pocket as the back-up ruckman to West Coast's Dean Cox.

Three players from a side that had finished down the bottom half of the ladder in the team of the year was an outstanding effort, and it was hotly debated in the media the following day.

There were a couple of other familiar faces on stage when the final 22 was revealed. Luke Ball was named as ruck-rover and another Saint, Nick Dal Santo, who I'd been in representative basketball squads with as a junior, was on the wing. The irony for Bally and I was that there was no C. Judd – although he already had an All Australian jumper, a Brownlow Medal and a best-and-fairest award from the previous season.

The Brownlow lead-up was interesting and eye-opening. The focus was on the fashion, but not what Lauren would be wearing. It was more about whether I would go with the traditional black tie or not. I didn't think anyone would care what I looked like, but suit retailers were keen to get their name up in lights by being linked to players. There was even a photo shoot for the media, with my final decision being a coloured tie and, controversially, bone rather than black shoes. Given that my teammates had for years hung it on me for wearing moccasins to training, they took great delight in seeing me attempt to be a fashion trendsetter.

It was a perfect night to let the hair down, and I didn't need much encouragement. We enjoyed a couple of drinks leading up to the start of the count. I was very relaxed about it all and thought about how nervous you would be if you were one of the favourites and had to sit through three hours of vote counting, limiting your alcohol intake in case you had to get up and make a speech.

From Round 3 onwards I popped up fairly regularly and managed a couple of three-vote performances. In the end I came in with 15 votes, two ahead of Spida and ironically the same number as Juddy, who was ineligible because of a suspension. West Coast, who were playing Sydney in the Grand Final, got the quinella, with Ben Cousins winning with 20 votes from Daniel Kerr on 19.

A couple of weeks later the suit was out again for Hawthorn's best-and-fairest dinner. I was required to make a speech this time, when I won the Peter Crimmins Medal with 173 votes from Spida and Crawf.

While it capped off a great season personally and may have silenced the great draft debate for a little while, individual medals didn't do it for me. You played footy for team success, and right now we were a long way from that. Give me a best-and-fairest medal in a premiership year and then you'd see some excitement.

My season still wasn't finished, as I'd been selected to play for Australia against Ireland in the International Rules Series. The team was being coached by Essendon legend Kevin Sheedy, and for the first time the selection hadn't been based around the All Australian team. The previous year Ireland had won easily, and it was decided to select an Australian team more suited to the hybrid game. This meant pace, pace and more pace.

I didn't bring that to the table, but as I'd already played the format as a junior, I was able to slot in nicely in a team led by co-captains Chris Johnson and Andrew McLeod. Also included was my former Geelong Falcons teammate Amon Buchanan, who'd just played in the premiership with Sydney.

The first test was in Perth and our new-look side blitzed them, scoring 100 points, which had never been done in the competition. A week later we were back in Melbourne at Docklands and, as tended to be the case with these games, tempers flared. Johnno was sent off early after taking on a couple of Irishmen, and Croady joined him in the third quarter. I found myself in a few scuffles, but the end result was another comfortable victory.

It was a fitting way to end what had been a massive year. I'd come far in a short period, but it was only the start of a long journey. Regardless of what I'd achieved personally, there was only one fact that really mattered – we'd finished 14th.

5

NOT ON MY WATCH

Something was happening. As I walked off Kardinia Park, I was feeling something I hadn't felt in a long time: we were a good team. We could be a very good team.

It was a weird feeling because it was so foreign – but I'd just had one of my more enjoyable afternoons in a Hawthorn jumper.

We'd travelled down to Geelong to play a team considered to be one of the 2006 flag favourites. In Round 1 we'd beaten Fremantle in Launceston, but we'd struggled the following week against Collingwood. This game against Geelong was going to provide us with a guide as to where we were at in the big picture.

And the answer was exciting. For the first time I could see the pillars in place. Plus, my attitude was also changing. Like every young player, in my first three years it had been about getting as many possessions as I could. That was my mindset because I thought it was the best way to measure success. The first thing you'd do on a Monday was get the paper, look up how many touches you'd got and compare your figure with others, and then celebrate if you'd made it into the best players. Now, I was thinking about the team.

We came out with a plan against Geelong and executed it to perfection, kicking nine goals to two in the second half to win by 52 points. We followed that game with wins over Carlton and Essendon, although we only beat the Bombers by a point after a late Mark Williams goal. After the opening five rounds we were sitting fifth on the ladder. It was new territory, and it continued our theme for the year.

We'd left our spiritual home of Glenferrie and moved to Waverley Park. While there was a lot of history and mystique linked to our traditional home, the facilities weren't up to the standards of the modern era and a plan had been hatched to resurrect the old Waverley Park ground as our training base.

Waverley had been the AFL's second main venue for almost 30 years and had hosted a Grand Final in 1991, which the Hawks won. The last official game out there had been in 1999, after which the AFL sold the site to developers who planned to build a housing estate. Most of the stadium had been demolished, except for the main members stand, before the decision was made to turn it into our headquarters.

The result was a state-of-the-art training facility and an excellent training ground. The only issues were that it was a 20-minute drive out of town on the South Eastern Freeway, and that it had a reputation as being the coldest and wettest place in Melbourne.

These issues were the furthest thing from our minds as we enjoyed our new status as the 'bolter' of the 2006 season.

Unfortunately, that status was short-lived – we won just one of our next 13 games.

It's hard to explain how that can happen. A young team loses confidence and everything just snowballs. You get caught in a trap of thinking 'Next week will be different' but then it doesn't happen and the hope moves to the following week. It was a vicious cycle that we couldn't break.

The club did the right thing and re-signed Clarko midway through the year, which killed off any speculation about his future. That was the last thing we needed. Through all the gloom we'd found a couple of players, with Grant Birchall slotting in nicely at half-back and Brent Guerra, who'd played at St Kilda and Port Adelaide, adding a strong body and much-needed experience. Brad Sewell, who'd started on the rookie list, was enjoying a break-out season through the midfield.

Finally, we found a way to stop the bleeding. A Round 19 win over Carlton kick-started an undefeated run to the end of the season. The irony of the four-match winning streak was that it finished with Geelong, the team who'd given us all false hope four months earlier. We again smashed the Cats, with Williams kicking eight goals in the 61-point victory. The highlight was the mobbing of John Barker when he kicked his final goal in AFL football; he'd already announced his retirement.

I played all 22 games but it was a struggle – a knuckle injury early in the season caused ongoing problems and an ankle injury late in the year saw me move from the midfield to half-back. Through it all, I managed to have a decent season, finishing second in the best-and-fairest behind Sam Mitchell and making the initial squad of 40 for the All Australian team. It had been a consistent year, but my patience was starting to wear thin. On top of my old mate

Amon Buchanan playing in a premiership, now Juddy had also won a flag – and been captain. Bally had played finals the previous three years and was also now captain of his football club.

At least I was getting closer in both areas. In the past three years we'd gone 15th, 14th and 11th, and I was promoted to co-vice-captain for 2007 alongside Mitch. There had also been a significant shift in the dynamics of the team and particularly for me personally. Spida, who'd been a major influence on me (some would say in a distracting way), had departed. He hadn't seen eye to eye with Clarko for most of the season. There was no doubt he was the best tap ruckman in the competition, in fact by a long stretch – whatever spot you nominated, he'd put it on your chest every time. But there were a couple of incidents off the field that ruffled some feathers among the playing group.

Spida would also do certain things that made you feel like he's the best teammate in the world. For example, he came down to Colac to help Dad out by speaking at the Colac Sportsman's Club and did it all for free.

It had all come to a head in the last month of the season, with Spida called in to front the leadership group. The question was thrown at him, 'Do you want to be at the footy club or not? If you don't want to be, then we're happy for you to leave.' Spida seemed taken aback that we'd even asked, and was adamant he wanted to stay.

Two weeks later he asked for a trade to Sydney.

Football seasons are all about routine. It's very hard to stop, take a breath and reflect. Each week keeps rolling into the next.

But in the lead-up to my 100th game in Round 12, 2007, moments of reflection were almost forced upon me because of the media interviews that were part of the deal around such milestones.

It wasn't in my personality to look back, and I certainly didn't want to see those famous photos of me sitting on a sand dune next to Juddy and Bally when we got drafted. Those pictures always seemed to get a run and they shocked me every time I looked at them. I was now a completely different person and, thankfully, I'd shed the puppy fat. I liked to live in the now and as far as I was concerned, coming into my 100th game my thoughts were simple: for the first time in my career at Hawthorn we had been competitive in every game of the season so far, and at the midway point we were in the eight. In fact, we were sitting third, with seven wins and four losses.

The Colac contingent was big for the milestone, which was on a Friday night at Docklands against Carlton. It happened to be my 23rd birthday and I was also the acting captain for the game – Vanders had been struggling with hamstring issues all season and Mitch and I were alternating in the role. It was fitting in a way, given my enjoyment of any sort of celebration, that the game turned into a party as we ran all over the Blues. The boys certainly looked after me – I kicked four goals and had 29 touches in the 100-point victory.

Two months later, the celebrations were on hold. With three rounds to go we found ourselves sitting second on the ladder. We were consistently playing at a high level, and the scenario heading into the Round 20 clash with Port Adelaide in Launceston, which was now our second home where we played four games each year, was simple. If we won, we were virtually assured of finishing in the top four and getting a guaranteed double chance in the finals.

Things were looking good with less than two minutes remaining and our lead at seven points. Then Port's Daniel Motlop kicked a goal out of nowhere with 43 seconds left on the clock. We flooded back to clog up their forward line, but they engineered the centre clearance and somehow got the ball to Brett Ebert. He was the last person I wanted having a set shot – every time I'd watched him play he never seemed to miss. He didn't this time either.

The loss was gut-wrenching in the circumstances. In the space of a couple of minutes, our status had gone from top four guaranteed to having to win at least one of our final two games to ensure we finished in the eight.

Thankfully, we ticked that off comprehensively the following week by pumping the Western Bulldogs by 84 points. The wind was taken out of our sails a bit in the final game of the season, though. A trip to Sydney to line up against our former teammate Spida Everitt didn't go according to plan, with the seventh-placed Swans doing a number on us to the tune of 12 goals.

We thankfully avoided a rematch a week later, as we finished fifth and played eighth-placed Adelaide at Docklands in the elimination final. Our recent history with the Crows wasn't great: we'd had a horror evening in Adelaide in Round 14 when they flogged us by 71 points. They clearly enjoyed playing us, because by quarter-time in the elimination final they'd kicked seven goals to four. Things got worse four minutes into the second quarter – I was crunched as I kicked the ball, with an Adelaide player falling across my left knee. The pain was immediate and extreme. I couldn't walk and needed two trainers to help me off the ground. The doctor didn't look too optimistic as he pushed and pulled on the knee, but I hadn't waited all this time to play finals for this to happen.

'Let's just go out there and see how it goes,' were my instructions, and ten minutes later I limped back on. The Crows lead had blown out to 31 points.

By half-time we'd got it back to a couple of goals, but we made up no ground in the third quarter as each team scored just two goals. The pressure was intense and it was obvious early in the final quarter that this elimination final was going down to the wire.

One of the main reasons we'd improved this season was on the back of the emergence of Jarryd Roughead and Lance Franklin in the two key forward posts. They were both in their third year and everything had clicked, particularly for Buddy. He was an amazing athlete at 199 cm and 100 kilos, with an incredible engine and unbelievable skills – all of which meant he was the type of player the competition hadn't really seen before. He'd had flashes of brilliance in 2006 with a couple of bags of six goals, but he'd also had a few off-field issues.

Buddy was no saint – he liked a good time, and had been suspended for breaking team rules by going out when he was sidelined with a foot injury. He was a risk-taker, and in big games you wanted guys with that mindset. Sometimes the ones who bent the rules off the field were the ones who were ballsy enough to break structures in a game, and the beauty of Buddy was that he had the ability to pull that off. While he was still on a learning curve, he'd clearly gone up a level – highlighted by a nine-goal haul against Essendon earlier in the season.

Roughy was a lot more laid-back and had taken a bit longer than Buddy to grasp AFL football. He was a good country lad who also didn't mind a beer. While he didn't have the freakiness of Buddy, he was mobile for his size and a lovely left-foot kick.

Or so I thought.

With a couple of minutes remaining in the elimination final, we were trailing by four points when Roughy marked on the lead 40 metres out. He'd already kicked three goals but had hit the post just a few moments ago.

He missed again. The Crows went short with the kick-in to midfielder Scott Thompson, who marked close to the boundary line in the back pocket. He was rushed after being called to play-on and went long towards the boundary line on the wing. Fortunately for us it drifted out on the full. Crawf took the free kick and went short inside to my old housemate, Rick Ladson. He had a beautiful left foot on him and managed to find a leading Franklin in among three Crows.

Buddy had already kicked six goals for the afternoon. This shot was from 50 metres out on the half-forward flank, and it never looked like missing. If anyone was made for the big moment, it was Buddy.

After the ball was trapped inside the centre square at the next bounce, the siren sounded while the umpire was reloading. The noise of the crowd was deafening as we jumped all over each other in the middle of the ground. Talk about a memorable finals debut.

Unfortunately, post-game adrenaline only lasts so long. When it disappeared, the reality of my banged-up knee hit home. By Tuesday I was able to shuffle around for a few laps, doing my best impersonation of one of Colac's famous products, the gumboot-wearing, ultra-distance runner Cliff Young. There was no way I was going to miss our semifinal match-up with the Kangaroos. That was never a consideration, and by the end of the week I was able to get through a light training session.

Given the euphoria of the Crows win, our confidence was high. Maybe too high.

The Kangaroos had been smacked by 106 points by Geelong in the first qualifying final, so we liked our chances. However, it was obvious early on that the Roos had arrived with the aim of annoying the hell out of us. Renowned tagger Brady Rawlings had been assigned to shadow me, which I wasn't thrilled about, and my displeasure grew as the game unfolded. I struggled even to get a kick. I couldn't get near it, and when I did, Rawlings was all over me. I was taught a massive lesson that finals football was different. Compared to the previous five months, it was a step up in all facets of the game.

While I was fighting my own battle, the side was having similar trouble breaking free. We managed only six goals to three-quarter time, and the Roos' lead was 17. Buddy came to life in the first minute of the final quarter to kick his third goal, but that was as close as we got. The margin was 33 points in the end, and a very disappointing way for our captain to finish his career. Vanders had been plagued by injury all season and had only got his body right in the previous six weeks. He'd decided before the finals that he'd come to the end of the road.

The postscript to the loss kept getting uglier. I had to front the tribunal after being booked for striking Rawlings and copped a one-game suspension, which meant I would miss the 2008 opener. Crawf also got reported and was whacked with a three-match suspension, and Jordan Lewis received a two-match ban.

Normally I welcomed the end of the season with open arms, but this time something wasn't right. I couldn't shake what had happened against the Kangaroos and found myself thinking about how I could atone for the semifinal performance.

It turned out I wasn't the only one.

*

'There have never been co-captains at the Hawthorn Football Club, and we're certainly not going to start on my watch.' Jeff Kennett was not one to mince words, and the former Victorian Premier was clearly not impressed with our submission. 'You three need to go into that room – you've got two minutes to decide who is going to be captain of this football club.'

The president was talking to Clarko, Mitch and me. We'd just presented a submission to the board about a player vote that had come up with a co-captaincy model to replace Vanders.

Earlier, ten players had met at Mitch's house and the vote had been split 5–5. This result was passed on to Clarko, who agreed to put our submission to the board recommending co-captains. But Jeff wasn't having a bar of it.

I knew we wouldn't need two minutes – I wasn't ready for the job. Mitch was the ultimate professional on and off the field, and he was what the team needed. He was 25 going on 40, while I was 23, still maturing and coming to terms with what I needed to do to play consistent AFL football. I had no doubt I could do my job on the field, but I still had some rough edges when it came to off-field behaviour.

On more than a few occasions I'd had to apologise to Vanders at recovery sessions. Even though my professionalism was on the improve, there had been times when I didn't adhere to the new standards at the football club.

Mitch was the perfect man to continue that work: he'd been living those standards from the moment he walked into the place. Mitch wasn't drafted from the TAC Cup, and had to ply his trade with Box Hill before getting a look-in. He was fastidious about his diet and training, and had followed Crawf everywhere he went because he wanted to learn from the best. My time would come.

The moment we entered the room I revealed my thoughts. 'We don't need to have a discussion. I reckon Mitch should do the job.'

Clarko nodded and turned to Mitch. 'Are you prepared to do it?'

He didn't need any thinking music. 'Yep.'

And with that, Hawthorn had its new captain.

6

DON'T BE A HERO

Disappointment drives people. Often, it's the best motivator.

This certainly applies to me.

It was obvious after the first week of pre-season training that we'd collectively come back in better shape than we had been in previously. The little things made a big difference, like going for that extra run you hadn't done in other years, or being more selective about your nights out. There was an expectation now about the pre-season. It wasn't fear – although you didn't want to be on the end of a spray from Jack or Clarko – but more a sense of responsibility for not letting your mates down. This was a new thing in my time at Hawthorn.

Training had a purpose about it, and it wasn't just about getting kilometres in the legs. Clarko had a new game plan he wanted to implement. It wasn't completely unfamiliar: we'd had a dabble with some of the new strategies in the 2007 pre-season, but these had failed miserably. Clarko and assistant coach David Rath had since refined the plan and wanted it to be our edge over the rest of the competition.

Clarko was always on the lookout for ways of getting ahead, travelling overseas to talk to people in other sports to see if any of their tactics could work in the AFL. He'd spent time at English soccer clubs, been to the States to visit NFL and NBA teams, and tapped into rugby organisations.

The end result was a system that would famously become known as 'Clarko's cluster'. It was a combination of a basketball zone and soccer formation, probably best described as a rolling zone. The theory was that if there was a great density of players in the centre corridor, then the likelihood of the opposition getting through was minimal – if one of our players didn't get them, there would be plenty of others who could.

Usually this would force the opposition to stay on the wings, and the zone would move over accordingly to suffocate there. Then, when the ball was turned over because of the pressure, the numbers in the cluster meant we suddenly had plenty of options – usually four on one side, four on the other, and two out the back to springboard an attack.

At stoppages, the plan was to funnel the ball out the back and then use the pace and skills of players like Chance Bateman, Michael Osborne, Crawford and Ladson to surge forward. Given our excellent inside midfielders, including Mitch, Sewell and Lewis, we knew we were a good chance to win the ball at the coalface more often than not.

The other bonus of the rolling zone was that it left our forward line open, which, with the athletic attributes of Buddy and Roughy and the evasiveness of sharpshooter Mark Williams, played into our hands.

Getting 22 players on the same wavelength doesn't happen overnight. Nailing down the cluster involved endless video sessions and hours and hours of match simulation on the training track. It was a long process but in Clarko's mind it was the tactic required to beat Geelong. The Cats had emerged in 2007 with a new free-flowing style focused on attacking through the centre corridor. It had revolutionised the competition and they rode it all the way to a stunning Grand Final victory over Port Adelaide by a record margin of 119 points.

There had been another significant development over the pre-season: I was going to be a father.

We'd found out just before Christmas that Lauren was expecting, with the baby due in July. And it was a double celebration, as I'd managed to convince her to marry me after a romantic evening at Crown Towers.

As part of this new set of circumstances in my life, I made another big decision, one that shocked my teammates more than the fact I was becoming a husband and father – I gave up alcohol. I wanted to support Lauren through her pregnancy and obviously she wasn't allowed to have a drink. So I wouldn't either.

I lasted ten weeks.

It wasn't actually my decision to break the vow – I was just following the orders of my captain. The problem with my well-intentioned stance was that when I was off the grog I couldn't get a kick. I struggled in the pre-season and then, after missing Round 1 because of the suspension out of the previous year's final, it was the same in the regular season. I couldn't get near it and as a consequence wasn't exactly a beacon of happiness.

After the Round 5 game against Brisbane at the Gabba, which we won to keep our unbeaten streak alive, Mitch pulled me aside. 'Look, you're not getting a kick, you're grumpy, you're a prick to be around . . . just go and have a couple of beers,' he said.

I was pretty surprised, mainly because this was coming from Mitch, who lived his life with alcohol bans. He wouldn't have a drink from New Year's Day to the last game of the season, and never missed a beat. I would try it for a couple of months and fall apart.

We got back from the game in Queensland on the Sunday morning and I was keen to follow the skipper's advice, so I roped in Brent Guerra as part of the exercise. Seven days later at the MCG, I collected 31 possessions against Richmond in easily my best game of the season.

The irony wasn't lost on anyone. For years, Vanders and Mitch had been on me about getting off the grog and improving my professionalism. They would always warn me about drinking on a Sunday and then rocking up hungover to Monday recovery, which set a horrible example for the younger players. Yet now I was being ordered to do just that.

My new-found happiness was short-lived. In Round 7 against Collingwood I pinged a hamstring early in the third quarter. I'd been driving the ball long into our forward line when my right hamstring gave way. I ended up missing three games, including our first loss of the season, in Round 10 against the Western Bulldogs.

What was even more disappointing was that I missed out on wearing the Big V jumper in the AFL's Hall of Fame Tribute Match. I'd been selected for Victoria in the one-off game at the MCG against the 'Dream Team', which was made up of star players who were born in other states.

One thing I timed perfectly to coincide with my stint on the side-lines was having my appendix removed. The lead-up was a comical turn of events that my wife hasn't ever been able to live down.

I started to feel crook the night before Lauren's final day at work. The baby was due in a couple of months' time and she was finishing up at Jeanswest, where she'd been working as a shop assistant. Given that her back was hurting all the time and she was permanently uncomfortable, I didn't get much sympathy about my sore stomach.

'Get over it,' she said.

I made dinner, which was a rarity, and even gave her a massage despite my own discomfort, which I was now trying to hide. The pain was even worse the following morning.

'Go to training and see how it feels,' was my wife's advice.

As soon as I arrived at the club I sought out the doctor, who immediately told me to get back in my car and go to hospital. On the way I rang Lauren to let her know what had happened.

'Hey, you've finished early,' she said.

'Yeah, well, I'm on my way to hospital to have my appendix out.'

I knew she felt bad, but I also knew I would be able to use this series of events to my advantage in the future. If she complained about being sick, I would be able to say, 'This is just like the time you made me cook dinner, give you a massage, go to work and then drive myself to the hospital to have my appendix out.'

During my absence, Clarko's cluster was the talk of the competition, with analysts falling over themselves trying to figure out the new Hawthorn way. On return, I played more forward than in the previous couple of years and managed three bags of three goals in a four-game stretch, which included our first win in 14 years at Football Park, against the Adelaide Crows.

In Round 15 I got an unpleasant surprise courtesy of an old friend. Late in the second quarter of the game against Sydney I was cleaned up. I didn't see the Swans player until it was too late and I was wide open. The hit rattled me and my head was still aching at the half-time break.

'Do you know who got you?' Guerra asked. When I said no, he told me it was Monty. Bloody Amon Buchanan. We had a laugh about it after the game – although he wasn't laughing on the Monday, when the match review panel handed him a four-game suspension.

The approaching birth of Lauren's and my first child was the main focus for the next couple of weeks. There was no way I wasn't going to be alongside her for it, and Hawthorn certainly had no problem with that. The timing for the Round 17 blockbuster against Geelong was going to be tight, though, as the due date was a couple of days before the Friday-night fixture. It was being built up as the game of the season, given that Geelong had only lost one game. They'd taken their dominance to another level and steam-rolled sides – the closest anyone had got in the previous five weeks was Port Adelaide, who'd been smashed by 59 points. We'd slipped up against St Kilda the week before, so it was third versus first at the MCG.

When we got to Friday there was no sign of the baby, so I started my pre-game routine. If there was any change, I would be out of there, but I was assured before I ran out that everything was under control.

Unfortunately, Geelong weren't. The Cats kicked six goals in the opening quarter. Thankfully they were a bit inaccurate in the second term and their half-time lead was just 17 points. Then our system clicked in. We'd created it for this opponent, and in the third term the cluster started to take effect. At the last break we were within four points.

Taking down Geelong would give us a massive psychological edge going into September. This was the moment, but it was going to take something special. These were the times when good players stepped up. I wanted to be the man. All I had to do was execute.

Unfortunately and uncharacteristically, I turned the ball over with poor kicks and poor decision-making three times in a row. The first time it happened was just a silly mistake. The second was stupid again, but alarm bells really started going off in my head when it happened a third time. Everyone makes mistakes, but three in a row like this was totally unusual for me. I was pushing too hard, but we had to win this game.

Then it happened again.

We were down by five points with three minutes remaining when Bateman passed to me on the edge of the centre square. Geelong had flooded back and we needed to switch the ball to the other wing. Stephen Gilham had made space, so I swung onto my right foot quickly to execute the 30-metre pass.

It never got there. Instead, the ball slewed off my boot straight to Ryan Gamble, who was 10 metres away standing in the centre circle and the only Geelong player in the vicinity. I couldn't believe it. Gamble then handballed to Tom Lonergan, who kicked it long into the forward line where Steve Johnson marked and then calmly slotted the match-winner.

I'd lost us the game.

To rub salt into the wound, in the final minute I took a mark in the middle and handballed it off, then got it back, looked up and saw Roughy leading towards the pocket, but my kick landed in the arms of Geelong defender Andrew Mackie.

I was devastated. I didn't know what had come over me. I was shattered after the game but the saving grace was the calendar – it was July and not September. While the 11-point loss stung, there was considerable optimism about our performance. Our game style had stood up, and for the first time Geelong had been vulnerable. They were beatable.

My brooding didn't last long, as at 5.36 p.m. the following day Cooper Jay Hodge came into the world weighing 8 pounds 12 ounces (just under 4 kilos). It was an amazing experience, with both mum and baby coming through like champions.

But it was back to business on the Monday, when I was summoned into Clarko's office. The review of the tape from Friday night wasn't pretty. 'What the hell were you doing, mate?' he asked. 'You don't have to be the hero.'

We spoke about how having an influence on games needed to come naturally by doing the simple things well. When you force something like that, it never works out. Being a leader of the team didn't mean the onus was always on me to come up with something special. Clarko urged me to look at Friday night as a valuable lesson. 'Just play by the book and it will come,' were my coach's wise words.

I'd played across half-back against the Cats and that was where Clarko wanted me to play for the rest of the season. He wanted to create more rebound from defence and figured I was better placed in that quarterback role leading into the finals – as long as I kicked the ball properly.

There was another small hiccup in Round 20 against Richmond. We collectively had an off day, going down by 29 points, and

I managed to get myself suspended again, copping one week for striking Brett Deledio.

The focus of the final game of the home-and-away season was on Buddy Franklin. He'd had an amazing year and was sitting on 98 goals coming into the Round 22 clash with Carlton. It didn't take him long to reach the magical 100 mark – he nailed a set shot in the final two minutes of the first quarter. It set off a stampede at Docklands. As soon as Buddy kicked the goal, security guards ran to protect him from the thousands of fans who swarmed the ground. These included my uncle Jason. He'd told me pre-game that he was coming, and as the players from both teams gathered in the centre circle surrounded by security guards, he lobbed next to me, taking photos with his phone to mark the historic occasion.

Eventually the guards got Buddy off the ground, which was the only way the fans were going to leave and let the game continue. It took at least ten minutes to get everyone off, and the funny thing was that we nearly had to do it again later. Carlton full-forward Brendan Fevola had come into the game sitting on 92 goals and initially didn't look like being a chance. But then he exploded in the second half and kicked seven goals. That left him one short, as the Blues weren't going to play finals. We certainly were, finishing second on the ladder and setting up a qualifying-final showdown with the Western Bulldogs.

Two 70-point-plus wins to finish off the season had us at the top of our game. It was almost an unspoken thing, a player's intuition that the planets were starting to align. We all knew it but didn't want to jinx it by saying it out loud. The team had evolved throughout the season, with some important additions.

Our first pick in the 2007 national draft had been an inspired selection of a kid from Darwin named Cyril Rioli. He was related to the great Maurice Rioli, who had been a star for Richmond throughout the 1980s. Cyril was a lightning-fast forward pocket whose tackling and pressure were standouts. Plus, he had some serious tricks.

We'd also gone for a left-field selection in the draft, selecting former Port Adelaide premiership player Stuart Dew at No.45 on a Clarko hunch. He'd coached Dew at Port and lured him out of retirement to have a second crack at AFL football. He was a fairly solid unit, in the 100-kilo range, and was a classy left-foot kick. The coach was banking on his finals experience being a key factor in the next few weeks.

The development of Buddy and Roughy had been crucial; they'd kicked 168 goals between them during the season. Xavier Ellis, the No.3 pick in the 2005 national draft, had also grown in stature. Left-footer Clinton Young was another youngster who'd started to blossom, and we'd found a good second ruck option in Brent Renouf.

There was another story bubbling behind the scenes that was driving us. Shane Crawford had given everything to the Hawthorn Football Club – he'd been at the club since 1993 and had played his 300th game against Brisbane in Round 19. We didn't know if he was going to play on, but regardless, winning a premiership with him was a motivating force for his younger teammates.

An eight-goal haul from Buddy in the qualifying final helped see off the Bulldogs, who were never in the game after we'd led by 44 points at half-time. The win gave us a week off before St Kilda emerged as our preliminary-final opponent. They'd been whacked by Geelong in the first week but rebounded to handle

Collingwood comfortably in the first semifinal. The Cats played the Western Bulldogs in the Friday-night preliminary and a comfortable 29-point victory meant they progressed to the Grand Final, having lost only one game for the year.

I had a bit of a scare with my foot in the lead-up to the preliminary final. Given what had happened at the start of my career with foot fractures, there were some anxious moments when I went for a scan. To be honest, they would probably have had to chop it off to stop me from playing, but thankfully no major problem was found.

A Saturday night at the MCG in front of 77 000 fans awaited us.

It was a brilliant atmosphere, although I didn't get to enjoy it for very long thanks to St Kilda big man Justin Koschitzke. I went back with the flight of the ball and he cleaned me up big-time with a knee to the ribs. The quarter-time siren sounded shortly after, and as the doctor was looking at me in the huddle I started coughing up blood. Any touch around my ribs brought shooting pain.

But if I could run, I was going back on. After a couple of minutes the doctor agreed.

I was back on the bench midway through the second after I attempted a hard spoil at full stretch and was immediately gripped by pain. I managed to hobble off, desperate to get some air into my lungs.

It felt better as the night went on, helped by the fact that we were in control. At half-time the margin was already 47 points and at the final siren it was 54. The bonus of the evening was that although Buddy had only kicked one goal, Williams stepped up with five and Roughy had four.

The thrill of making the Grand Final was tempered because the ribs were sore – very sore. I also knew I wouldn't be telling anybody.

I didn't have to wait long before the first question about the injury came, with Channel 10 boundary rider Mark Howard bailing me up shortly after the siren. 'It's all right,' I said. 'I've got a bit of padding through there, so it wasn't too bad. We'll be fine.'

The coughing-up of blood was the issue for the medical staff, but they figured it could have just been a burst blood vessel. We agreed there was no point getting a scan because regardless of the outcome I was going to play. That was never in question.

It was easy to find the problem area by touch and feel, and before the main training session of the week the physios devised some padding to assist. I managed to survive a few bumps and that was all I needed.

I wasn't the only one who was the focus of speculation, with full-back Trent Croad managing a foot problem he'd sustained in the qualifying final against the Bulldogs.

In many ways the ribs were probably a good distraction, as they didn't allow me to think too much about the occasion – playing in an AFL Grand Final and fulfilling a lifelong dream. This was all I'd thought about as a kid, and that I could be a premiership player. It was good that I wasn't thinking about any of those things.

One of the biggest traditions of Grand Final week is the Friday parade through the streets of Melbourne. For this we were divided into pairs and each pair perched on the back of a Toyota Hilux. Guerra and I soaked up the beautiful sunshine, although the media were soon alongside, keen to quiz me about the ribs. I'd watched the parade on TV plenty of times and wondered what it must feel like to stand on the steps of the Treasury Building and look out at the sea of people dressed in team colours.

It was as good as I'd imagined.

The best part of the day was when I got home, away from the cameras and crowds. Hanging out with Lauren and Cooper was the ideal way to keep relatively calm. Sleep wasn't a problem, as they slept in the spare room.

My morning ritual was the same as it had been before every game of football since I was a kid: a bowl of Weet-Bix and then some toast, watching an episode of *The Simpsons* on TV.

7

KILLING THE SHARK

'What happens if sharks can't go forward?'

Clarko was standing at the front of the coach's room in the bowels of the MCG. On the whiteboard he'd drawn a picture of a shark. We were less than an hour away from running out onto the ground for the 2008 Grand Final.

I had no idea where the shark story was going, but thankfully we had a couple of experts in the playing ranks. 'They die,' someone said.

'That's right,' Clarko said. 'Sharks need forward momentum. Sharks die if they get caught in a net, because there is no water and oxygen running over their gills. So as soon as they stop, they die.'

This was very interesting stuff, but I wasn't sure what the coach meant.

'What has that got to do with this?' Clarko asked. 'They're trying to come through us like a shark. Well, good luck to them. Good
luck to them in the Grand Final, on the big stage with lots of pressure. They're coming up against the best defensive pressure side in
the competition.'

He started tapping at the whiteboard. 'We have to kill this shark
as early as we possibly can, because if it sits there, it's just going
to die.'

He was saying that the key was to deny Geelong the centre corridor and force them wide. Clarko's cluster had been invented for
this day, and our coach was adamant it was the way to bring down
Geelong. Importantly, his players were also believers.

'Let's kill the fucking shark,' he said. And with that, the meeting
was finished. The coach had done his work. It was now time for the
players to do theirs.

One of the main things Stuart Dew had spoken about during the
week was making sure you took everything in during the warm-up,
and enjoyed it. 'Don't be too nervous and don't be too serious doing
that – save that for the game. Smile, laugh and wave to the crowd –
get that out of your system so when it's time to play, you're ready.'

It was good advice and by the time we ran out through the
banner, the nerves were there but we had a businesslike mindset.

We linked arms for the national anthem; Geelong didn't. While
that mightn't have meant much to most observers, for us it reinforced the sense that we were one. We weren't individuals – we
were a team who were ready to go into battle. I was next to Mitch,
who belted out the anthem, but I wasn't much of a singer so I just
stared straight ahead.

We'd discussed in the lead-up how Geelong might set up.
There was a thought that Max Rooke might be my opponent

as a defensive forward, but he was nowhere to be seen. Instead, Mathew Stokes stood alongside me. I wasn't surprised about the first thing on his mind – and it wasn't a handshake. He tried to land a couple of short jabs to my ribs, but I laughed it off and pushed him away. He clearly hadn't done his research as he was poking the wrong spot.

All you want at the start of a big game like this is an early touch. Feeling the Sherrin in your hands and then making a good decision is all you're thinking about. Luckily, both of those things happened to me inside the opening minute.

Geelong's first forward entry came our way, and Guerra ran across to help the spoil. The ball then sat up perfectly for me and I ran onto it and kicked down the wing to Michael Osborne.

We were away.

I took a mark in front of Stokes a couple of minutes later, which helped to ease the nerves further. It was a fast and physical game early, and by the end of the opening 30 minutes there was only a point between the two sides.

Our task got a little bit harder midway through the second quarter when Croady went down with a foot injury. He was running towards a contest when the stress fracture in his foot gave way. While this was a big blow, we'd become used to Clarko's philosophy that if one soldier goes down, another steps up. Campbell Brown was the one who shuffled back to help the defence.

Normally, most of our focus was on how our own system was working, but there were some things about Geelong that were raising our eyebrows. They did a couple of out-of-character acts, and from their opponent's point of view this was very positive. In the second quarter they blew a number of chances in front of goal.

The moment I started to think we could get them came midway through the second quarter. There was a turnover in the midfield that caught all of us out, and a Paul Chapman soccer off the ground ended up close to ruckman Brad Ottens, who had no one near him. He gathered the ball, took one bounce and ran to within 20 metres. He had two teammates inside him – one already in the goal square by himself and the other running into it, also by himself – but instead of a simple handball over, Ottens took the shot. And missed.

For a team who'd preached all year about goal assists, their mindset had changed. Geelong hadn't been put under this much pressure for a long time and cracks were appearing. As long as we could keep up the pressure, we'd get them. We'd kill the shark.

At half-time our lead was three points, but that was mainly thanks to Geelong wasting chances; they kicked one goal and nine behinds for the quarter. Their worst blunder came after the siren, when Cameron Mooney somehow missed a set shot from 3 metres out.

They were rattled.

Mooney's opponent, Stephen Gilham, was going to have a go at him but I grabbed Gilham and pushed him away. My thinking was that we didn't want to poke the bear. The last thing we wanted was a fired-up Mooney getting on a roll.

It was an intense Clarko who met us in the rooms. He had Mitch in the gun, as he'd been blanketed by Cameron Ling. It was an impressive spray and sent a message to the rest of us that if the captain was copping a bake, then no one was safe.

All year our number-one team rule had been 'Go when it's your turn.' The theory was that a player must sacrifice his body and risk injury if the moment arrived. Clarko was emphasising that a moment would arrive in the next two quarters for each one of us. If we embraced it and followed the team rule, Geelong would have no answers.

'Boys, no matter how tired you are feeling, they will be feeling worse. We have to take this game and screw our guts up and find something extra.'

The early highlight of the third quarter was Mitch responding to his coach by running through Ablett. It was out of character and got him reported, but there was a statement in the skipper's actions and we received it loud and clear.

The game remained in the balance for most of the third quarter until a man who had been recruited for this very moment presented himself. Stuart Dew changed the Grand Final in a five-minute burst.

We were clinging to a slender lead coming into time-on of the third quarter when Dew started to do his business. A long bomb to full-forward was gathered brilliantly by Cyril, who strolled into an open goal. A couple of minutes earlier, the teenager had received a standing ovation after taking on three Geelong players on the members wing, pressuring and tackling them before eventually earning a free kick.

Dewy's first goal was a trademark bullet from 50 metres after he'd pounced on a Geelong error. Then a minute later he took on three Cats and managed to release a handball to Williams for another goal. Our sixth successive goal of the quarter came from Dewy courtesy of a brilliant snap, and suddenly the scoreboard had us leading by 30 points.

They were rattled.

Two Geelong goals in the final minute of the quarter brought us back down to earth, but there was no way we were going to let it slip now. We were two men down, with Clinton Young joining

Croady on the sidelines, but setbacks like that, which would normally cause concern, weren't even registering. There was something about us that had been there all day – a confidence, an inner belief that if we continued to work for each other, then something special could happen.

Clarko drew on our Kokoda experience during his three-quarter-time address. 'This is when you think about things like Kokoda and how hard we've worked as a group and how much you blokes want to be mates for life.'

My biggest fear was a Geelong burst at the start of the final quarter, but when that didn't eventuate in the opening ten minutes, the confidence rose. A Buddy Franklin goal midway through the term helped that, and then Mitch got one. When Laddo nailed a shot with eight minutes remaining, the lead was out to 33 points.

The shark was nearly dead.

But still I wouldn't allow myself to relax. I even sprayed Crawf when he dared to declare the premiership ours.

'Relax – we've got it! We've got it!' he screamed.

I snapped straight back. 'Stay focused, Crawf. Get back over there!'

There was no way I was going to break my intense focus until I heard the official siren sound. When it finally came I was alone in the centre of the MCG. I raised my arms in the air and my next thought was to find my best mate, Guerra. We'd made a pact beforehand to get to one another when the business was done. I spotted him 30 metres away and started sprinting. I hadn't run this fast in the game yet here I was moving like Cyril.

We started laughing as we hugged like long-lost relatives meeting for the first time. Then it was on. More screaming, more laughing and lots more hugging. People were coming from everywhere.

The rest of the guys on the list must have started sprinting in their suits as soon as the siren sounded, because they were onto us before Guerra and I even parted.

The look of pure elation on the faces of so many people was what stood out. Plenty had tears in their eyes, including Crawf, who looked to be in shock. Croady was there on crutches with the biggest smile on his face. I couldn't stop shaking my head as we all gathered in a large group and waited for the official presentations to start.

My daydreaming was interrupted by an AFL official. He said something to me but I had no idea what he was talking about. 'Mitch is the captain, mate,' I said.

He just looked at me and smiled before walking off. Then it hit me, and suddenly my whole body tightened. I realised he was talking about the Norm Smith Medal.

I hadn't given it a thought until that moment. We'd had a lot of good players on the day. Clinton Young was probably best-on-ground before he went off injured, Sewelly had been outstanding in the middle of the ground, and Ablett and Steve Johnson had got plenty of it for the Cats.

It's weird where your mind takes you in these situations. All I could think about was that it would be the best stitch-up of all time if they read someone else's name out. I could see Collingwood legend Tony Shaw on the stage and figured he was the man who would be handing over the medal. What was I going to say? I couldn't remember what the AFL guy had just told me.

It wasn't a stitch-up. Shaw read my name out and immediately a dozen hands were rubbing the top of my head. What is it about footballers messing each other's hair?

That was the least of my worries as I walked up on stage. What was I going to say?

I gave Shaw a big hug and then, as he stepped back, the Pies' 1990 premiership captain almost fell off the stage, which was a nice distraction, albeit a brief one, from the dread I was feeling.

'First of all I'd just like to thank Geelong,' I said. 'The last two years you guys have been what we have been aiming to be. Thanks very much for the game today – you have been superb.

'To the AFL and Toyota, thanks very much for putting on not only today, but the whole season.

'And also just to the boys and all the Hawks supporters out there, it has been sensational. I'm looking forward to next year. Well done, boys.'

I was back on stage a few minutes later to receive my premiership medallion from a little Auskick kid to whom I handed a Hawthorn cap, which I thought was a pretty good deal. As I walked off the stage I kissed the medallion.

When I got back among my teammates, I quietly slipped the Norm Smith Medal underneath my jumper. The premiership medallion was what today was about. There hadn't been any individuals during the game and there weren't going to be any now. We'd won as a team and we'd celebrate as a team.

After the traditional photo on stage with brown and gold confetti raining down on us, we started the slow lap around the MCG, taking it in turns to hold the cup. Along the way I embraced Clarko again and confessed that the end part of my Norm Smith speech had been a lie. I didn't care if there wasn't a next year.

'Mate, I'm done,' I told Clarko. 'We've won a flag. I'm done.'

8

THE HANGOVER

It was the perfect time to reflect – on the back of a horse and cart with your best mate.

Guerra and I had spotted the ride as we were making our way from Hawthorn's official function to get changed at a city hotel before heading out to continue the celebrations, which so far had been chaotic.

One of the highlights after the game had been the team coming together in our suits in the centre of the MCG. The stands were empty and it was hard to fathom that not that long before, 100 000 people had been in the stadium. We linked arms again, surrounded the premiership cup and belted out the Hawthorn club song.

'We're a happy team at Hawthorn, we're the mighty fighting Hawks . . .'

It was impossible to count how many times I'd sung that song in the six hours since the final siren. And there was certainly no let-up in the ensuing days, which included a fans' day at Glenferrie Oval and a trip to Tasmania to fulfil our sponsorship commitments. By the time the best-and-fairest night came around the following Saturday, we were all running on empty, but we managed to get up again for a few more renditions of the song.

Buddy took home the Peter Crimmins Medal to cap off his incredible season. The boys were leaving the next day on the footy trip, and even though I loved nothing more than getting away with my teammates (as evidenced by my enthusiasm for previous trips), I was pretty happy to be staying put this time with Lauren and Cooper.

We headed to Cairns for our first family holiday together, and it was fantastic. I just sat around eating and drinking with a permanent smile on my face. I was a premiership player. How good was that to say? I was a premiership player.

That scenario, the eating and drinking part, was on constant rotation. Back in Colac it was certainly a daily ritual, as my mates revelled in the fact that the Hawks had won the flag. I had a hit of cricket while I was down there and fitted in the odd run, but the ratio of exercise to enjoying myself was probably a little bit out.

I found it was a lot out on day one of the new pre-season. My weigh-in for the start of training was just over 93 kilos – I'd managed to find an extra 5 kilos over the break. The problem was that I wasn't the only one. As a group we'd certainly celebrated in style. In addition, we already had a long injury list, with a lot of players recovering from post-season surgery.

I knew I had a bit of work to do, but that task was about to get a lot harder. A week into the pre-season we were doing a match simulation drill and I ended up on Roughy. He led out on a lead and I tried to get there but was too late to get near the ball, so I decided to give him a clip around the ears instead.

It was a bad idea. In the process of hitting Roughy's hard head, I managed to tear the rotator cuff in my shoulder. I'd had shoulder issues previously and figured this one would only cost me a few weeks, but scans revealed more damage. A complete shoulder reconstruction was required.

I had a partner in rehab: Jordan Lewis was forced to have the exact same procedure a few days later. Our injury list was ridiculous, with Franklin, Robert Campbell, Croady, Gilham, Ellis, Laddo and Young all having post-season surgery. We were already without Crawf, who'd realised there was no better way to end his brilliant 305-game career than by winning a premiership medal.

I was staring at three months on the sidelines, which wasn't ideal. Nor was the fact that I continued to eat and drink as if I was in proper pre-season training. Sure, I was getting into a sweat on the exercise bike, but that clearly wasn't enough. The balance was out and I got told as much by an unlikely source.

We'd been working with a leadership consultancy company called Leading Teams for a couple of years, focusing on creating good leadership and values around the club. Part of the program included promoting open and honest feedback in the group.

Jordan Lisle had arrived at the club via the 2008 national draft. He was a big bloke, a potential key forward, who was given the task of delivering the feedback from the younger players about the leadership program.

'You are elite on the field, but off it you're not,' he told me.

I had to do a double-take. Who the hell did this kid think he was? I gave him a Clarko-like glare and said, 'Okay, can you explain?'

'Look at your skinfolds,' Lisle said. 'They're around 60, whereas most of the other guys are between 40 and 50.'

I knew it wasn't the time or place to bite back. This was the sort of thing we were promoting, and if I jumped down the throat of the first young kid who said something, then the whole program would collapse.

The more I thought about what Lisle had said, the more I realised he was right. I'd thought that because I was injured and not training I had a good enough excuse for not being in mint condition. That was a cop-out, and it had taken guts for an 18-year-old to call me on it. I was glad he had.

Things had to change, and the first thing on the list was my diet. I had the perfect solution. After having Cooper, Lauren had started Lite n' Easy to lose weight. It was a healthy eating program with all the meals sent to your doorstep at the start of each week. Not having to cook was a massive bonus and having dinner planned out each day worked a treat as I managed to gradually shed a couple of kilos.

One pre-season game was all the preparation I managed to fit in before the start of our premiership defence. It didn't get off on the right foot, with consecutive losses to Geelong and Sydney.

Unfortunately, this was going to be a constant theme. Going into Round 7 we were just inside the eight with three wins and three losses. We kept telling ourselves that our ordinary start was all about our interrupted pre-season. Once we got players back and got kilometres in our legs, everything would click.

Surely, everything would click. Surely.

An abductor strain, which I carried for a couple of weeks before eventually conceding, cost me three weeks on the sidelines. On my return against Sydney in Round 11, Clarko threw me to the wolves by having me play on two-time Brownlow Medallist Adam Goodes.

It didn't get any easier the following week in Tasmania, when I had to spend the day standing in front of Brisbane Lions centre half-forward Jonathan Brown. We were both Western District lads, given he was born in Colac and then grew up in Warrnambool, but that didn't stop him from threatening to cause me serious harm if I tried to cut off his leads.

Brown had been a part of the great Brisbane team who'd won three premierships in a row from 2001 to 2003. My first experience of this incredible outfit had been an interesting one. It involved their inspirational captain, Michael Voss, who took over as the Lions' coach in 2009.

My first meeting with Voss was back in 2005. I was standing in the middle of the ground before the first bounce, waiting for everyone to get into position. I'd known for a few days that I'd be lining up on Voss, who was one of the best players of the modern era, and I was shitting myself. He seemed so calm and assured as he walked up, looked straight at me – and then elbowed me in the guts.

I was caught by surprise, but instinct kicked in and I elbowed him back. We traded a couple more elbows before going on with our business. I knew he was sending a 20-year-old a message: 'You're playing with the big boys now, and physically you need to be ready.' It's no wonder the Lions won three in a row with a leader like that.

My bad Lions' experiences kept coming on what became a dark afternoon in Launceston, with Brown kicking five goals to engineer a 42-point win. It was a bad loss, but two more followed in the next couple of weeks, including an embarrassing 88-point flogging by the Western Bulldogs.

We slumped to 11th and the history books were being consulted. No reigning premiership team had failed to make the finals
the following season since Adelaide in 1999.

The natives were restless, in particular our president, Jeff
Kennett, who penned a letter to the members apologising for the
football department's performance against Brisbane. It was a direct
attack on Clarko and the media had a field day with it.

Finally, we did something to help the coach. In Round 15
against North Melbourne in Launceston, we came from behind,
kicking five goals in the last quarter to win.

The following week something else happened. It clicked again.

Collingwood were a quality team, sitting fourth on the ladder.
At half-time they led by 11 points, and then the old Hawthorn
returned. Big time. We kicked seven goals to two points in the
third quarter, producing football that hadn't been seen since
Grand Final Day ten months earlier. Buddy kicked five goals, and
I appreciated a return to the midfield by having 34 possessions
and kicking three goals. Mitch also booted three.

The final margin was 45 points, and I left the MCG that
night convinced we'd turned the corner. The injury curse that had
weighed us down in the first half of the year was finally disappearing. The band was getting back together and it looked like it could
still play some good music.

This warm and fuzzy feeling lasted for one whole week.
A heartbreaking one-point loss to Geelong in Round 17 sent us into
a tailspin again. We'd been 28 points up early in the last quarter but
crashed, with Jimmy Bartel kicking a point after the siren to win
the game.

We lost our next three games before regrouping against
Richmond in Round 21. Remarkably, that win meant we could still

make the finals if we defeated Essendon, currently sitting eighth, in the final game of the season. We still had the belief that we could beat any team at any time, so the finals would effectively be the start of a new season.

The only thing was . . . we had to get there first.

At half-time we had one foot in the door courtesy of a 22-point lead. Enter Matthew Lloyd. The Essendon full-forward wasn't the player he had once been, and it wasn't the scoreboard where he hurt us. He came off the line and crudely hit Sewelly when he had his head over the ball, knocking him out cold. It resulted in an all-in melee, with tensions understandably boiling over.

Unfortunately, it was Essendon who settled better after that. They reduced the lead early in the final quarter, and then kicked away to win by 17 points.

Ninth.

It sucked.

I'd received an interesting phone call leading into our final game. Clarko had rung and said he wanted to catch up.

It wasn't unusual to be summoned to the coach's house for a chat, but this one was more interesting than most as it was about my contract, which was ending that year. My manager, Paul Connors, had been in discussions with the club for a while but they hadn't come to an agreement.

Clarko wasn't one to muck around, and as soon as I sat down he hit me with it. 'I need to know what you're doing,' he said. 'Are you going to sign? I want you to stay here because my goal for you is to play 300 games and be a three- or four-time premiership player at this club.'

I thought he was crazy but there were a few balls in play. A new franchise on the Gold Coast was entering the competition in 2011, and they were in the market for a marquee player. They'd made contact with Paul and were interested in my thoughts on heading north. I actually had no interest, but you never say never to these things, and negotiations with Hawthorn had stalled, not over the money but over the length of the term due to me having a young family.

Normally I liked to know exactly what I was doing ahead of time. It was part of my personality. Both of my previous contract extensions had been finalised early in their final year. But this would be the biggest deal of my career, so there was a lot riding on it. Paul had even suggested signing a one-year deal and then backing ourselves to get an even bigger contract down the track.

'We need an answer,' Clarko said.

Two days later, at training, he asked me again. 'What's your decision?'

I laughed at him. 'What are you talking about? We only spoke two days ago.'

After yet another inquiry after the last game, my new three-year contract was sorted a couple of weeks later, much to the delight of Clarko, who then went about improving our list by luring classy Port Adelaide midfielder Shaun Burgoyne. He was a super talent who'd played in the Power's premiership but had some injury issues in recent times. We also bolstered our defence by bringing in Josh Gibson from North Melbourne.

The most telling departure was Grand Final hero Stuart Dew, who was one of many who had struggled with injury in 2009.

*

In a year devoid of highlights, I managed to find one on 24 October: my wedding day.

The lead-up was amusing, although Lauren probably didn't see the funny side. My groomsmen, who included Guerra, Koppy, Daniel Elstone, Jake Carmody and Ben Harris, had dinner at Tokyo Teppanyaki in Chapel Street the night before the wedding. A couple of my uncles and mates also showed up and we shared plenty of laughs. We went back to Guerra's to prepare for the big day.

Lauren and her girlfriends were getting picked up by a stretch limousine at 7 a.m. to start the long process of preparing themselves for the wedding.

We woke up at around 10 a.m. and quickly put on our suits. The ceremony was at St Joseph's Church in Port Melbourne. We actually got there early and decided to sneak across the road for a couple of nerve-settlers.

The highlight of this brief session was when Koppy, who was 26 years old but small in stature, was asked for ID by the security guard, while my brother Dylan, who was just 13, sailed in no worries. It was one of those priceless moments that we all knew would be retold over and over again.

We thought we did a pretty good job of pulling ourselves together by the time we got back to the church, but Lauren instantly saw through us. 'You stink of alcohol and you look green,' was my future wife's opening line, although at least it was said with a smile.

Happy days.

9

FINDING FAITH

'I want to be captain.'

It was the first time I'd said it out loud. Brad Sewell had asked the question and I didn't think I needed to hide my aspirations.

'Well, keep going along these lines,' he told me. 'The boys are starting to see a real change in you.' He then added the money line. 'The senior guys are starting to have faith in you.'

Boom. There it was.

In football clubs, faith and trust are vitally important. If you don't have them, you can't be successful. I hadn't even had them in myself for years, so it's no wonder my teammates hadn't either. But I was a different player and person in the lead-up to the 2010 season, helped significantly by being 5 kilos lighter than 12 months earlier. I was eating better, had been injury free and was running better.

All of this was music to the ears of fitness boss Andrew 'Jack' Russell. In terms of trust, he was emerging as the most influential person in my career. After having taken a while to size each other up, which was my style, we now had a unique understanding. I was in his office every day before training, wanting to know what drills we would be doing and what the session required of me. Again, that was my personality. I liked to know exactly what I was doing and why we were doing it.

Jack and I had what could be described as a love–hate relationship. Shane Crawford actually told me he'd gone to see Jack in 2006 because he was afraid that Jack was going too hard on me. Crawf was worried that if Jack kept pushing, the same thing that had happened to Crawf's younger brother, Justin, would happen to me. After starting his career at Sydney and then joining Hawthorn in 1997, Justin had retired at the age of 21 after 46 games because he found the demands of the AFL too much and they ultimately drove him away from the game.

Apparently Jack listened but told Crawf that he had to take the risk with me, because if he didn't continue to push, I wouldn't reach my full potential.

The relationship between Jack and Clarko was one that fascinated the boys, particularly early on. Clarko had so much trust and faith in Jack that we often joked that Jack must have had something over the coach, like nude pictures of him, or something like that.

Clarko hated handing over power to anyone – Jack was the exception. He was the only person who seemed to be able to stand up to Clarko if it was required, and who wasn't intimidated by him. They worked brilliantly together and always talked the same language. If a player wasn't training properly or his intensity wasn't where he wanted it to be, Jack would load the gun and get Clarko to fire the shot.

There were plenty of shots being fired in the opening two months of the 2010 season.

A six-goals-to-zip opening quarter against Melbourne was the perfect way to start the new year, and it flowed into a 56-point win. Another nailbiting loss to Geelong followed, which meant we hadn't beaten them in three meetings since the 2008 Grand Final.

After playing midfield in the opening two rounds, I returned to half-back in Round 3 against the Western Bulldogs after new recruit Josh Gibson injured his hamstring. Unfortunately we had no answer to the Dogs' spearhead Barry Hall, who kicked six goals in his side's 16-point victory.

Having no answer became a common theme over the next month as we slumped to 1–6 and 14th position on the ladder. A flogging by Collingwood was followed by a loss to North Melbourne in Launceston, where injuries bit us, but when Essendon torched us by 43 points after we failed to score in the final quarter, the jungle drums started beating.

A trip to Perth didn't help, and neither did losing Mitch and Buddy for the game – although Roughy stepped up and kicked six goals against the Eagles. We again came up short, by eight points this time.

Then came our football club's sliding-doors moment.

With 50 seconds remaining in the final quarter of the Round 8 clash with Richmond, we were clinging to a three-point lead. The ball was in the hands of Tigers midfielder Shane Tuck, who'd gathered it just outside the 50-metre line. As he was streaming towards goal and just as he went to kick, Mitch came from nowhere and dragged him down. It was an incredible effort and a game-winning tackle.

Rumour had it that Jeff Kennett had been considering sacking Clarko if we lost that game. Sensing that the walls were closing in on him, Clarko called for a change of routine and we all went away together for a night. The reason for the getaway was to talk about our game plan, which was outdated and being exposed.

Clarko hated change and hated negative football, but in this case he knew he had to relent. Collingwood had emerged as the best team, and they played a style that was focused on kicking long down the line and then getting bodies to the contest to hold in the ball.

The days of us being able to come out the back and flick it around were over. Opposition teams had figured it out, and our personnel had also changed. Our strength was now more inside, where Mitch, Sewelly, Lewis and I could hold our own. We needed to start playing to it. It was decided that we were no longer going to spread the field and run all day – the battle was going to be won in tight, and that's where we had to focus our energies.

The other significant change centred around the interchange. We'd been the team that had the fewest rotations, but now we would use the bench more so we could have the constant fresh legs required to alter the state of our season.

Changing a game plan mid-season was a huge risk, even if we didn't really have a choice. If we pulled it off, Clarko said, it would tell him that this group could be open to anything in the future. That excited the coach.

A 50-point thrashing of Carlton was a good way to start our 'new' life, and the wins kept coming. By the end of Round 11 we were in the eight, and it was six wins on the trot by the time we got a week off for the split round.

Once again the draw had been kind to me. My 26th birthday fell three days before our Round 13 contest with Essendon. We had the week off after the game, which we won by 16 points, so a celebration was planned.

I didn't know exactly what it would be. All I was told was that it was a joint celebration with Guerra's partner, Rachel, whose birthday fell in the same week, and that they'd pick Lauren and me up at 1.30 p.m. on the Saturday. There was no other information, which worried me given what I'd done for his birthday. Guerra was petrified of heights, so we'd taken him skydiving.

Thankfully my fears of payback weren't realised, although he certainly caught me off guard. I found out later he was working in cahoots with Lauren and after we went to a couple of different locations and had a nice dinner, they'd directed us towards a friend's bar in Richmond. I didn't think twice about why we were going there until I walked in and found 80 of our friends and family inside for a surprise birthday party.

There was no repeat of the shenanigans of my party experience in Melbourne a few years earlier, and we returned from the break to hold off the Western Bulldogs by three points.

Our seven-game winning streak was once again broken by Geelong. Another epic game, another loss – this time by just two points.

So how good were we? That was the debate that raged as we continued to pile up the wins, importantly proving our worth against the top sides. St Kilda was one of those, and we didn't lose any fans in what was an incredible Friday-night contest in Round 17. It was the first draw of my AFL career.

Not that I celebrated, given the circumstances surrounding the result. The AFL had cracked down on players going on and off the interchange bench, and if you stepped out of the box in front of the bench before your teammate was off the ground, it was an infringement. Even if there was only a few centimetres in it, a white flag would be raised by an official and the result would be a free kick against your side. I felt it was an over-the-top reaction – teams weren't deliberately trying to get an advantage by having 19 men on the field but it was the buzz rule of the season, and it screwed us.

With two minutes remaining against the Saints, Cyril had the match-winning goal denied because of an interchange blunder. This meant our lead remained at seven points and the ball was brought back to the middle of the ground, where St Kilda were awarded the free kick. They went forward and scored a behind, making it just one goal the difference. In the frantic final minute we failed to clear our defensive half and the ball ended up in the hands of Saints ruckman Ben McEvoy, who somehow dribbled through a goal with 12 seconds remaining.

It was a bitter pill to swallow, but the result further fuelled talk about our emergence as legitimate premiership contenders.

That wasn't the only discussion point, with the captaincy back on the agenda. Calls for change had been bubbling along since early in the season, with a number of prominent media commentators leading the charge. What they didn't know, and neither did any of our teammates, was that it had already happened. Mitch and I had sat down with Clarko and mapped out the changeover, which would occur at the end of the season.

Mitch had become a father for the first time earlier in the year, and he'd also just found out that his wife, Lyndall, was expecting twins. He was going to have his hands full next year, which is what he said when he approached me about the captaincy handover. Importantly, he also felt I was ready for the job.

While we were very different in many ways and had butted heads a lot over the journey, Mitch and I were actually good for each other. The reason we clashed was because we were different personalities and both brutally honest.

Sometimes we didn't like what each other said but we both knew, even though it may have been tough to hear, it was always for the benefit of the club. That's the environment you need in a strong club and if you're in a football club where players aren't butting heads, then blokes aren't being honest with each other.

We came from different directions with a lot of things. For example, Mitch was a bookworm while I would never pick up a book. He was an astute student whereas I just loved playing sport, but we did share one common goal, which was our love for the game and the Hawthorn Football Club.

His professionalism had finally rubbed off on me and I'd helped him become less intense, which had made him a better leader. We'd spent a lot of time together recently as we'd embarked on a business course together. Former club president Ian Dicker put three of us – Ellis, Mitch and me – into a course at Monash University. It was part of an MBA program, and even though none of us had an undergraduate degree, they'd found a way to get us involved.

Xavier lasted two lectures, but I thought I'd try to stick it out.

The first unit was 'Change Management', which centred around looking at different management styles. It was interesting to examine how different personalities managed situations, such as how Jeff would do something compared to Clarko.

I ticked off that subject with a little bit of help from Mitch along the way, and was pretty proud of my achievement. I got halfway through a second subject when it became obvious once again that I just wasn't cut out for studying.

It was my second attempted venture into the workforce.

A few years earlier, Jordan Lewis and I had spent some time with the police force. Learning that will amuse many people, but we both had a keen interest in the men and women in blue. The club was pushing players to think about life after football and organised a work placement for us. It was a good experience and we covered a number of different aspects of the job, having a look around the St Kilda Road headquarters, going cruising in a patrol car, and even doing a day with the water police. We also went to the police academy and met former Essendon player Aaron Henneman, who was going through the training to get his badge.

My budding business and police careers were the furthest thing from my mind when we hit a small snag, losing two games in a row for the first time in three months. However, victories over Melbourne in Round 20 and Fremantle in Round 21 ensured we would be playing finals.

The Dockers had looked after us by resting some of their players for the game, which was in Launceston, as they were already assured a finals berth. The result was a confidence-boosting 116-point victory to us, although I finished the game on the bench after wrenching my knee.

It was nothing serious, but enough to see me rested for the

final game of the home-and-away season, against top-of-the-ladder Collingwood. Our position in the final eight couldn't change, so the match became a free hit against quality opposition. We caused an upset with a six-goals-to-three final quarter and got home by three points.

The draw with St Kilda came back to haunt us, though – it meant that we finished two premiership points behind Fremantle and Sydney. We had a better percentage than both of them, and if we'd collected the full four points against the Saints we would have finished fifth rather than seventh and had a home final. Instead, we were headed to Perth for the elimination final.

The last time we'd played in a final we'd been assisted by the inaccuracy of our opponent. This time, ironically, we were the ones gripped by issues in front of goal. Kicking one goal and 11 points in the opening half of any game is a problem; doing it in a final is a disaster.

While our second half was better, we were never really in the hunt and trudged off Subiaco Oval having suffered a 30-point loss. It was a tough day at the office for most of us, and I was at the head of that queue. The knee caused more problems than I'd anticipated, and after slightly tweaking it early in the game, I was in trouble.

My afternoon wasn't helped by Docker Adam McPhee shadow-ing me all day and, because I couldn't change direction due to my injury, my chances of out-running a tag were minimal.

In the end, it had been a very disappointing day at the office. A loss like that sits in the guts, and I struggled to shake it even though I was required to put the suit on and do the rounds of the awards dinners.

The All Australian was first, where I got a pleasant surprise when I was named captain and in the centre for the team of the year. Then, at the AFL Players Association awards night, I managed second place behind Collingwood's Dane Swan.

There had been a buzz around me about the Brownlow Medal throughout the second half of the season, but I hadn't bought it for a minute. I'd definitely had a consistent season, but Swan and Gary Ablett were way ahead in my mind.

The hype around the event had always made me uncomfortable, and it was worse when you were considered one of the favourites. Channel 10 were hosting the night and they requested that Swanny, Gaz and I stand up on the stage with a spotlight on us to start the broadcast.

I hated public speaking, and the thought of standing up there, which to me screamed 'Look at me! Look at me!', just didn't feel right, so I politely declined. Gaz was annoyed afterwards, because he hated doing that sort of stuff as much as I did but had been coerced into it. 'You're an arsehole,' he said with a smile, giving me a slap on the back for good measure.

It became pretty clear early on in the proceedings that we were going to be able to enjoy ourselves as a speech wouldn't be required. I'd been thinking about Clarko's comments to me a couple of years back when he was selling me the move from the midfield to half-back. 'I will coach a premiership player before I will coach a Brownlow Medallist,' he'd declared.

The irony was that the person he was referring to when he made that statement was Chris Judd, who came from nowhere to win his second Brownlow Medal. He was now captain of Carlton after coming home to Victoria in 2008. It was funny because I'd always said the comparisons made of us for years because of the draft order should have been between him and Ablett. They were the best players in our draft and their careers had followed a similar path, with both winning premierships and being awarded the Brownlow Medal.

This time Juddy came out on top, with a flurry of best-on-ground honours to win with 30 votes, from Gaz on 24 and Swanny on 21. I came in equal seventh, on 16 votes.

I had a bit more luck a couple of weeks later at Hawthorn's best-and-fairest count. It was a big night in more ways than one. The captaincy handover was made official by Jeff Kennett and I managed to win my second Peter Crimmins Medal, getting home from Buddy Franklin, with Mitch third.

This was classified as a double celebration, and we didn't hold back as the night progressed. Lauren and I found ourselves with a few teammates and friends from Colac in Crown Casino's Mahogany Room, which was the VIP room for high rollers. We certainly weren't high rollers but we didn't mind a game of roulette.

The topic of conversation became unusual as the night wore on. There was a dispute over daylight saving – the clocks were changing and we were trying to figure out if they were going forwards or backwards an hour. The reason for this was because we had to be at St Kilda Beach at 5 a.m. We were required to do an early-morning swim because a number of players had returned from the break with significantly increased skinfold readings. It was the perfect opportunity to send a message to the group about our professionalism.

I didn't share this theory as I struggled to get out of my suit in the darkness on the beach. Some of the boys had been home and even had a couple of hours of sleep, and were there in their bathers. I was in my jocks, and was coming to the realisation that a few of us had still been out just half an hour earlier.

We all jumped off the pier into the freezing water and some-how swam back to the shore. If I thought that was bad, things were about to get a whole lot worse.

'Hodgey, do you want to address the boys?' Clarko asked.

'Of course not, coach,' is what I wanted to say. I was pretty sure I wouldn't make any sense. But I began with, 'Look, boys, it's not good enough.' That was the gist of what I attempted to say, but my slurred speech meant it didn't exactly hit the mark. I was trying desperately to avoid Clarko's stare but the more I looked away, the more I saw the boys pissing themselves laughing.

'Just look at you,' Clarko said. 'Your first day as captain, where you could have set a prime example of how we should be better as a group, and look at the state you're in.'

Later, when I got back to my hotel room, I realised the session hadn't been without incident. I'd lost my wedding ring during the swim and also managed to misplace my wallet and watch. And I had sand all over me, which Lauren was less than impressed with when I climbed into bed.

If I had've been in better shape, my speech for Clarko would have been gold.

'When you appointed me you said I was captain for a reason and it was important that I didn't change. You said if I wanted to have a beer with the boys, I should have a beer. You said, "Don't change, because that's why they've voted you in."

'Well, coach, I've followed your advice to the letter.'

IO

THE CURSE

The first five minutes were always the worst.

Getting out of bed. A simple thing you'd never really thought about before that suddenly required intense focus and concentration. The stiffness complicated the issue. And of course it wasn't isolated to one side, it had to be both. The first step sent a message to the brain to remind it that getting to the bathroom wasn't going to be easy.

In the end it was a hobble. If anyone was watching, they would think it was a 76-year-old pensioner crossing the room rather than a 26-year-old AFL captain. This impersonation had been happening for most of the summer. Both my Achilles were shot. Well, the technical term was that they were inflamed.

It had been a tough couple of months. Just before we were scheduled to take off for a post-season getaway in Bali, I got a call from Lauren that rocked my world. She was shopping at Chadstone when she rang.

'You have to come and get me,' she said with desperation in her voice.

My heart immediately sank. I knew what had happened. Lauren had suffered a miscarriage. She'd been nine weeks along and we'd been so excited about having a baby brother or sister for Cooper.

It was a horrible few hours and straight away I figured we'd postpone the holiday. But after getting medical advice, it was thought going away together was probably a good thing to do in the circumstances.

And Lauren insisted we do it. I just had to be there for my wife, a shoulder to cry on or the person to get a smile back on her face. I knew I had to appear strong and positive even though that wasn't how I was feeling, but for Lauren's sake I needed to portray that.

In my own private moments I was hurting, and once again I went back to my childhood ways of dealing with matters of the heart . . . I turned to sport. Every day I would train over there, each day harder than the one before. I was running a lot of kilometres as I found it was my escape.

It was my way of clearing my mind, almost like the harder I pushed, the better I thought everything would be. Did I overdo it? In hindsight, maybe it contributed to the latest injury setback which had flared around Christmas. It came out of nowhere really.

Every Tuesday we'd do a recovery session that was an easy jog. By early December, for the first 20 steps I'd be tiptoeing but then everything would warm up, and there would be no problem. This continued until early January, when I started to pull up really sore. It got to the point where the medical staff suggested scans were required. The scans came back with a couple of answers:

both Achilles tendons were inflamed, and there was a slight tear on the left one.

My new teammate David Hale, who'd crossed over from North Melbourne in the trade period, had recently gone through a groundbreaking procedure for the condition that involved having blood removed from the Achilles, spinning it in a centrifuge to increase its oxygen content, and then reinjecting it. With this procedure, they said I'd be back running in just over a week and would return to training after two weeks at the most.

That had been two months earlier. I tried everything, including sleeping with green teabags strapped to my Achilles – I'd heard somewhere that this would work. It showed the desperation I was feeling. As I searched for the magic cure, I also wore special socks when I was sleeping that effectively pulled the foot back.

The start of the 2011 season was closing fast and I wasn't even able to run laps. It wasn't exactly a good start to my captaincy reign.

Proving my fitness came down to a VFL practice match with Box Hill before Round 1. I played just over a half and got through, which in my mind was enough. 'I'm going to be all right to play,' I told Clarko.

He didn't share my enthusiasm about making the trip to Adelaide for the season opener. 'We're taking over 22 fit blokes. Have another game at Box Hill.'

While every player knows the Round 1 game is only worth four points – the same as the rest of the home-and-away season – there's no doubt there's a greater emphasis on it than on other games. Everyone is desperate to play in it and put into practice everything they've worked on for the previous six months.

For me, the fact that it was my first year as captain added another layer of urgency, plus there was still some angst in the pit of my stomach about what had happened in the final against Fremantle. In hindsight, I probably shouldn't have played in that match. I thought the knee was ready, but I struggled and I felt like I'd been a liability. Since that final it had been a long time to wait to start the process of making up for what had happened in Perth. And now Clarko was making me wait another week.

A 20-point loss to the Crows wasn't an ideal start to the new season, but we got rolling and won three in a row before another epic public-holiday showdown with Geelong. It was on a Tuesday, as that year was the rare occasion when Easter Monday and Anzac Day came together.

The lead-up centred around Paul Chapman, who'd revealed that the Cats had made a pact after the 2008 Grand Final, pledging they would never lose to Hawthorn again.

This was on top of what our president, Jeff Kennett, had done on the eve of the 2009 season: he'd accused the Cats of not having the 'mental drive' of Hawthorn. This statement had since grown legs and become known as the 'Kennett curse' because we hadn't beaten Geelong in two years.

We thought it was all a bit of a joke, and four goals to zip in the opening 15 minutes had us on track to debunk the myth. But that was short-lived, with Geelong hitting back and going down the path these contests regularly followed. Unfortunately, on our part, a couple of sloppy late errors opened the door for the Cats, who won again by 19 points.

I was struggling. Having had no pre-season was hurting me big time. I'd slotted back across half-back as I tried to build my fitness, but I just wasn't myself and felt like I was a second behind everything. I could see the play unfold but just wasn't getting there like I usually did. It was every footballer's nightmare.

Speaking of nightmares, our record in Sydney had been just that, in particular at the Sydney Cricket Ground. This fact was playing on the mind of Clarko, so he reached into his bag of tricks in the lead-up to our Round 9 clash with the Swans. Just after we arrived in Sydney on the Saturday and checked into our hotel, we had a team meeting. There was a box on the table at the front.

'Boys, get your mobile phones out. They're going in here,' Clarko said, indicating the box.

We all looked at each other and frowned. What was the coach up to?

'We're here to play footy, and we don't want any distractions,' he told us.

Panic swept the room, given that many of us had arranged tickets to the game for family members, and suddenly our means of communication would be gone. Also, we would be cut off from loved ones back at home, which was sure to cause some angst.

You've never seen grown men move so slowly to give up their devices. We all quickly sent text messages alerting our friends and family to the situation. But Clarko didn't care. He threw his own phone into the box too. His theory was that everything had been too comfortable each time we'd been to Sydney. The hotel was in a beautiful spot, the stunning harbour was close by, and the trip always had a 'weekend escape' feel about it.

Now, every time we instinctively felt in our pocket for our phone, we got a subtle reminder that we were here to play football and nothing else.

It was a genius move. Our seven-goal third quarter blew the game apart, Buddy Franklin kicked six goals, and our Sydney hoodoo was buried with a 46-point victory. The win was part of a five-game winning streak that came to an end at the hands of . . . Geelong.

Once again we put ourselves in a good position, leading by 17 points at three-quarter time, but then we failed to score in the last term and when the siren sounded the ball was in our forward line but we were five points behind. The Kennett curse was getting more traction.

Adding to the frustration of the day was a bad Achilles injury to Roughy. He'd been chasing after the ball and then gone down as if shot by a sniper. His season was over.

Geelong and Collingwood were the pacesetters of 2011, and in Round 15 we came up short against the Magpies, getting beaten easily by 41 points. It was our last loss of the season. We won the final eight games, and the bonus of the way we were playing was the injection of some youth. Isaac Smith, Luke Breust and Paul Puopolo all added good leg speed, and Liam Shiels and Matt Suckling had improved significantly.

It's funny that while the team was flying, from the outside it appeared that I was enjoying a dream debut as captain. In reality I was finding it quite tough.

Clarko and his two main lieutenants, football operations manager Mark Evans and head of coaching and development Chris Fagan, had decided to part ways with Leading Teams after 2010, as they felt we knew what we were doing now after five years. That was good in theory, but in practice it wasn't ideal for a new captain.

Included in the 'new way' was the scrapping of the leadership group in favour of a floating model, where various senior players and younger guys would be involved at different times.

There had also been a significant change to the club's development program.

This involved the setting up of a leadership forum broken into 'Lethal groups', named after Hawthorn legend Leigh Matthews, who played in three different decades and then became a premiership coach in two more. He made his debut in 1969 and finished up in 1985 after 332 games and four premierships. He then coached Collingwood to the 1990 premiership before moving to Brisbane, where he led them to three consecutive flags from 2001 to 2003.

The Lethal groups were: the 60s, which contained the first- to third-year players; the 70s, who were the young developing players starting to play senior football; the 80s, who were the regular senior players, including the likes of Roughy and Jordan Lewis; and the 90s, the veterans who were starting to prepare for life after footy. The guys in the 90s would act as role models for the other groups. Mitch was in there, along with Shaun Burgoyne and Chance Bateman.

It was an excellent set-up, as it helped teach young players how to adapt to the life of an AFL player while assisting the more senior players to think about life after football.

I wasn't as glowing about the leadership set-up. There were lots of moving parts in the structure, and it was hoped that if more people felt like they could have a say, or more people were listening to others, then there might be more buy-in. It was a good idea, but in my opinion it simply didn't work, and as captain I felt it left me out on my own without someone by my side to bounce things off.

Clarko and Mitch had both figured that the best way to approach the captaincy handover was to leave me alone and let me do it how I wanted. The trap I fell into was to try to do everything.

Finding the balance between mate and captain was another challenge. I certainly encouraged the guys to go out and have a beer, but I put the emphasis on doing it at the right time. Given that I'd personally stuffed up so many times, I was able to have the kind of relationship with the younger guys where I could help if they made a mistake. They knew I'd been there and done that, so whatever advice I gave them came from the right place.

The shift was most noticeable in, of all places, the spa. I used to be in there with the young boys and hear all the tales from the weekend. When you're captain it's a different story: everyone stops talking and there's silence as you get in. Understandably, the boys were worried that if they were on the borderline with something, blabbing it to the captain in the spa wouldn't be the smartest move.

Clarko pulled a smart move in the final round of the home-and-away season.

We were scheduled to play the Gold Coast Suns at Carrara and he decided to rest eight players, including me, Buddy and Cyril. We were already guaranteed to finish third and get a double chance, with Collingwood on top and Geelong second.

The Pies adopted a similar strategy in the final round, resting a number of players against the Cats. Unfortunately this resulted in the reigning premiers' second loss of the year, to the tune of a whopping 96 points.

It set up an enticing finals series, and we had our third date for the year with Geelong in the qualifying final. Naturally, the Kennett curse got another run-around in the lead-up and we couldn't do anything to stop it.

Cyril got the first goal of the game and then Buddy kicked a ripper to ensure we led by 11 points at the first break. But as usual,

Geelong found a way to get going and capitalised on a brief lapse in concentration by us, which had become a pattern. Late in the third quarter, they kicked four goals in five minutes to take the game away from us.

To cap off our 31-point loss, Buddy had to be helped off in the last quarter after hurting his knee. He was diagnosed with bone bruising, and the lead-up to our semifinal against Sydney was all about whether our gun forward would play. Most observers wrote him off, but for all of his amazing skill and freakish ability, Buddy is a warrior, and he got to the line.

There was no way we were going to exit again like the previous year, and at quarter-time the Swans had only scored one point and we were on 23. Three goals in the first half from goal sneak Puopolo helped push our lead out to 40 at the main break.

Sydney closed in the third quarter, and when they scored the opening goal of the final term the lead was only 19 points. But by that stage Buddy had warmed up, and his three last-quarter goals propelled us into the preliminary final.

All that stood between us and another Grand Final was Collingwood, the team who'd won the 2010 premiership in extraordinary fashion after a draw in the first Grand Final against St Kilda. They'd actually looked even better throughout 2011, but we didn't fear them. Our best could beat anyone, and we'd shown in the past couple of months that we had all the right ingredients.

Leading out the team on a Friday-night preliminary final at the MCG in front of 87 000 people was when the honour of the job I'd been given hit home. This was the stage you wanted to be on; this was when you wanted to perform; this was where reputations were made or broken.

The first goal of the game was important and we got it, through Lewis. Importantly, in the opening 30 minutes we more than held our own.

Some Buddy magic then gave the Pies serious concerns. He'd once again taken out the Coleman Medal for kicking the most goals in the season, but none was more important than the two he kicked midway through the second quarter to extend our lead to 13 points.

It was always going to be an arm wrestle, and that's what it settled into in the second half. We kicked the opening two goals of the third quarter only for the Pies to hit back with two of their own. A brilliant pressure goal from Cyril ensured that our lead was 17 points at three-quarter time.

Collingwood hadn't been under this sort of pressure all season. We knew they'd respond, but the key for us was that when they went up a level, we had to be able to do so too. As predicted, they surged, with goals to Chris Dawes and Leon Davis inside a minute. This was why they were the reigning champions. A response was needed.

I found myself deep forward when Bateman sent the perfect kick in my direction, allowing me to have a run and jump at the pack. The mark stuck, which left me with a 40-metre shot from a slight angle, which suited my left foot.

Talk about the old cliché: a captain's goal. This was it. All I kept thinking about as I walked back was routine. I had to find a way to block out the surrounding noise and just think 'routine'. I'd done this thousands of times – one more wasn't a big deal.

My technique had usually been sound with set shots, and thankfully the body and mind combined to strike this one perfectly. It never looked like missing. The lead was ten points with 14 minutes remaining. There was still a long way to go.

Seven minutes later, we were behind. A Dane Swan snap goal had been followed by a Travis Cloke mark and goal, which put the Pies two points up. The stage was set for something special, and it was no surprise who put his hand up.

A hurried kick into our forward line gave Buddy a chance to run onto it towards the boundary line, but the problem was that he was running in the wrong direction for a left-footer, and his opponent, Chris Tarrant, was right on his tail.

For a normal human being such obstacles would have been too much, but not for Buddy. He did a banana kick with the outside of his foot to dribble the ball through from 25 metres out. It was the goal of the year and it came with less than four minutes remaining in the preliminary final. We were back in front by four points.

There was too much time left to try to shut the game down, so we had to find a way to hold firm. Collingwood surged forward and created a stoppage in the forward pocket. Going third man up in the ruck contest and bashing it away from the congestion was a tactic we'd used effectively, and young defender Ben Stratton attempted to do that.

The problem was that the ball only went as far as Luke Ball. His and my careers had been linked since the 2001 draft; he'd crossed over to Collingwood last year from St Kilda and played in the premiership. Now, he was about to deny me a chance of winning another one.

Ball's left-foot snap was shepherded through on the goal line. They were back in front with two minutes and 49 seconds left.

I was in the middle for the centre bounce along with Sewelly and Burgoyne. Hale managed to get the tap down in my direction and I had it momentarily before a tackle knocked the ball free and allowed Swan to quickly throw it on his boot. An ugly bounce allowed Cloke in, but his shot from 60 metres luckily bounced into the post. We were still alive.

Through sheer willpower we managed to get the ball into our forward line with 90 seconds remaining, but Puopolo was called for holding the ball, which seemed a very quick whistle from the field umpire. Collingwood managed to get it back to their half-forward line – but with a minute remaining we got one more chance.

A big third man up from Lewis knocked it in our direction and he followed up with a handball to release Cyril. He was in the centre of the ground but he had nothing ahead. Everyone had been sucked towards the contest. He hesitated and was run down from behind by Collingwood's Dale Thomas.

Game over.

Season over.

Premiership gone.

TROUBLED TIMES

'Can I have that?'

Brent Guerra looked at me smugly and shook his head.

'Can I have a beer?'

That got the same response.

'A red wine?'

My teammate smiled and reached over to pour me a glass. 'Yes, you can.'

We were in Croatia in the final stages of our European vacation. Lauren and I had started in Barcelona and then met up with Guerra and his girlfriend, Rachel, in Paris.

The reason I was asking my teammate what I could eat or drink as if he was my dietitian was because he'd actually taken on that role to save me from myself. I'd embraced Europe with all of its delicacies on the food and drink front. The problem was that indulging for 28 days hadn't done great things for my waistline.

Earlier in the trip the shoe had been on the other foot. We were only a week or so in when we arrived in Venice, Italy. Guerra jumped on the scales and the reading came up as 94 kilos.

'Hey, fatty, look at you,' I said.

I'd actually been crook for a couple of days and had struggled to eat before the weigh-in, which helped me to register only 89 kilos. We were generally always pretty much the same on the scales, playing at around the 91–92 kilo mark.

However, things were a lot different a couple of weeks later. At this weigh-in, I came in at 94.5 kilos and Guerra had dropped down to 91.

'What's going on? You're fat,' he said.

The problem was I'd been enjoying everything that Italy provided, whereas Guerra had stuck to the lower-kilojoule options of red wine and vodka soda. There may have also been an issue with my love of crepes for breakfast.

'If you keep going like this, there's no way you're going to drop your skinnies in time,' he continued.

Guerra had a plan. For the last week and a half of the trip I would eat and drink exactly what he was having. We would still go out and enjoy ourselves, but everything we ate and drank had to be the same. There could be no deviation. I had to have what he was having for breakfast, the same alcoholic drinks and the exact same dinner. Guerra was loving the power, and I played along because I knew he was right. I couldn't afford to turn up overweight to the start of pre-season training.

It worked. I checked back in at the footy club at the start of

November weighing 91.5 kilos and with my skinfolds at an acceptable level.

I'd had an interesting relationship with skinfolds over my career. Early on, some teammates and I created a scam with the skinfold testing.

How the scam worked was always going into the dietitian for your skinfold test with a teammate. 'Never go in solo' was the golden rule. With two players in there, one would get tested while the other would type the results into the computer as they were relayed by the dietitian. If a reading was 10.2, you'd type in 9.2. Distractions like asking how the dietitian's family was going were crucial, because it was easy to get caught typing in the wrong figure. The best strategy was to wait until your partner in crime ran interference and the dietitian's attention was elsewhere before you entered the falsified figure.

Five spots are measured, so you also had to be smart about where you cut corners. Trimming every one could raise alarm bells, so half a point here or there was the way to go. The stomach was always my problem area; if it came up as 17.6, then it got typed in as 15.6.

Unfortunately those fun times were behind me, because scamming the skinfold test probably wasn't at the top of the leader's handbook.

The European adventure had been important on a number of levels. While it was obviously hard to leave Cooper at home, his grandparents and my sister, Bianca, certainly loved having the opportunity to look after our three-year-old, and the time away with Lauren was significant given that it had been a full-on year. The captaincy had been a bigger job than I'd imagined in terms of the requirements outside of the regular day-to-day running of the team. There were endless functions for sponsors and appearances where the captain was required. That meant I wasn't home as much as I should have been to help Lauren, so a trip away together was definitely needed.

In my absence, there was support at home from my uncle Jason, who'd been living with us for the past few years. Cooper loved hanging out with him, and his presence certainly helped the house run smoothly. He played many roles, from babysitter to drinking buddy to football coach reviewing my performance. His biggest role, though, was as resident handyman. Jason installs air-conditioning units for a living, and the running joke in our house was about how bad I am with any sort of tool. In fact, hammering a nail into a wall is something I can find a way to stuff up.

Getting away on holiday also helped force my mind to move on from the preliminary-final loss. Collingwood had been beaten by Geelong in the Grand Final. I'd attended because I had a commitment with one of my sponsors, Toyota, before the game. I then spent the afternoon with some of the retired players who'd done a pre-game lap of honour, including Brisbane's Daniel Bradshaw and Sydney's Tadhg Kennelly.

It had been tough to watch. I had to get away.

The heartbreaking loss had certainly been felt across the group, but it was exciting to turn up to pre-season training knowing that the team was a contender. It certainly made the 2.2-kilometre time trials in 30-degree heat easier to take. Well, for some people, anyway.

After lengthy debate, the traditional leadership group was rein-stated, with Buddy Franklin elevated to the nine-man panel courtesy of the coaches' input. They figured it might help his development on and off the field if he was engaged in the group. Importantly,

Mitch was back in an official capacity while Jordan Lewis and Jarryd Roughead were joint vice-captains.

Unfortunately, Lewy and Roughy got more action in their new roles than we wanted.

As part of the introduction of another franchise, the Greater Western Sydney Giants, for the 2012 season, the AFL's official launch was held in Sydney. The captains from every club assembled up there, with an all-in media day the main event. It meant I missed a training session leading into the season opener. Round 1 was to be a repeat of the preliminary-final match-up with Collingwood, and I'd been waiting six months for it.

I'd had a tight calf for a couple of days and it was still there when I got off the plane from Sydney, but I wanted to make up for the missed session. Even though it was our day off, I did a repeat speed session with Jack Russell. It probably wasn't the smartest idea to jump straight into that off the plane. When I cooled down, the tightness in the calf was worse.

The next day I spoke to Mitch, who had a history of calf problems, and he said that with some of them you were still able to play but you couldn't go flat out. I figured mine wasn't that bad and thought I'd be able to cruise around.

We had a light training run the day before the Friday-night blockbuster against the Magpies, and as I was doing the warm-up some doubt entered my mind. The calf still wasn't right, and it got tighter as I started training. I thought about walking off, but that would definitely mean I wouldn't play. Was my heart overriding what my head was saying?

All summer I'd thought about this game, so a little niggle wasn't a good enough reason to pull out. I stayed on the track and it seemed to start to warm up – or so I told myself.

The next drill was a set play off half-back where I had to run and receive the handball. As I was waiting for it to unfold, I kept telling myself not to run too fast. I took off and straight away the calf went pop. It felt like I'd been shot. I looked up and saw Jack staring at me. I shook my head, handballed the ball away and slowly walked off. I couldn't believe I'd been so stupid. I was not only going to miss Round 1 – I was probably looking at three or four weeks on the sidelines.

The other frustration was the fact that I'd ruined my family's holiday plans. I was coming into the season on 195 games, with my 200th-game milestone scheduled to be played in Launceston against Sydney. Mum, Dad, Bianca and Dylan, plus a heap of family and friends from Colac, had locked in airfares for the trip to Tasmania.

I've never been a good watcher, but there were many layers of disappointment as I walked into the MCG for the start of the 2012 season. I'd so wanted to be out there. I know it wasn't revenge, and it didn't make up for losing a preliminary final, but at least getting out and venting some of my built-up anger towards the Magpies would have made me feel better.

Thankfully, my teammates did it without me and did it in style. An eight-goal second quarter set up a 15-point half-time lead. It stayed around that mark until the final term, when we kicked another six goals to record an impressive 22-point victory. Buddy was brilliant, with five goals.

Geelong were next, and if I thought watching from the stands was hard normally, this was a whole different level.

We controlled the Easter Monday game for most of the afternoon and led by three goals at three-quarter time. Then driving rain struck the MCG, which normally means it's hard for the team chasing to make up ground. Geelong forward James Podsiadly had been lively all day and proceeded to kick three goals in the final term. With six minutes remaining, they were in front.

There were so many 'nearly' moments after that – the biggest coming in the final 20 seconds, when Roughy flew high and got two bites of a mark just 20 metres out from goal. It looked like it had stuck until the last second, then from the spillage Jack Gunston kicked a point. It was our fifth for the quarter; we'd gone goalless. The two-point loss made it eight consecutive losses to Geelong.

I did get back for that Round 5 game against Sydney in Launceston, but it was game number 196 and not the double century. And it was a forgettable one. We gave up a 20-point lead at half-time and conceded seven goals in the final quarter to lose by 37 points. The Swans were undefeated while we slipped to 11th, having won just two of five games.

It was the third time for the year we'd been overrun late in a game. Something wasn't right, and the leadership group called a players-only heart-to-heart meeting. It wasn't crisis time by any stretch, but sometimes an open and honest conversation among teammates can clear the air quickly and regenerate a group. Who knows whether it worked or not, but at least we got back on the winner's list the following week against St Kilda.

I certainly wasn't smiling afterwards – in fact, I was in pain. There had been an incident in the second half when St Kilda's David Armitage moved back into me as I went for a mark. I put my knee up to block the space, but something went wrong. The impact on the knee was significant and it was instantly sore. I hobbled around for a few minutes on it but had a sense there was something amiss.

Three days later, I was sitting in the medical room at Waverley Park as the club's medical staff discussed my future. Scans had revealed I had a tear to the posterior cruciate ligament in my left knee, as well as some medial ligament damage. Initially I didn't particularly like where the conversation was going: one course of action was for me to have reconstructive surgery, which would end my season. The other option, which was far more appealing even though there was an element of risk to it, was to rehab the injury and see if it healed. There were no guarantees, but at least it would give me a chance.

I wasn't allowed to do anything for six weeks. There was to be no running. We just had to be patient and let nature run its course.

Nature had certainly come through for Lauren and me – we had another baby on the way. We were both as relieved as we were excited. Lauren had experienced a second miscarriage, this time after six weeks, which led to her seeking some answers. Thankfully, there were things we could do. She went on medication to help with the problem and it was all worth it, although the new baby had an interesting due date of around late September or early October. Potentially that could throw up a curve ball, but there was one minor detail that had to be taken care of. I had to get back playing.

'I think Hodgey is in trouble.'

I was sitting upstairs with my uncle Jason watching Fox Footy's *On the Couch* program. Those words were being spoken by the *Herald Sun*'s chief football writer, Mike Sheahan.

'I think he might be finished.'

Jason seemed as shocked as I was at what we were hearing.

Sheahan went on to suggest that my body had taken such a pounding over the years that I would struggle to come back from the knee injury. His theory was based on how fast the game was becoming – he figured I'd struggle to adapt when I got back.

I was stunned. The shock then turned to anger.

'Fuck off, Sheahan,' I said. I'd had two unfortunate injuries. The calf was a stupid mistake that I had to take responsibility for, but the knee was a collision injury. It had nothing to do with my age or the speed of the game.

I couldn't get Sheahan's words out of my head over the next few days. I'd already missed a couple of months, and there hadn't been a lot of improvement in the knee.

The truth was that, like Sheahan, I had doubts. Andrew 'Jack' Russell was the only person who knew about them, as I'd had many conversations with him in recent times on the subject. Maybe Sheahan had a point: I was 28 years of age, and for a decade the body had taken a battering.

Jack was brilliant. He wouldn't have a bar of the talk that my career was over. 'I guarantee you this is not going to be an issue,' he said.

After riding a rollercoaster of emotions for a while, I decided to channel my anger in a good way and turn it into motivation. I typed Sheahan's words into my mobile phone and saved them in the notes section so I could look at them any time. I'd always loved proving people wrong. It was that competitive streak in me. If someone said I couldn't do something, I'd move heaven and earth to do it.

Sheahan had started something.

There was one unexpected benefit of my time out: I learnt to become a better captain. When you watch games from the coach's box, everything looks easier and mistakes are magnified. Initially

I would go down at half-time or at the next week's leadership group meeting and question the boys. Why didn't you chase then? Why didn't you push to pick up the loose man?

Lewis pulled me aside and said, 'Your feedback is a bit harsh. Mate, it's not as easy as it looks sitting up there.'

It was a good reality check.

As he explained it, what looked like an easy kick from the grandstand was anything but when you had someone defending you, pressure from all sides and voices everywhere. And often the failure to push 50 metres to man up was because the player had five efforts in a row and was genuinely stuffed.

I gained more understanding and sympathy from my time on the sidelines. In many ways I was a very demanding leader on the field, but after what Lewis said, I understood that I had to improve the way I gave feedback. You always had to look at both sides – not just go on what you saw, but think about what was in the player's mind as well.

My mind was gripped by frustration. The knee problem had lingered and lingered. Initially we thought it would be a six-to-eight-week recovery, but it was pushing three months before I got the all-clear to have a run around with Box Hill. I'd tried to return a few weeks earlier but the knee had swollen up and I'd had to have fluid drained from it.

It was certainly an interesting return. I forgot my boots so had to drive out to Waverley to get them, and then I ran out wearing number 75, given Box Hill had their own list numbers with number 15 already taken. We were playing against Collingwood at Victoria Park and I managed to kick one goal and get 24 possessions.

Fortunately, Clarko had seen enough. He told me he had a special job for me on my AFL return. We were playing Essendon in Round 18 at Docklands, and he wanted me to tag veteran defender Dustin Fletcher. Fletcher had been a dominant figure in the Bombers' structure for several years and the springboard for a lot of their attacking moves.

I didn't care where I played – I just wanted to run out again. Defensive forward worked fine for me.

Something pretty impressive had been happening while I was out – we were on a seven-game winning streak and sitting third on the ladder. Essendon were sitting seventh, so it was built up as the match of the round, given it was in prime time on a Friday night.

With an eight-goals-to-one first quarter, we blew the Bombers out of the water. They never recovered and we enjoyed a night out. The margin was 11 goals at half-time and a stunning 94 points at the final siren. It was the perfect type of game to return in, and I was lucky enough to get on the end of a few and kicked five goals.

A loss to Geelong was next, and this could have been the worst of the lot. With 75 seconds left on the clock, the play was 15 metres out from our goal with a ball-up, and our lead was three points. Surely, this time.

The ball spilled out towards centre half-forward and into the hands of Clinton Young, whose snap from 40 metres cleared two players near the goal line and then bounced into the post.

Geelong went straight down the middle, but a great tackle stopped Podsiadly from going long into their forward line. Rather than go back and steady, we hurried the ball forward and it ended up in the pocket, where Paul Puopolo attempted a miracle goal out of midair. Instead, the ball went across to the other side of the goals, where Geelong defender Andrew Mackie marked. The clock was down to 35 seconds and the Cats were surging, with free men out ahead. The centring pass was marked by Joel Selwood a second before Brad Sewell flew in to try and spoil. Selwood played on immediately and his kick found Tom Hawkins on the lead.

I watched all this unfold from the interchange bench. In my second game back, I couldn't get near it and was subbed off. The AFL had introduced a rule the previous year where teams were only allowed three on the interchange and one substitute. When the sub was activated, the player he'd replaced wasn't allowed back on the ground and, to rub salt into the wound, he was required to wear a red vest to make sure everyone knew who was the sub.

Not being able to be out there during those frantic moments, especially as captain, was excruciating. Hawkins had already kicked five goals for the night, and as he started his run-up the siren sounded. He was 60 metres out and it never looked like missing.

The Kennett curse had now reached nine consecutive games, and even the non-believers were starting to think there was something weird going on with Geelong–Hawthorn matches.

Ironically I did end up playing my 200th game in Launceston, but it was three months after I'd planned. We celebrated in style by thrashing Port Adelaide by 72 points and our push for a top-two spot gained momentum.

A ten-goal win against the Gold Coast followed the next week, before a top-of-the-table clash with Sydney at the SCG in Round 22. We were boosted by the return of Buddy, who'd missed six games because of a hamstring problem. He proved to be a fairly handy inclusion, kicking four goals as we rallied from an early deficit to win by seven points.

A strong performance against West Coast in the final round ensured top spot and a showdown with Collingwood in the qualifying final. The Magpies had finished in fourth, just a game away from us.

Our confidence as a team was certainly up, and I was starting to get some sort of touch back. The only major issue was Guerra, who tore his hamstring in the final home-and-away game. We also lost Young, and Lewis was a late withdrawal for the first final. And then Brendan Whitecross seriously injured his knee at the five-minute mark.

It was a typical pressurised opening and no goals were kicked for almost half the quarter. I started forward again, spending time on my former Geelong Falcon teammate Nick Maxwell. He'd turned into an excellent intercept-mark player and a great leader. It helped that I hit the scoreboard, scoring the first goal of the night with a quick snap out of a stoppage. We slowly gained the ascendancy and when Buddy kicked a goal after the half-time siren our lead was 18 points.

It was one of those nights where we seemed to have the answers. Every time Collingwood looked like building some momentum, a Hawthorn player would stand up. Buddy came to the party with four goals but there was an even spread of contributors behind him, with Breust, Gunston, Hale, Rioli, Shane Savage and I all kicking two goals.

In the end it was a comfortable 38-point win, which ensured we would get the opportunity to right a few wrongs after our last visit to the preliminary final, 12 months earlier.

Well, Hawthorn got the opportunity. I didn't.

On the Tuesday leading up to the preliminary final, in which we were playing Adelaide, I started to feel a bit crook after training.

We had Wednesday off. I still wasn't right on Thursday but forced myself to get out on the track. By the time I got home I was in serious trouble. I was sweating profusely and experiencing bouts of diarrhoea and vomiting. Lauren was heavily pregnant and due at any time, so obviously she couldn't afford to catch whatever bug was attacking me. I rang the club and the doctors quickly arranged for me to get to hospital, where I was put on a drip for a couple of hours.

It seemed to stabilise a little bit overnight, but I wasn't eating anything. And the scales were telling me a scary tale: I'd dropped 4 kilos in 24 hours. I knew if I was to play in the preliminary final, I had to train the day before the game. Somehow I managed to find a way to complete the session, but it was through gritted teeth with my fingers crossed.

My normal pre-game routine involved a bowl of pasta the night before. I figured I needed to stick to the routine and went to Fasta Pasta with Grant Birchall. I ordered my normal big dish with loads of sauce, wanting to try and put some of the weight back on. It was a big mistake. I couldn't keep anything down. Even if I had a sip of water I would spew it up. The sweating and diarrhoea got worse that night and I couldn't stop them. I'd never been so sick in my life.

The thought of not playing in a preliminary final because of illness just didn't make sense in my mind. I would have to be almost dead not to play – but the problem was that I felt like I was dying.

My mind was cluttered, but when it clicked over with its captain's hat on, I started to think about the team-first mentality we were trying to instil in the group. It was up to me to set the example. If I played, at best I'd get through a half. But at what level? Was that the best thing for the team?

I decided to sleep on it. Well, I decided to *try* to sleep on it. But the sweats came back and I was virtually living in the toilet.

By morning, I knew I had no choice. I was almost in tears as I dialled Clarko's number. From that point on, the day seemed to go ridiculously slowly. I couldn't believe what had happened. I was sad, then I was angry, then I was frustrated. But most of all I felt helpless.

It was a twilight final at the MCG, starting at the strange time of 5.15 p.m. I was nervous knowing there was nothing I could do and that for the next couple of hours I just had to sit there and pray that my teammates could get it done. My anxiousness rose when I saw how Adelaide started the game. They looked 'on'.

Lauren and I were watching the game together upstairs at home. I'd obviously not watched many Hawthorn games with her, and it was soon apparent that this wasn't a good time to start. She was a very animated viewer, groaning and jumping around if there was a close call or when Adelaide kicked a goal. At quarter-time I'd had enough. 'Either you're going downstairs or I'm going downstairs. You're giving me the shits,' I said.

It was an interesting choice of words, given what I'd gone through over the past 48 hours, but Lauren knew I meant it in the nicest possible way.

The margin was seven points their way at quarter-time, and they were still in front at half-time after Tex Walker kicked a ripping goal from 60 metres on the siren.

My virus sweats were getting worse because of my nerves. Four goals in a row by us during the third quarter at least brought the heart rate down. A 16-point three-quarter-time lead was good, but it wasn't enough. When Kurt Tippett kicked truly for the Crows, they were within 11 points and I was starting to get seriously worried. Surely my season couldn't end like this, alone in my bedroom, saturated in sweat and on the verge of vomiting.

With six minutes remaining, Crows forward Jason Porplyzia collected David Hale, which earnt the big man a free kick. It had been a late hit and youngster Ryan Schoenmakers wasn't impressed, so he gave Porplyzia a nice bump to let him know we didn't appreciate those types of actions. Porplyzia went down as if he'd been shot, which opened the door for one of the worst decisions I've ever seen.

I couldn't believe it when the field umpire ran in and reversed the free kick, handing Porplyzia a shot at goal from 45 metres. As the ball sailed through to reduce the margin to five points, I lost it. After delivering a torrent of abuse at the TV, I stormed into the bathroom. I couldn't watch any more and decided to take a shower. The water was almost hypnotic as it soothed my aching body, which had taken a battering over the past few days.

I was too scared to go back out and see the score. If we lost, I wasn't sure how I would handle it. The fact that a tummy bug had kept me out of a preliminary final was embarrassing. As I turned the water off, I stood still, trying to make out the sound coming from the bedroom. I couldn't wait any longer. I grabbed a towel and charged through the door.

The first thing that struck me was the sound. It was familiar . . . it was the Hawthorn club song! We must have won!

Oh my God. I was going to be playing in another Grand Final.

Lauren heard my carry-on and raced upstairs. We hugged as my illness was momentarily forgotten.

It was a while before I saw the highlights and filled in the blanks between Porplyzia's goal and the siren. The Crows had actually hit the lead with five minutes remaining but then Cyril had come to life. He kicked a goal to put us back in front and then, with three minutes left, handballed to Buddy for an easy goal. This put us ten points up. Then Walker got one back for the Crows with just under 30 seconds left on the clock. Thankfully, we found a way to defend it and the final score was Hawthorn 13.19 (97) to Adelaide 14.8 (92).

My phone started going nuts with messages. There was a theme to them all. 'Hurry up and get well!'

We were going to the big dance again, and there was no way a dodgy tummy was going to stop me from playing this one.

12

HEARTBREAK

The irony wasn't lost on me.

I was in a meeting talking about putting weight on, not getting it off, which was a career first. It's fair to say I'd never been more engaged in a conversation with a dietitian. I knew getting my body back to normal operating order in just a few days was crucial. I was going to need some magic from Simone Austin.

It was the Monday of Grand Final week and my quarantine from the team had been lifted. I'd lost 4 kilos and hadn't even been able to get out of bed two days earlier. Rebuilding my energy stocks was the priority.

Vegemite on toast and Gastrolyte were about all I'd been able to consume. I couldn't just go out and have five Big Macs in an eating binge to try to get the weight back on, so an eating plan was put in place. Hopefully by the end of the week it would have me back to as close to normal as possible.

On Tuesday I took part in a light training session, and it felt good just to be kicking the footy again. I never got out of second gear, but that would happen in the main training session on Thursday. I also had a new nickname courtesy of Mitch, who started calling me 'Sniffles' because I'd missed the biggest game of the year so far through illness.

'Are you all right, Sniffles?' Mitch would constantly ask.

What I was doing a lot of was sleeping. My regulation eight hours a night had turned into 12 as my body was still fatigued from what the virus had done to it. It was all part of rebuilding the energy levels, which had certainly improved enough by Thursday for me to show Clarko and Jack that I was going to be able to play in two days' time.

The illness certainly took care of any Grand Final week nerves. I didn't really have time to think too much about Sydney and the challenges they presented. I had enough challenges of my own to deal with.

Defender Tom Murphy was the unlucky one who had to make way for me in the team. There were 12 new faces compared to the team of 2008, as Guerra's attempt to come back from his hamstring injury had failed. The key defensive posts were overhauled, with Josh Gibson, Ben Stratton and Ryan Schoenmakers the new faces. Left-footer Matt Suckling had also emerged. There was a new look at the other end too, with Jack Gunston, a leading forward we'd got from Adelaide, adding a different dimension, along with goal sneaks Breust and Puopolo. The midfield had been injected with pace from Isaac Smith and class from Shaun Burgoyne, plus we had new additions in Liam Shiels, Shane Savage and ruckman David Hale.

Sydney were a consistently strong team and played a hard, contested style of game. We knew what we were up against. We'd split our two meetings during the year, so it looked like it was going to be an old-fashioned dogfight.

The weather supported that theory: it was pouring rain as we assembled in the city on Friday for the Grand Final parade. Instead of sitting on the tray of the ute, this time we had to be inside. I had Cooper sitting on my lap, waving to the crowd. It was incredible in its size, given how wet it was.

Lauren had got in early about the pending arrival of our second child, declaring that if the baby came on Saturday, she would have all the support she needed, and that I was to try to win the family a second premiership. This meant a lot, but I was praying it wouldn't be an issue. All the indications suggested that next week was the more likely arrival time.

Luckily the rain eased by the time we got to the Old Treasury Building, where my first major official gig as captain took place. The premiership cup was sitting in the middle of the stage with brown and gold streamers attached to one handle and the red and white of Sydney on the other. The role of the two captains was to hold it up together and present it to the crowd. Sydney had co-captains, and it was Adam Goodes who had the job of lifting it with me. There was a fair bit of awkwardness about the whole exercise, and the photographers wanted shots from all angles.

A press conference inside was next, with the two coaches and two captains. I sat at the end of the table and didn't offer much. There was one question about my health, which I answered simply with, 'I'm fine.'

I was fine compared to where I'd been a week ago. The eating hadn't come as easily as I'd thought, and I'd only put a couple of kilos back on. I was definitely a lot more tired than normal, but once I crossed that white line there would be no excuses.

Sleep certainly wasn't an issue on Grand Final Eve, as I still had lingering fatigue from the virus. My pre-game jog through the streets of Glen Iris was achieved, surprisingly, under blue skies, although in typical Melbourne fashion it was raining when I drove into the MCG. It was a different feeling from that of four years earlier. The nerves were obviously still there, but just the fact that I knew what to expect brought with it an air of confidence.

Did I have confidence in my body? I knew I was fit enough to play, and I also knew I wouldn't let my teammates down. That had been the main issue in the lead-up to the preliminary final. I'd made the right call then, and I knew I'd made the right call this time.

The theme throughout the pre-game was all about playing the same way as we had all year. The Hawthorn way had got us to top of the ladder and Clarko just reinforced the need to deliver on that again – there was no need to go outside it.

Leading the team out was a special moment. As we stepped outside the rooms there was a line of Hawthorn's premiership cups on display along the walkway to the ground's entrance. The club had won ten, the first in 1961. Number 11 had a nice sound to it.

I had an early victory as captain: the toss.

Sydney's other co-captain, Jarrad McVeigh, called and got it wrong. I decided to kick to the city end because it felt like the wind was blowing more in that direction. While it always seemed to swirl around inside the magnificent stadium, the warm-up proved that there was an advantage at that end.

Clarko wanted me to play the quarterback role again across half-back, and we were going to try to orchestrate a loose man in defence by starting seven in their forward half. It was a tactic Richmond had used successfully against the Swans in recent times and we'd studied what they'd done.

The search for that elusive first touch in the opening minute saw me come up with something different. I went third man up in a ruck contest and managed to get the tap. A soccer off the ground soon followed and then I put myself in position to get my first clean possession. The problem was that I didn't get a chance to take it. I'd earnt a free kick after I was taken high at a throw-in and quickly went back and played on, but just as I was in the kicking action, the umpire blew his whistle.

'Blood rule, Hodgey,' he said.

I hadn't noticed anything but blood was streaming from a cut above my right eye. A couple of minutes later I was back on with a bandage over the eye and all the way around my head.

As anticipated, the game was an arm wrestle for most of the first quarter. We got moving in the final three minutes. Buddy nailed a set shot from 50 metres, and then in the final 40 seconds we kicked two goals. Breust delivered a clever dribble goal after a good passage of play and from the re-start we got the centre clearance through Mitch. His quick kick lobbed to centre half-forward, where Gunston roved the pack perfectly and then slotted a snap over his shoulder from 50 metres.

We certainly needed the late spark. With the wind, a quarter-time lead of 19 points was only a pass mark.

The second quarter was anything but that. We scored one point for the entire term, while Sydney kicked six goals straight and went into half-time leading by 16 points. I went into a few centre bounces to try to get something happening, but the Swans seemed to be playing to a plan. They were certainly limiting our space, and the extra spare in their defence seemed to be working. Every time we looked up and inevitably headed towards Buddy, they would have two or three near him. One thing was obvious: they'd done their homework.

Physically I got through, although I didn't find much of the ball and was one of many who needed to lift. Sewelly was clearly our best player, but he didn't have enough friends.

Nothing really changed at the start of the third quarter – in fact, it got worse. Josh Kennedy, who had started his career at Hawthorn, kicked the opening goal and then Lewis Roberts-Thomson scored another. Three minutes in, their lead was 27 points. This wasn't how the script was supposed to go.

But history showed that we couldn't panic. Momentum would swing our way again – we just had to be ready for it.

Finally, with ten minutes remaining in the quarter, Hale got a free kick and nailed the shot from 50 metres. In the next five minutes we kicked four goals. It was exhilarating football. Buddy kicked two, both off one step from 55 metres, Gunston nailed a tough set shot, and Smith burst through the middle of the ground and kicked a beautiful long goal to put us in front. An undisciplined 50-metre penalty against Mitch for not throwing the ball back properly took the wind out of our sails, handing McVeigh a goal and the Swans a one-point lead at three-quarter time.

There wasn't going to be a magical move by Clarko to win the game – this one was on the players. A premiership was within our grasp and we just had to do the work required to grab it properly.

Before we left the huddle, I dragged all the boys together. You never know what to say in these times, and I'm not sure if anyone listens, but I decided to stress a couple of points. 'The momentum is ours. Let's just keep running, keep playing on as much as we can,' I said. 'We're going to get them.'

And we did. Inside the first minute.

Breust again got on the end of a brilliant Cyril Rioli handball to kick his second goal. And then, 30 seconds later, Hale snapped one out of a stoppage and suddenly we were 11 points in front. The game then hung in a holding pattern for about ten minutes.

Unfortunately, we didn't break the deadlock. It was Swans midfielder Dan Hannebery. With ten minutes left, there was only a goal in it.

My cut head again caused a distraction, with the umpire sending me off to get a new tape job. As I returned, Sydney drew level in the most unfortunate circumstances. Swans midfielder Kieren Jack was chasing a soccered ball towards goal but Clinton Young got in front of him to defuse the situation . . . or so we thought. Young fell over, and as he lay sprawled on the ground, Jack ran onto the ball and kicked the easiest of goals.

A minute later I was back on the bench. More blood. I'd managed to get through three and a half quarters without an issue, and now I'd been off twice in three minutes. I was waiting to get back on when Sydney took the lead. A long bomb deep into their forward line was roved off the pack by Goodes, and his quick snap bounced through. We had just over six minutes to win back the Grand Final.

Often in these situations you need a lucky break or you need Buddy Franklin. He pulled down a big mark at centre half-forward, 55 metres out. It was in range for him but he decided to do the unselfish thing and kick it to Gunston, who had got free in the forward pocket. Gunston was easily the best shot at goal in the club – possibly even in the competition – but he hit the post.

We knew more chances would come, and managed to form a wall with the ball living in our half of the ground. A couple of left-foot snaps by Sewelly registered behinds, and with three minutes left the margin was four points. At some stage the Swans were going to get a break, and sure enough, they managed to get it to half-forward where Lewis Jetta marked. He soaked up a bit of time and then kicked it long towards the goal square. The ball hit the deck and bodies went everywhere to trap it in. We had a lot of numbers back, but the clock was our enemy and we needed to move it quickly. I was on the defensive side of the ball-up and we managed to force the ball away from goal.

Then, through a mass of bodies, I saw a Swans player somehow get the ball to his boot. It was Nick Malceski. He was a left-footer, and it was on the perfect side for him. I knew instantly he'd made good contact and almost didn't want to look up. It was very high, it was floating . . . it was a goal.

With less than a minute left, Sydney pushed all their players back. We needed a miracle. We didn't get one. The ball pinged around the centre square for a couple of moments and then I was chasing a couple of Swans when the sound I'd been dreading erupted around the MCG. It was over. We'd lost the Grand Final.

Ten points. Ten bloody points.

I hunched over with my hands on my knees as a group of Sydney players jumped on top of each other a couple of metres away. I felt numb and couldn't help but think we'd blown it. The Swans had obviously played well, and they'd come with a plan and executed it. Why hadn't we done the same? What had gone wrong? It was 26 scoring shots to 21, so we'd had plenty of opportunities.

I was still in a world of my own when Hawthorn legend John Kennedy approached. He'd coached the club to three premierships, and if we'd won today he would have been handing over this year's cup.

'Bad luck. It's part of football,' he said. 'Hold your head up high and just go and get them next year.'

As much as I wanted to leave the field and sit alone in a darkened room, I had an important job to do. The losing captain always speaks first at the presentation. I'd been given some sound advice about jotting down a couple of notes before the game that would work whether we won or lost. I retrieved them from our media manager on my way up to the stage.

The Swans were first on my list of acknowledgements, then the AFL and its sponsors, Hawthorn's sponsors, Clarko and the coaches, and the players' partners and parents. The final word went to my teammates. 'I know with the group we've got we will be back here next year,' I said.

The next few hours were torture. We had to attend an official dinner and everyone tried to put on a brave face. We had a couple of beers but it certainly had a different taste to it. My head was elsewhere.

Fortunately, I had an excellent reason to excuse myself from the wake over the next couple of days. Lauren was ready to pop any second. The added bonus of the pending birth was that I missed Clarko's review of the game, which by all reports wasn't pretty. Fingers were pointed, as they needed to be.

The whole season had been a train wreck for me because of the knee. I'd only played ten games and felt like I was at a crossroads in my career. But before I could worry about that, I had much more important things to take care of. On Wednesday 3 October, we welcomed our second son, Chase Brady, into the world. He arrived at 12.15 p.m. and weighed an impressive 3.9 kilos.

Lauren was again amazing and it was good to have a reason to smile again.

However, I wasn't much of a help when they came home. We traded places and I headed to hospital for two rounds of surgery. We'd sought out leading orthopaedic surgeon Julian Feller and I'd had further scans on the knee that showed there was an ongoing issue. We had to make a call about it. I could push on and probably get through to next season with some swelling and soreness here and there, or I could go in and get it fixed properly. We decided on the second option.

The operation was a posterior cruciate ligament reconstruction and the recovery was at least six months, which would put the start of the 2013 season in jeopardy. I went in on the Monday for the surgery and, while I was in there, decided we might as well knock over two birds with one stone. I'd been carrying a problem with the knuckle of the little finger on my right hand for a while. It was bent out of place and surgery was required to fix it. So, two days after the knee operation, I went under again to fix my busted finger.

This all meant that when I eventually got out of hospital I wasn't much help to Lauren and the boys. I wanted a fresh start physically and mentally. Things had to change – and Mike Sheahan had to be proved wrong.

13

CHANGING WAYS

'I won't have lollies or chocolate until the end of the season.'

It was New Year's Eve and 2013 was only hours away when I made this resolution to Lauren. She raised her eyebrows, knowing how much of a sweet tooth I was.

'But there's one allowance,' I quickly added. 'I'm allowed to have an M&M McFlurry. They're not something you have every day, only on a special occasion. I'm going to need at least one release.'

This got a laugh out of my wife, but I was deadly serious about my 2013 makeover.

Call it an epiphany, call it a light-bulb moment, but something had clearly shifted in my brain. The realisation that football wouldn't last forever had hit me like a ton of bricks. It was almost like I'd seen the dark side, had a peek at life without football when I was out injured, and been scarred by the experience. I wasn't ready for it to end yet, and to ensure that didn't happen I had to change. I had to be elite with my preparation.

I'd had an interesting conversation with one of our assistant coaches, Adam Simpson, about the year ahead. He played 306 games for North Melbourne, was captain for five seasons and was a member of two premiership teams. Simpson explained how when he turned 30, he started to drop 1 kilo in weight each pre-season. He found that this helped him to continue at the same level, whether it was a mindset thing or because his body felt lighter and more free. He figured he had to be proactive and do as much as he could to delay the wall that every AFL player hits at some point. That's the moment when the game passes you by, when you realise you can no longer do what you used to be able to do and that there are faster, stronger, younger players who can. I was only 28, and I wanted no part of that wall.

There wasn't any overseas footy trip. Instead, Lauren and I took the two boys down to Sorrento for a couple of weeks. I wasn't allowed to run until January because of the knee injury, so I walked everywhere – and I mean *everywhere*.

Beer was out, red wine was the drink of choice if we were having one, and I was religiously sticking to the Lite n' Easy program again. It was a completely different mindset, and it showed when I returned to pre-season training in November. My weight was down to 88 kilos and my skinfolds were around 50, which was more than satisfactory considering I was only walking and doing light gym exercises.

*

The lingering hurt of the Grand Final loss had played on the minds of most of us, in particular Brad Sewell, who'd made contact with me when he returned from an overseas holiday. He'd done a bit of soul searching and wanted a meeting with Jack Russell, player development manager Jason Burt and myself.

This was one of the reasons I loved Sewelly. We were a good combination – he was a deep thinker who brought a lot to the table, things I would never have even contemplated. We met at a cafe in Camberwell and Sewelly said he'd jotted down notes while he was on holiday because he was worried about the direction the team was headed. His main point was that he felt there was something missing in the relationships the players had with each other. The bond we required to be a special team was missing. 'We need to have more of an interest in each other,' he said.

He talked about incidents in the Grand Final as examples of players going outside team rules. He put his own hand up about taking a shot at goal instead of centring the ball; I was also guilty of ignoring that basic rule. There were a number of other undisciplined acts, like Sam Mitchell giving away that crucial 50-metre penalty by not throwing the ball back properly.

Sewelly felt that our care for one another, that immeasurable element, wasn't there when the heat was on in a game. There was a disconnect.

We agreed we needed to become a more selfless, team-first football side. Changes were already in motion – we were going back to Ray McLean's Leading Teams model. It was decided that the perfect environment to further discuss and work on implementing change was the pre-season training camp in Mooloolaba, Queensland, in early December. Clarko and the coaching panel had come up with a set of behaviours and team rules they wanted to enforce.

McLean attended the camp and was explaining expectations at a team meeting when a hand was raised at the back of the group. It was Luke Lowden, a 206-centimetre ruckman who'd been at the club since 2009 but was yet to play a senior game.

'What's wrong, mate?' I asked. Something was obviously weighing on the big man's mind.

'This is all good, and I understand why we're doing it, but we've heard this all before from the leaders. Nothing changes,' he said. 'You keep saying you're going to do this and going to do that, but when are you actually going to follow through with it?'

Whack.

He wasn't finished. 'When it comes to big games, that's when all these behaviours and standards get thrown out the window. And it's you guys as leaders who aren't sticking to them. What do you expect the other players to do?'

The outburst stunned all of us. I was actually momentarily lost for words, but we'd wanted feedback and we'd most certainly got it.

After the meeting finished, the leadership group, which included Jordan Lewis, Jarryd Roughead, Josh Gibson, Mitch and Sewelly, stayed behind. The more I thought about what Lowden had said, the more I realised he was right.

'You know what? He's got a point,' I said. The others around the table agreed.

The on-field discipline wasn't there. We were all guilty of giving away silly free kicks and going outside team rules. The kicker was that many of us thought this was the reason we'd just let a premiership slip. Lowden clearly thought so, and I'm sure he wasn't alone.

What was needed was an honesty system among the players.

Coaches can have trademarks for out on the ground, which are essentially things that a team live by. Whether that is a certain style of play or an attitude, it's a trademark where every player in the team knows what's expected in connection with it and understands they are judged against it. However, the reality is that unless the players come up with these and have ownership of them, they're not going to stick to them. McLean and Clarko both agreed that from now on, the leadership group, and by extension the whole playing list, had to take on the responsibility of enforcing the team's values and rules.

'It's not my job to police it – it's up to you guys,' Clarko declared. 'You guys set it up and I'll follow what you say.'

After much discussion, six behaviours were identified as the foundation for the team's values, four of them on-field and two off.

The off-field behaviours related to how elite and respectful a player was away from the footy field, the difference between the seen and the unseen. Are you as good away from the club as you are inside the four walls? Do you respect everyone at the club – not just your teammates, but the staff upstairs and the people making you lunch every day?

The on-field behaviours took in a number of obvious areas, with the difference that now your teammates would be holding you accountable. We borrowed some of the language for the trademarks from legendary coach John Kennedy.

The first was 'Commando football', which involved going when it was your turn, putting your head over the ball and showing courage.

Next was 'Ego on the hook', which meant putting the team first. Did you take the shot from the boundary line instead of centring the ball? Did you try to dodge through two opponents instead of giving off the first-option handball?

Then there was 'Selfless', which included acts like running 30 metres to cover for a teammate and giving a block or a bump, or if someone knocked over your teammate and then going in and flying the flag.

The final trademark was 'Open and honest communication'. Are you having the difficult chats? It had to be two-way communication, so if you give feedback, then you have to accept it as well. There also had to be an understanding that it wasn't personal. The tough conversations were to benefit your performance and the club's.

A rating system was set up as the vehicle for change. After every game, each player would rate himself out of ten, with seven seen as a pass mark. We all also had to rate the four key on-field value areas with either green, which was a pass, or red, for a fail.

Each behaviour had a buzzword associated with it that, in time, would become second nature and enable players to recognise it on the field and act accordingly.

The leadership group would review each other's ratings, and Clarko would then give his assessment. Often he would have the benefit of watching a recording of the game, so he'd come armed with more information, which could be either good or bad for the player's own rating. This way, the leaders were being held accountable for their actions just like the rest of the playing group.

What soon became obvious was that the new system led to some tough discussions. For example, if a player rated himself an eight with four greens, yet you recalled him failing to centre the ball or the vision showed him ducking his head in a contest and also not pushing over to help a teammate, then you would call him on it.

The key to the system was open and honest communication, which also applied to Clarko and the leadership group.

It was decided that for leadership meetings, which would happen every Monday morning, the eight blokes around the table – six players, Chris Fagan and Clarko – would be on equal standing. There would be no hierarchy. Clarko wouldn't be the boss. He was just one of the eight and, like everyone else, subject to honest and open feedback.

It's fair to say there were some teething problems in getting to this stage. Originally only Fagan had sat in the leadership meetings and taken notes. He would relay messages to Clarko if there were any concerns about what he was doing at training or an issue on game day that the players weren't happy about.

Sometimes the message could be misconstrued when it was being delivered second-hand, and I'd already butted heads with the coach a few times during my captaincy stint. One big moment in our relationship came when we lost the preliminary final to Collingwood in 2011. Afterwards some players voiced concerns about a few things they didn't like about what Clarko was doing, so I called a meeting with the senior players to nut them out and figure out the next course of action.

We told Fagan that we needed to chat with Clarko to sort some things out.

As the coach walked in, he declared, 'Right – this would want to be good.'

I knew that wasn't a good way to start, so I told him to come back in a few minutes when we were ready to go. We were actually ready, but the discussion had to be on our terms. It was a gutsy call from me and, given the death stare I received from the coach, I wasn't sure it was the right one. He stormed out and slammed the door behind him. 'He's going to kill you,' was the consensus around the table.

Clarko was boiling when he returned, and later admitted he'd wanted to punch me that day. But the beauty of our relationship was that we moved on quickly and we both knew that everything we did was for the benefit of the team. Hopefully this new system would instil that mentality in the rest of the group.

We needed to be better in big games, because as far as I was concerned we'd choked in 2011 and again in 2012. I was sick of choking.

14

BREAKING THE CURSE

'Look, mate, we know there is a lot of pressure on you.'

Buddy Franklin was moving uncomfortably in his seat as I spoke to him. Around him was the rest of the leadership group, plus Clarko and Chris Fagan.

'We want you to stay, but whatever decision you make at the end of the year, that's not the priority right now. As long as you play Hawthorn footy now, focus on that, because we're in prime position to contest for a flag.'

Buddy was out of contract at the end of the season and had put negotiations on hold until the end of the year. This was never a good sign.

Adding to our nervousness was the fact that the AFL's new franchise, Greater Western Sydney, who'd joined the competition in

2012, had targeted Buddy to be their marquee player. There were rumours of a $10 million, five-year deal on the table, which we all knew was too good for him to refuse.

Buddy was the best player in the game. His athleticism for his height was unbelievable. He was 199 centimetres yet he ran like the wind, and for pure talent there was no one like him. He played the hardest position on the ground and often had two or three defenders dropping off him but still couldn't be stopped.

Buddy had won our best-and-fairest in the 2008 premiership year and finished second in 2010. He'd led our goal kicking for the past six years and had won the Coleman Medal for the most goals in the competition in 2008 and 2011. He was also a four-time All Australian.

But off the field it wasn't easy being Buddy Franklin. He was the biggest thing in town, which didn't match up well with his personality. He was a very private person who couldn't go out without being constantly harassed for photos and autographs. Rumour was that if he went out for lunch or a coffee, it always had to be at his local cafe, where the owners looked after him with an area off to the side away from prying eyes.

The amount of scrutiny he was under had reached a ridiculous level. If he sneezed, people would ring the club, and the number of things he was supposed to have done that got reported in the media was staggering. These would inevitably find their way to the leadership group, and when we spoke to other players they'd say they were with Buddy on the night in question and there was no way he'd done what was being alleged.

It was when he was out with people not connected with the football club that he seemed to find trouble. In saying that, he was only doing what most 20-something males did. But sometimes he got caught up in the moment. The thing we all figured out pretty early was that Buddy never liked being told what to do. If you went hard at him, he'd get defensive and annoyed.

We'd decided to call Buddy in after the first month of the season because we knew the speculation would continue to build. We figured that by laying all the cards on the table, by addressing the elephant in the room, Buddy would feel more comfortable and be able to focus on our 2013 campaign.

There were certainly no early signs that things were weighing on his mind. Our star centre half-forward kicked 15 goals in the opening four games, three of which we won convincingly. The one loss came in Round 1 against . . . guess who?

Geelong chalked up win number ten in a row against us since the 2008 Grand Final after mounting a second-half comeback to win by seven points. At one stage in the third quarter we led by 20 points, but then Geelong captain Joel Selwood carried his side back into it.

Unfortunately his opposite number was unable to respond because he was sitting in the coach's box. I'd run out of time in my recovery from the knee, but not by much, and actually played in the VFL that weekend. The original timeframe back in October was that I'd miss the opening month of the season, but a couple of days after the Easter Monday loss to Geelong, Clarko was on the phone.

'What are your thoughts about going to Perth?' he asked. We were playing the West Coast Eagles at Subiaco in Round 2.

I didn't have to think twice, especially when the coach explained that I wasn't going to be thrown to the wolves. The Eagles had a couple of impressive key-position forwards in Josh Kennedy and

Jack Darling, but Clarko was planning to have me play on the resting ruckman.

A six-goals-to-one first quarter set the tone for an enjoyable return. I managed to find a bit of the ball and collected 25 possessions as we blew the home side away, kicking 23 goals for the day and winning by 50 points.

From there we started rolling. Physically I felt the best I had for some time, and the team were also in a healthy space as we went on a 12-game winning streak. It's amazing what hunger combined with confidence can do to a side.

My game preparation became an obsession. Every spare moment was spent on it – before training, after training, at home, on my day off. Stretching, massage, physiotherapy, chiropractic work . . . anything that helped was getting utilised.

One of the keys to the whole program was the hands of a DNS specialist.

A what?

That's exactly what I said when I was first introduced to Mark McGrath.

The non-scientific description is that he's an expert in body movement. At the start, I had absolutely no idea what he was on about, and Jack Russell even warned him not to overload me with his philosophy because he thought that would instantly turn me away.

He was right, but Mark and I survived our introduction phase and my knowledge was expanded.

DNS stands for dynamic neuromuscular stabilisation and it's about making sure your whole body is balanced evenly. It's based on how infants' and children's nervous systems develop. The theory is that you're born with a perfect nervous system and then life stress takes over and gets you away from that. Our movement patterns are ingrained, and as we grow up, simple things like sitting on the couch or doing weights throw the body out of alignment. What Mark does is focus on going back and doing movements that babies and children do.

Some sessions involved Mark treating my body with his hands, while others were a series of exercises basically involving complex stretching. They certainly made me feel better, and if this was the 1 per cent I was looking for, then it would be worth it. I started seeing him three days a week, including on my day off.

I also got Maria, a masseuse from the club, to come to our house every Monday night for an extra two-hour session. I also had my own chiropractor, Michael Crane (not linked to the club), who I saw every Monday.

The biggest problem area was my back. All the other problems – with my groin, hips and glutes – would stem from something going amiss with my back. That's why I required so much massage and manipulation. I needed everything loose to keep it all working.

I even got a sauna put in at home next to the pool to assist with my recovery. The heat of the sauna helped relax the tension in the muscles of my back and that meant I slept better. I normally used it a couple of nights a week. The process would go something like this: sauna for 15–20 minutes, jump into ice-cold pool, back into sauna, then pool to finish. Go inside, have a shower, a cup of tea and go to bed.

There was little time for anything else in my life. It was tough on Lauren, because I wasn't exactly the life of the party. All the training, extra recovery and body management were exhausting. She was stuck in the house with a couple of young kids while I was off at my appointments.

Our social life declined rapidly because I was basically too tired. If we arranged a rare date night out at the movies, there was a pretty strong chance I'd be asleep before the movie was half over. And going out for dinner or having people around just became too hard. There were a couple of close friends who Lauren would call on when she sensed we needed some interaction with society. They were the type of friends you didn't have to get dressed up for, who were happy with dinner and a glass of red wine on the couch in tracksuit pants.

I knew this lifestyle was far from ideal, but, more importantly, I knew I had to sacrifice a lot if I was going to keep my AFL dream alive. And that premiership flame was certainly flickering strongly after the way the first half of the season had progressed.

Our biggest change in personnel was the introduction of tall defender Brian Lake from the Western Bulldogs. He was a two-time All Australian who had seemed to fall out of favour at Whitten Oval, so we swooped.

Brian was a different unit. One of my first dealings with him came when I got a Sunday-morning phone call from Brian in January informing me that he had been locked up after a big day at the Portsea polo.

While he had his own way of doing things, Brian's ability to intercept-mark was right up there with the best in the competition, and he became another weapon for us.

We also added some outside speed with the introduction of Brad Hill, who'd cemented his spot in the team after getting a taste in 2012. He was the younger brother of Fremantle's Stephen Hill, and his pace on the wing added an important dimension.

*

Our biggest test of the home-and-away season came in Round 15 at a blockbuster Saturday-night MCG clash with Geelong. It was first versus second on the ladder, and we couldn't have been better prepared to break the Kennett curse. Thirteen wins in a row would also be a club record.

Unfortunately a five-goals-to-two opening quarter by the Cats again had us on the back foot. The game was virtually a mini-final, with the pressure intense, but we managed to hang in there despite Geelong's lead getting out to 27 points at one stage early in the last quarter.

A miracle goal from the boundary by Jack Gunston gave us hope, and then with eight minutes remaining Jonathan Simpkin, another former Colac boy, snapped a beautiful goal to get us within three points. We had all the momentum, and all the signs pointed to this being the night we would end the curse – but one constant in all of the losses to Geelong was that in the key moments they didn't make mistakes and we did.

Two goals in two minutes – one a set shot from the boundary line by Josh Caddy and the other from Jordan Murdoch, who'd caught fire and kicked three last-quarter goals – saw Geelong prevail by ten points.

It was getting ridiculous.

Chris Fagan had certainly had enough. He wasn't able to sleep in the aftermath of the loss and made some notes that he presented to the leadership group. He had collated comments made by our players after the last few losses to Geelong, and we were always very complimentary, praising them for being the better side each time.

'The Kennett curse is a load of crap. The results in these games have nothing to do with a curse,' Fagan wrote. 'The simple fact is that Geelong want to beat us more than we want to beat them. Let's not kid ourselves. It means more to them, so they get the job done. Don't forget the disappointment from this game. Don't let time and other victories wash it away.'

The following day I addressed the team regarding Fagan's thoughts and suggested we all take a step back and think about what Geelong was saying about us right now. We were a laughing stock in their eyes.

'What would Paul Chapman be saying?' I asked. 'Or Stevie J?'

We were almost certain to get another shot at the Cats in September. In the meantime, we got back on track until a surprise slip-up in Guerra's 250th game against Richmond in Round 19.

It was a dirty day, wet and cold, and things were made even worse for me in the last quarter when I copped a knock to my thumb. I could hardly feel my hands anyway because of the terrible conditions, but when I cooled down it was obvious this was more than just a knock. Scans on Monday confirmed as much, and later that day I was in hospital having surgery to correct a small fracture. I trained after one week off with a protective guard and it felt pretty good. We looked at it as a blessing, as it gave me a week off to freshen up. I returned against Collingwood in Round 21.

We faced an interesting scenario coming into the final-round game against Sydney. Earlier in the year we'd extracted some revenge against the Swans, if you could call it that, but even though we'd won the Round 7 encounter at the MCG there was still a hollow feeling about what had happened the previous year.

The Round 23 clash was at Stadium Australia at Olympic Park in Sydney, and the Swans were set to finish fourth regardless of the result. If we won, it looked like we'd finish first, which meant that we'd clash with them again the following week in the qualifying final.

A quick start from the Swans had us on the back foot for most of the night but in the final term we clicked into gear and kicked six goals to three to get home by 12 points. The talking point to come out of the evening wasn't a good one for us, with Buddy reported for a high bump on Sydney's Nick Malceski. It didn't look great, and that view was reinforced when Buddy was given a two-week suspension, which could be reduced to one week if he pleaded guilty.

Normally, the thought of going into a finals series without your best player would throw up visions of wheels falling off. But there was something different about this group. The pre-season heart-to-heart and new values system had definitely had an impact. While we would be put to the ultimate test in the coming month, there was a belief and resolve about the group that hadn't been there before.

That's why Buddy not being there for the qualifying final wasn't the catastrophic event others thought it would be. The forward line still had a fairly handy target in Roughead – he was actually the one who'd taken out the Coleman Medal this year, kicking 68 goals for the season compared to Buddy's 58. We also lost Cyril Rioli just before the game with an ankle injury, but we owed Sydney one and a couple of injuries weren't going to get in our way.

The first half went as expected: hard, tough, contested football with not much space for anyone to move. It was no surprise that the scores were level at half-time.

With no Buddy, we had a number of unlikely goal kickers who stood up. Full-back Brian Lake drifted forward to kick the opening goal of the third quarter, and that kick-started a five-goals-to-one term. Matt Spangher, who'd started his career at West Coast and then spent a couple of years at Sydney, had come in as our makeshift centre half-forward, and he kicked a goal. Ruckman Max Bailey also got on the scoreboard; he was another feel-good story of the year who amazingly had fought back from three knee reconstructions. He'd managed to cement the No.1 ruck position this season, and his partnership with David Hale was proving a winner.

As we continued to put the foot down in the final quarter, one word kept popping into my mind: focused. That's what we looked like in our impressive 54-point victory against the team who'd stolen a premiership off us a year earlier. We were in a good position to make sure that didn't happen again.

The make-up of the rest of the finals was turned on its head the following day when Fremantle travelled to Geelong's home ground of Kardinia Park for the second qualifying final and upset the home side. That meant Geelong crossed over into our half of the draw, and the following week after they got over Port Adelaide it was confirmed that we'd be playing them. Sydney had managed to defeat Carlton and were travelling to Fremantle for the second preliminary final.

There's no prize for guessing what the public's topic of conversation was in the lead-up. The Kennett curse certainly got a good run in the media, but we were well and truly over it. The only thing we discussed that had anything to do with the past was about standing up in the big moments.

We were all experienced enough to deal with the week off in between games, but I was a little bit on edge about what I ate. I didn't want any repeat of last year's horrors. Thankfully my

TOP: Getting in early. A quiet Christmas coldie in the nappy.

ABOVE: Big unit. Primary school days at Sacred Heart.

LEFT: First Victorian jumper, the state primary school team, which baby brother Dylan's clearly excited about.

Dad and me rocking the big V. I think mine fit better.

ABOVE: My first footy team, the Tigers at Colac Youth Club (me top left).

BELOW LEFT: A Colac Tiger in my teens. Given I was a Richmond fan, I was pretty happy that my local team wore the yellow and black.

BELOW RIGHT: Sporting family. My sister, Bianca, and me trying to keep Dylan under control.

TOP: Pathway to the big time – I joined the Geelong Falcons.

ABOVE: Proud to win the Ron Barassi Medal in the 2001 International Rules Series against Ireland.

LEFT: My mum, Leanne, and me on draft day, 2001, where I became a Hawk.

ABOVE: The famous sand dunes picture: Chris Judd, me and Luke Ball in the lead-up to the 2001 National Draft.

BELOW: Addressing the media at Melbourne Park after the national draft in 2001.

Dad, Bianca, me and Mum back at the Colac Imperials clubroom to celebrate getting drafted, with family and friends.

ABOVE: With Lauren, not long after we first got together – she's been there for all my big moments.

LEFT: A new Hawk. Not sure about the pyjama shorts!

Enjoying our first best and fairest night, in 2002.

Best day of my life, marrying Lauren and sharing it with the Hodge clan on 24 October, 2009.

ABOVE: My first official AFL photo as a Hawk.

LEFT: Former great Kelvin Moore presenting me with my first Hawthorn football jumper, number 15, which he'd worn in 300 games.

Getting a kick in my debut season in 2002.
My first game against Richmond, at the MCG.

ABOVE: Cooling off in New Zealand in 2005 with Ben Dixon and Richie Vandenberg.

LEFT: My best year of footy so far came with some nice silverware, including the Peter Crimmins Medal.

OPPOSITE: Representing Australia in a 2005 International Rules test match in Subiaco against Ireland.

ABOVE: Tangling with my old mate Buddy Franklin in Round 19, 2017.

LEFT: Fighting out of my weight division with St Kilda champion Nick Riewoldt in 2006.

Starting to shed the puppy fat. At training in 2008.

ABOVE: Winners are grinners. Celebrating my first premiership, in 2008, with two good mates, Brent Guerra and Brad Sewell.

LEFT: Not a fan of public speaking, but managed to get a few words out after winning the 2008 Norm Smith Medal.

The dream shot . . . confetti and the 2008
premiership cup.

LEFT: As good as it gets. Only wanted one, but more than happy to take home two medals from Grand Final Day 2008.

BELOW: The boys' reaction when my name was read out as the Norm Smith Medal winner in 2008.

A rare launch. Getting airborne against Geelong in 2010.

ABOVE: Doing the hard yards out at Waverley Park in 2011.

BELOW: Milestone man . . . ticking off my 200th game, down in Launceston in 2012.

ABOVE: Sick in the guts. The pain of losing the 2012 Grand Final, with Brad Sewell.

LEFT: Breaking the curse. Celebrating beating Geelong in the 2013 preliminary final with Jack Gunston.

ABOVE: Pure relief. After the pain of the previous year, the sound of the siren in the 2013 Grand Final was an amazing moment.

RIGHT: Words of wisdom. Always enjoyed my chats with coach Alastair Clarkson.

Celebrating the 2013 premiership victory with the team, and then in the rooms with the family.

OPPOSITE: The best moment of the day . . . the siren sounds in the 2014 Grand Final.

ABOVE: The kiss with my former teammate Buddy Franklin during the 2014 Grand Final.

BELOW LEFT: Two is better than one. Lucky in 2014 to win my second Norm Smith Medal.

BELOW RIGHT: Celebrating our triumph over Sydney with Grant Birchall.

King of the kids. Sharing the 2014 win with the Auskick kids who'd handed over our premiership medallions.

ABOVE: Going to war. On the way out to tackle West Coast in the 2015 Grand Final.

BELOW: The moment after the goal of my career at the MCG.

ABOVE: The lucky six. The 2015 premiership cup made it four flags for Cyril Rioli, Jordan Lewis, Sam Mitchell, Jarryd Roughead, Grant Birchall and me.

INSET: Notes from my speech at the 2015 Grand Final.

BELOW: Celebrations begin after defeating West Coast.

LEFT: Walking out for my 300th game, with my three boys, Cooper, Chase and little Leo.

ABOVE: Special Puma boots to mark my 300th game, featuring the names of my three boys.

BELOW: The big lift. Jarryd Roughead and Grant Birchall struggle to keep me up as I leave the MCG after my 300th game.

It's over. Lauren and the boys were with me when I announced that I would retire at the end of the 2017 season.

THANK YOU HODGEY

TOP: Saying goodbye . . . leaving Etihad Stadium for the last time on 25 August, 2017. Honoured to do it with fellow retiring champions Bob Murphy and Matthew Boyd from the Western Bulldogs.

ABOVE: Celebrating a long career with my management team Paul Connors and Melissa Oberhofer.

LEFT: Final farewell.

stomach made it through, although there was the odd butterfly, given the enormity of the occasion. A Friday-night preliminary final at the MCG with 85 000 fans – it doesn't get much bigger.

Clarko certainly lifted for the occasion in the team meeting the previous day and brought some props. At the front of the meeting room, he'd poured some flour in a straight line. He was just standing there talking away normally to us but then he'd step over the line and go ballistic. Then he'd step back and be calm again. He repeated it a couple of more times.

'There is the white line,' Clarko said. 'You can be as happy as you like tomorrow but as soon as you cross that line tomorrow night you're an animal. You'll do anything for your teammates.'

He also had an oval drawn on the whiteboard and when we walked out he got us to cross over the white line and then write our number inside the oval. The message was clear: we were in this together. These were a couple of simple things but sometimes those are the ones that register the best.

It was at the forefront of our minds as we faced off against our nemesis in what was an electric atmosphere. The first goal through Jack Gunston certainly helped to calm things.

The contest quickly settled into its rhythm, where the lead bounced around as both sides enjoyed good patches. Unfortunately one of Geelong's came late in the third quarter, which meant that at the final break they had a game-high 20-point advantage.

Despite the scoreboard, there was a confidence about our huddle. Clarko was emphasising that our time would come, the momentum would shift. 'We've made it tough for ourselves, but we are not out of this by a long shot,' he said. We knew we were the best last-quarter team in the competition and this was highlighted a number of times. As we started to disperse, Grant Birchall made a point that really hit the mark. 'This could be Gooey's last quarter of football. Let's give it everything.'

My best mate, Brent Guerra, had let a few of us know a little while ago that this would be his last season. He was 31, the preliminary final was his 254th game, and it was becoming harder and harder for him to get his body up. Going out with a bang with a premiership was the plan, and if we were going to help him out, then we had to find a gear – and fast.

I was hoping to find one myself. It had been one of those nights when things hadn't fallen my way, and sometimes the harder you try, the worse it gets. I had to live what I preached and play my role.

Luke Breust certainly did that at the start of the final quarter, with a beautiful tap setting Buddy free for an easy goal from the goal square. Suddenly there was a different feel about the game, and it was the little things that were standing out.

Burgoyne's pressure on the goal line resulted in a hurried clearing kick from Geelong that landed in the lap of Brad Hill, who snapped truly. Then it was Burgoyne again with a handball to Gunston for another goal, and with seven minutes left we were within four points.

Ninety seconds later it was Burgoyne again. This was the exact reason why we'd recruited him to the club. He was a big-game player, and right now he was living up to his reputation. A series of handballs ended with him in the forward pocket, and he made no mistake to put us in front.

Word got out to us that there were under five minutes remaining. It was too early to save the game, so we just had to keep doing exactly what had got us rolling in the last quarter. We locked the ball in our forward half, with the result a couple of behinds, but what this did was instil something in Geelong that hadn't been seen in our previous 11 encounters: panic.

Twice they just bombed it long into the centre, almost praying for something to happen. This was really unusual for a team who had cut us down late so many times with cool heads and precise ball movement. It was playing into our hands, because we had plenty of numbers around the ball.

Where was the siren? Trying to calculate time while you're out in the heat of battle is virtually impossible. We just knew Geelong were going to get at least one chance, and as I saw the ball land in the hands of Stevie Johnson near the wing, I sensed this was it. He turned onto his left foot. I was in no-man's-land, stuck right between him and where the ball was going to go.

Johnson kicked it back inside towards centre half-forward, and when I looked to see where it was headed, the only person I could see was Geelong's Travis Varcoe. How was there no one near him?

After an initial fumble, he gathered. He was 40 metres out, directly in front. I couldn't get there. Sewelly dived at his boot but didn't make it in time. As I looked up, the ball headed towards the right goalpost. It was drifting . . . to the other side.

A behind.

Burgoyne took the kick-in and his pass landed on my chest, 25 metres away. I soaked up as much time as I was allowed before going long towards the wing. There must be only seconds left, surely.

We managed to win the stoppage and the ball was going our way. Roughy ended up with it and went long to Cyril, who was on his own just 20 metres out.

Siren.

Or at least I thought it was the siren. Cyril played on and kicked it to Buddy, who was in the goal square. Then the umpire blew his whistle. It was over.

I raised my arms to the sky. We'd broken the curse.

15

TIME TO HUNT

'They might talk about it, but what are they like when they come up against a team who is just as good?'

Chris Fagan was posing the question about the Fremantle Dockers at our Monday team meeting. We'd been given the weekend off to get the adrenaline out of our systems after the epic preliminary final, and on Saturday night, Guerra arranged for the 'country crew' – Lewis, Birchall, Roughead and myself – to go to his friend's restaurant where we watched Fremantle take on Sydney at Subiaco.

A lot of the buzz around the Dockers was about how good they were as a defensive unit. They certainly seemed to strangle Sydney, who had managed just two goals in the first half. In the end the home side won comfortably by 25 points.

Fremantle's defence was the key topic at the team meeting. Already the media commentary was casting doubt on how our precision-kicking game and ball movement would be able to get through the Dockers' zone. Fagan quickly put an end to that. He came armed with statistics that painted a very different story. The figures for our defensive areas showed that we were not only right up there with Fremantle across the course of the season, but No.1 throughout the finals.

'They're going to panic,' Fagan told us. 'We will be able to turn the ball over and the game is going to be played in our half.'

There was a quiet confidence about the match-up. We'd finished on top of the ladder, we hadn't done anything wrong, and my feeling had always been that a hard-fought preliminary final provided the perfect build-up. There was a danger that if that game had become a blow-out, the players might have got ahead of themselves.

In my mind we were ticking a few boxes. We were healthy, a lot of our players were in good form, and we had plenty of motivation courtesy of what had happened the previous year.

The unlucky player this year was Brendan Whitecross, who had seriously injured his knee in the last quarter of the preliminary final. Simpkin had been best-on-ground in Box Hill's VFL premiership win on Sunday, which earnt him a call-up.

The week ticked over without too many issues. The Grand Final parade was again a lot of fun, although there seemed to be plenty of support for the Dockers, with lots of purple and white in the crowd. Once again I got to hold the premiership cup at the end of the parade, this time with Fremantle captain Matthew Pavlich. I kept looking at it and thinking that surely the next time I was in its presence there would only be brown and gold Hawthorn ribbons attached to it.

*

Sticking to routine was the focus for the next 24 hours. I'd already started by having pasta on the Thursday night, which became a routine two nights before a game. The night before was always a Lite n' Easy meal.

Passing the time wasn't an issue with two kids under five, but ensuring the right amount of sleep was a potential problem. This was where Lauren was a champion. If Cooper or Chase woke at any stage during the night, she would go straight up to them and, if required, lie with them in the spare room or go downstairs and sleep on a mattress.

Life as a footballer's wife isn't easy. Many see the Brownlow Medal ceremony and other occasions and think it's all glamorous. The truth is it's anything but, given that your partner rides the highs and lows more than anyone. It's certainly an emotional rollercoaster dealing with injuries, the frustration of losing, and the fact that their man isn't usually around for birthdays or important family stuff because of football.

I am an organised person and I particularly like to stick to a routine on the morning of game day. There's a point where there is a changeover and I go from father and husband to football player. Lauren says she can tell whether I'm going to play well or not by my mood. Her theory is that I play well when I'm relaxed, but if something pops up unexpectedly in my routine, it puts me on edge and impacts my preparation. I know that behind the scenes Lauren, her parents and my mum do a lot of work to ensure this doesn't happen. The in-laws and Mum regularly turn up on game morning to take the kids away for a couple of hours.

The regular routine starts with taking Chase in the pram to get coffees. Mid-morning I go for a run, which I find helps wake up the body. After a quick shower, I check again to make sure

I've got all my gear, and then it's into the car for the short drive around the corner to the local milk bar, where I get the same sandwich before every game. I don't even have to order it now as they know what 'the usual' is: ham, carrot, avocado, cheese and a dash of mayonnaise on white bread. It gets consumed in the car along with another coffee as I drive to the ground, with music usually from the Wiggles or some other kids' show playing on a DVD in the back seat.

That day the routine was followed to the letter, which was a good thing according to Lauren's theory. I made it to the MCG with plenty of time to spare, and as always was the third physio spot at 12.30 p.m. Jordan Lewis was always the first. There are usually three or four of us who are there early and get dressed first. I get into my full kit straight away and after the physio I have my ankles strapped. The on-ground warm-up is different on Grand Final Day. Because of the pre-game entertainment, a lot of it is done indoors. Another massage is next before some drills with Andrew Russell to get the reflexes up and firing.

I'm not a headphones guy like a lot of the boys. I don't need music to pump me up; in fact, I'm pretty cruisy compared to some and I don't talk a lot in the warm-up. I'll get over to the younger guys and remind them to focus on doing the simple things and that's all we expect from them. We don't need anything special.

It's very difficult to judge what's going to happen out on the field from the pre-game atmosphere. Over the journey I've seen it throw up many different results but, out of all the scenarios, I figure calm and focused works the best. There was definitely an air of control about the rooms that day.

*

That cliché about goosebumps on the back of the neck? Well, think of that and multiply it by 100. That's the feeling that pulsated through my body as we emerged onto the MCG. When I saw the message on the huge Hawthorn banner, I was impressed – whoever had come up with that was on the money. It read: TIME TO HUNT.

Suddenly, there was a lot to get through before the actual bounce: team photo, quick warm-up, national anthem, coin toss (which I lost) and then the final rev-up address, which didn't really have any planning go into it. I'm not sure the boys even heard it. They were all well and truly ready.

The conditions were on the cool side and it was certainly blustery inside the MCG cauldron as I walked to half-back.

A lot of the talk in the lead-up had centred around Fremantle tagger Ryan Crowley, who was the best in the business and had claimed a lot of big scalps. I'd had a couple of run-ins with him previously and he'd actually got to me in an unusual way: he didn't fight back.

When I got tagged during my midfield days, I enjoyed the physicality of it, but Crowley gave me the shits because he wouldn't fight me. My plan was always to start fighting with my opponent so he would respond at the wrong time. This would work to my advantage, particularly if we were wrestling at a stoppage.

But Crowley did sportsmanship acts like picking me up off the ground or patting me on the back when he ran past. It drove me nuts! I'd watch him against other opponents and he'd bash into them all the time. The behaviour was actually pure genius by him because this Mr Nice Guy routine clearly put me off my game.

Thankfully he was nowhere near me for the start of the Grand Final. As anticipated, he was standing next to Mitch.

The ball avoided me for the first five minutes, during which time we scored the opening goal through Gunston. Eventually we did a switch in the last line of defence and I got in the chain, which relieved the anxiety associated with not having touched the ball.

During the middle of the term, Fremantle had a good patch but wasted opportunities and missed three relatively easy shots, including two by their rising star Nathan Fyfe. We made them pay when Dockers defender Luke McPharlin went over the mark as Buddy was shooting for goal, which resulted in a 50-metre penalty and a certain goal. Interestingly, when the quarter-time siren sounded, the much-hyped Fremantle defence had allowed two goals and, as Fagan had predicted, we'd gone even better, with the Dockers scoring just three behinds.

There was no letting up in the second quarter, which followed a very similar theme to the first. Gunston kept kicking goals and Fremantle kept missing. At half-time our lead was 23 points, with the Dockers having kicked just one goal. The game was going exactly as we'd planned, and the message during the break was all about keeping the pressure on. At some stage Fremantle would have a run – we just had to be ready for it.

My prediction was on the money. Well, the first bit at least.

They came with a rush and for five minutes were in total control, kicking three goals to get within three points. We couldn't get our hands on the ball, particularly out of the centre, and they were 'running on top of the ground' – one of the new buzz phrases that had entered the footy vernacular. In other words, they were running harder, quicker and for longer than we were.

Roughy stopped the rot eventually, but then Michael Walters, the Dockers' livewire goal sneak, kicked his second for the third quarter to bring the margin back to three points. Thankfully Gunston was running hot and brought up his fourth goal for the day a minute later. Ten points was the lead at three-quarter time.

As the defenders formed our own small huddle, I grabbed assistant coach Luke Beveridge. I thought a change had to be made, and I'd already had a quick chat to him about it when I'd come off briefly during the third quarter. We had to swap Brian Lake and Josh Gibson. Brian was playing on Pavlich, with Gibbo as the loose man. Their roles needed to be reversed. Gibbo's strength was as a one-on-one defender; if Lake was spare, he could fly for as many marks as he liked, which was his strength.

Beveridge agreed, but before we got a chance to explain it to the group, Brian went on a rant about what was required with Pavlich. He wouldn't stop.

'Shut up, Brian!' I shouted at him.

Steam was coming out of his ears and I thought he was going to punch me right then and there.

'You're not playing that role any more,' I said. He seemed confused, but then Beveridge stepped in and spelt it out.

Brian could be a space cadet at times, and probably the most frustrating player to play with against a lesser team, because his mind would wander and he'd make horrible mistakes. But put him in a big game and you knew he'd back himself. That was the type of player you needed alongside you, and we needed 'good' Brian for the next 30 minutes.

After Clarko had finished his speech, I called the boys in for one last word. We had finished off well in last quarters all year and I wanted to point that out. 'There's a reason for that, and it's because we've worked hard. Let's go and do it one more time.'

Once again, Fremantle got the centre clearance to start the final quarter, and the ball went to a one-on-one between Gibbo and Pavlich. Gibbo marked it. The genius move was already working.

Isaac Smith then produced a brilliant 55-metre set shot to give us some breathing space early in the final term. And when Luke Breust roved a throw-in and snapped truly, our lead was back to 24 points and we were only 15 minutes away from a premiership. A couple of minutes later, Brad Hill ran onto a bouncing ball to kick another goal. Fremantle had kicked six goals for the afternoon and now needed five goals in just over ten minutes.

They got two of them back quickly, which caused a flicker of concern, but once we managed to slow down the game for a minute or so on the outer wing, the job was nearly done.

When it was officially finished and the siren sounded, what flushed over me was more relief than anything.

I was relieved it was over.

I was relieved we hadn't choked.

I was relieved that all the work we'd put in had paid off.

I was relieved I was now a premiership captain.

Hale was next to me and he pulled my head into his chest. Then I was off in search of Guerra. What a way to go out. My best mate was finishing as a premiership player. Total mayhem broke out. So many hugs, so many tears, so much love.

The first person I saw when order was finally restored for the presentations was John Kennedy. The legendary coach was back again this year, and this time I'd be getting the cup from him. Even though my speech was a winning speech, it still made me nervous. I'd written my notes earlier in the week and got them from our media manager, Leah Mirabella.

Carlton legend Greg Williams was presenting the Norm Smith Medal, and I figured it would be a close call, given how many players had had big moments.

The winner put a smile on my face. It was Brian. Talk about genius moves. He'd taken several telling marks in the final quarter and that had obviously tipped the judges his way.

One by one we went up to get our premiership medallions. I was last because I was captain, and the little Auskick girl who put the medal around my neck made my smile even bigger when she said, 'You're a champion.' I thanked her and moved to the back of the dais to wait for Clarko to arrive and give his speech. I was to follow him, and then Kennedy would finally hand over the silverware.

My opening words were to thank Fremantle, and then I slowly made my way through my checklist, which included the AFL, Clarko and the other coaches, and all the players' partners and parents.

Finally I said, 'To my boys, I couldn't be prouder. The resilience, the courage, just how much you stood up from last year and fought through a long pre-season. And coming up with such character. Well done, boys. Fantastic effort.'

I turned and looked out at the sea of brown and gold around the stadium. 'Lastly, to the most important people, the heart and soul of our football club – all our supporters, the 63 000 members. That over there, which John Kennedy is holding, is the reason why we are always Hawthorn. Thank you.'

Nailing speeches wasn't usually my forte but I'd made the marketing department happy by getting that last line in, given it had been the club's catchcry for the season.

My best moment of the day was yet to come. As we started the traditional lap of honour to high-five the fans and take endless photos with the premiership cup, I was on a mission. I wanted to share this moment with some special people, and it didn't take long for me to find Lauren, Cooper and Chase in the crowd.

My wife got a big kiss and hug, as did Chase, and then Cooper, who had his football boots and Hawthorn guernsey on, jumped into my arms and we wandered into the middle of the MCG. It was a magical moment.

It was *the* moment.

16

MAN DOWN

'How about Bud leaving?'

It was the week after the Grand Final and Brent Guerra was on the phone.

'Yeah, I thought he would,' I said.

It had been obvious the longer the season went on that Buddy Franklin was going to leave. I didn't have a bad word to say about the way he'd handled himself through the whole saga. In fact, he'd been sensational. He was one of our best case studies for the new values system, and there was no doubt he had become a more team-oriented player.

In the preliminary final against Geelong, he'd got a laugh out of Clarko when he put up his hand to play further up the ground. He figured that was the best way to deal with Cats full-back

Tom Lonergan, who had a good record on him. Buddy had actually come into the leadership group meeting to voice his theory.

'I'll run him around,' he said.

His strategy was something Clarko had been trying to implement for years, but previously Buddy had been less than enthused.

He did it again in the Grand Final, suggesting he should drag McPharlin up the ground and away from the action. McPharlin was the leader of the Dockers' defensive unit and kept their structure in place. Moving him out of the way exposed our ex-teammate Zac Dawson in one-on-one contests with Roughead and Gunston.

'Do you know where he's going?' Guerra asked me.

'No. Where?'

'Have a guess.'

All year the speculation had been that it would be the Greater Western Sydney Giants, but given Guerra was posing the question, I sensed something was different. 'The Giants,' I said.

'Nope.'

'Fremantle.'

'Nope. Keep guessing.'

I was quickly losing interest in the game.

'He's going to Sydney,' Guerra eventually revealed.

I nearly dropped the phone. Sydney had just paid millions to lure ruckman Kurt Tippett away from Adelaide.

'How did they get him?' I asked. 'They just got Tippett on a shitload, plus they already have a lot of quality players.'

Guerra's lack of surprise made me think he had known for a while but he still didn't have an answer to my salary-cap questions.

The next day I got a call from the man himself. I could tell Buddy was nervous. He wanted to explain why he was leaving and also how much he loved the club.

'Mate, I understand it was probably a contract you couldn't knock back,' I said. 'You've won a couple of flags. I've got no issues with you leaving.'

Losing your best player isn't the ideal start to a premiership defence but it was something we'd worry about later. There was still some celebrating to be done.

First off there was Guerra's bucks party in Thailand. Seven of us, including his brother Luke, former Carlton player Luke Livingston, who'd been his best mate since school, and Grant Birchall, hired a house in Koh Samui. We figured it was a great way to celebrate the premiership as well.

Before we left, Lauren and Rachel, Guerra's soon-to-be wife, had some advice for us: don't get a tattoo.

So what did we do?

Guerra always answers the phone with 'Hey boy', and that was the tattoo we got in the same position on our right hip. We thought it was hilarious at the time, but the women in our lives didn't see the funny side when we sent back pictures on our phones.

I already had a couple of tattoos. I had a tiger on my shoulder, which I'd got on the Gold Coast. I don't why I did that, but I always say it's linked to the premiership I won with the Colac Tigers under-18 team and the fact that I was a Richmond supporter growing up. The symbol underneath my right arm was done in Cairns and, again, I'm not sure why other than it illustrates why I don't like having spare time. I end up doing stupid things like getting tattoos!

We celebrated Lauren's 30th birthday with a trip to America, which happened to coincide with Guerra and his now wife being over there. Some genius planning by my best mate and I ensured that we were all in New York at the same time. It was a great trip, and the batteries were certainly recharged by the time pre-season training came around.

The elephant in the room was what had happened in 2009, the year after our previous premiership win. We'd had the hangover to end all hangovers and it actually saw us lose our way for a couple of years. They say you learn from your mistakes, and it was pretty obvious we all had. I was certainly in far better shape physically and mentally than five years ago.

Clarko was all over it. He hadn't been happy with how the coaching panel had handled the premiership hangover either, and was searching for any sign of complacency in the group.

In a smart move, the club organised a two-week training camp in South Africa in December. Getting everyone together, outside of their comfort zone, was the perfect way to kick us out of celebration mode and zero in on our new challenge.

For the first week we stayed at a sports camp an hour and a half's drive north of Johannesburg. The England soccer team had used the camp as its base for the 2010 World Cup and it had all the facilities we needed. We moved to Cape Town for the second part, and that was when Clarko called a meeting with the leadership group.

'I reckon you blokes have come back too entitled,' he said.

Poor old Roughy copped it – earlier he'd made a joke about how we'd all received miniature premiership cups after 2008 but he hadn't seen any for 2013. Clarko was on a roll. 'You think you deserve this, you think you deserve that. This attitude – you didn't act like that last year when you were coming off a loss.'

There was one particular incident that had been the final straw for the coach. When we'd arrived in South Africa, all the boys had grabbed their bags, put them underneath the bus and then got straight on. We were all sitting up there when I looked down and saw Clarko and the rest of the staff struggling to carry multiple bags and get the equipment, including massage tables, onto the bus.

'Look out. We're going to cop it here,' I said to the boys.

Clarko just had a look in his eye. He was searching for any sign to jump on us and we'd just loaded the gun for him. The boys tried to spin that they'd been told by security, who were travelling with us, about the dangers of South Africa and were just obeying instructions by sticking together and getting on the bus as quickly as possible. It was an innocent mistake, but it wasn't good enough. It certainly didn't wash with Clarko, who let us have it with both barrels.

It's fair to say that for the rest of the trip, Kenny and Bobby, who were in charge of the equipment, had never had so many helpers offering assistance. I also made sure I was one of the last ones to get on the bus – and I definitely got on after Clarko, every time.

We also had a couple of meetings about the Fat Club. This was a select group of players whose skinfolds weren't at an acceptable level. I'd been a member previously but not since 2009. This year's line-up was headed by Cyril Rioli and Brian Lake. Their punishment for not being under the required skinfold number was not being allowed to have a drink on the final night in South Africa with the rest of the team. It mightn't sound like much, but after two weeks of intense training, the thought of a couple of cold beers at the end was what had kept a lot of us going.

The final day of the South African camp was the hardest training I've experienced. It started with a three-hour skills session and continued with a trek up the famous and steep Table Mountain. We started at 8 a.m. and were still going at 4 p.m. in 32-degree heat.

It was serious torture, and when we got back Jack and the medical team informed us that there was a condition attached to the evening's activities. We weren't allowed to drink any alcohol until our hydration reading was back at a certain level.

This threw the cat among the pigeons. It was funny to watch guys desperately trying to get their levels up. Matt Spangher had to keep going to the toilet, which didn't help his cause; it took him three or four hours to reach the level required.

The South African trip was as much about life experience as training, even though the training was intense and rewarding. We arrived just two days after Nelson Mandela died, and found a country in mourning. Later in the trip we got to visit Robben Island, the prison where Mandela spent 18 of his 27 years behind bars. We also got the chance to get up close and personal with African wildlife on a safari tour, and did some shark diving, which was certainly an experience.

When I got home, Lauren and the kids were in Geelong visiting her parents, so I decided to reward myself with another tattoo to mark the premiership success. The illustration used to represent our players' trademark is a hawk with a premiership cup at the top of a pyramid. I decided it was the perfect image to put onto my ribs – although I was rethinking that location about halfway through, given the pain.

My tattooist asked if I wanted to put the year on the premiership cup. 'Nah. Hopefully we'll be putting another premiership there,' I said.

The next morning I got a text from one of my cousins. 'Did you get a tattoo last night?'

I was shocked. 'Yeah, I did. How the hell do you know that?'

He explained that the tattoo artist had put a picture up on his blog saying he'd done work on Luke Hodge and that the Hawthorn captain didn't want the year put on the premiership cup 'because he believes they're going to win more premierships'.

I lost it. I thought it made me sound arrogant, and that was the last thing I wanted to come across as. I sent the tattooist a message straight away. 'What the hell are you doing? Take it down.' All I could think about was how it would come across to others. The camp had specifically worked on trying to erase any arrogance or entitlement.

When I spoke to the tattooist later, he was genuinely remorseful. He honestly knew nothing about football and had put the picture up on his blog because he thought he'd done a great job. I actually felt bad for spraying him, but it showed my mindset for the new season. I was on edge. I wanted more success, more premierships, more tattoos.

Given how well my chocolate and lolly ban had worked, I figured I'd go again. This time the New Year's resolution was no soft drink. This was also a big call – I didn't mind a fizzy drink, and back in the good old days when I lived with Dan Elstone soft drink accompanied most meals.

A groin strain halfway through the Round 2 clash with Essendon stalled my enthusiasm, and I didn't play the next week against Fremantle.

The traditional Easter Monday clash against Geelong was again an epic, with both teams undefeated coming in. They controlled the game for most of it, but we kicked two goals early in the final quarter to hit the lead. Then Cats spearhead Tom Hawkins kicked three of his five goals for the day to give them the victory by 19 points. We didn't play well and were probably flattered by the scoreboard. The one saving grace was that at least the Kennett curse wasn't a talking point any more.

What was a talking point was our first showdown against Buddy Franklin, which came in Sydney in Round 8. I flew up but was still troubled by hamstring soreness so I wasn't going to play, and we already had Sewelly and Mitch missing because of long-term injuries. At the team meeting the night before the game, Clarko delved into his bag of tricks. We were all gathered in the meeting room when the door opened and the coach marched in dressed like a member of the Queen's Guard at Buckingham Palace.

'What am I doing?' he asked us.

The boys lost it and we all reached for our phones to video what was turning out to be one of Clarko's finest moments.

'What's this?' he continued, as he marched up and down the front of the room. 'There is no Hodge, no Mitchell, no Sewell. It's a changing of the guard. Roughead and Lewis, you are now in charge.'

As crazy as it looked, the message got through – which wasn't always the case. Clarko had had some hits and misses along the way. At one meeting he brought in chopsticks and started off by snapping one of them in half. 'What happens if you get 22 chopsticks together and try to break them?' he asked us. 'You can't.' His point was that if we played together as a 22 and not as individuals, we wouldn't be broken.

One stunt that bombed spectacularly involved a video of a pair of ice skaters dancing to classical music. I figured it was something to do with working in unison, but we never actually got a chance to find out. The giggling started in the back row, which contained

Guerra, Birchall, Lewis, Gibson, Buddy and me, and we quickly came up with a plan to give the video a standing ovation when it finished.

'Yeeeaahhhh!' we roared, as the six of us got up out of our seats and started clapping loudly. The rest of the boys cottoned on and followed suit. It was hilarious, and we couldn't stop laughing.

He'd put so much time into that presentation, which he thought was a masterpiece. When he turned around he saw the boys laughing and told us to piss off with a smirk on his face as everyone left the theatre still laughing.

Clarko was fuming after the opening bounce of the Sydney game. Buddy had run straight off the line and dropped his shoulder into Lewy just as Lewy released a handball. Buddy was sending a message, but no one had run in to remonstrate. If it had happened to anyone else, Lewy would have been the first one over there getting into the offender. From the coach's box it looked as though Buddy could do whatever he wanted and no one was willing to get in his face about it.

Later in the game it happened again. Birch was over the ball and Buddy came through and bumped him in the head. Gibbo walked past and gave Buddy a bit of a push, but it wasn't much, and no one else did anything.

You could tell it was eating away at Clarko. The scoreboard didn't help his mood, as Sydney kicked six goals to two in the final term to win by 19 points. Things would be a lot different the next time.

The bye came at a good time, as our injury list was growing by the week. Mitch had torn his hamstring tendon and was out for a couple of months, while Sewelly hadn't played all year because of persistent hamstring issues, and Cyril had done his hamstring again. Brian Lake had been missing with a calf problem and Gibbo had just torn his pectoral muscle, which meant ten weeks on the sidelines.

I returned against Port Adelaide at the Adelaide Oval in Round 10. They were the hottest team in the competition, a game clear on top of the ladder. We hung tough for most of the match but couldn't quite get our noses in front, and in the end we went down by 14 points.

The loss wasn't what worried me – I was more concerned about my own patch. I again struggled to have an impact on the game. My form was fluctuating all over the place. I'd have one good game or one good quarter and then the next week I'd be average again.

It really hit home after the Power game, because if ever there was a time when my team needed me to stand up, it was then. We were down on experienced bodies and I needed to fly the flag, but I couldn't. Instead, Jordan Lewis did. He was outstanding, collecting a game-high 38 possessions and kicking two goals.

Was it time to hand over the captaincy? This type of question was running through my mind. I'd had a good run for three years and captained a premiership – maybe it was time for someone else to a have a crack. I felt more like a liability than an inspirational leader.

I wasn't the only one feeling under the weather. On the Monday morning, I was at the club early as usual when Clarko arrived. As he walked in, he tripped and nearly fell over. I started laughing and hung it on him.

'I can't feel my feet,' he said.

I thought that was a bit weird but didn't think more about it until I got a message that night saying Clarko had been rushed to hospital. It turned out that at the game on Saturday night his feet were numb and he feared he was going to fall down the steps as he made his way from the coach's box to the ground.

The diagnosis wasn't good. Clarko had what is called Guillain-Barré syndrome (GBS), which is an autoimmune disorder. There was no timeframe on his recovery or even any certainty that he would get better. GBS can leave people paralysed for months or years.

So the premiership defence looked something like this: the coach was in hospital with an uncertain future, and the captain was questioning his own.

17

BACK-TO-BACK

'Be reliable, not remarkable.'

Brendon Bolton was addressing the team ahead of his debut as senior coach against GWS. The assistant coach, who didn't have much of a profile outside the four walls of Hawthorn, had been elevated to the main gig in the absence of Clarko, who was still in hospital.

His motto resonated with the playing group. Be reliable as a teammate. If you try to go over and above, it won't work.

There were similarities between Bolton and Clarko, and not just that they were small in stature. They were both former school teachers and shared the same philosophies about football.

Bolton was originally from Tasmania and had been a successful captain-coach with North Hobart before moving to Victoria to take over as Box Hill Hawks coach in 2009. After a couple of seasons there, he'd been upgraded to assistant coach with Hawthorn in 2011.

When he got the nod to take over as senior coach, Bolton addressed the leadership group. 'I'm not Clarko,' he said. 'I don't want to be Clarko. I don't coach like Clarko. I'm going to be myself.'

That was exactly what we wanted to hear, and we told him to preach whatever he wanted to preach. The game style was going to stay the same, but one of Bolton's strengths was to narrow the focus, make things clear and get everyone on the same page.

We nearly made his first game memorable for all the wrong reasons when we just fell over the line against the second-last-placed GWS. The good news was that Clarko had been given the all clear. However, he was ordered to stay at home and rest for at least a month.

Bolton made it five from five and had us on top of the ladder for Clarko's return in Round 16 against North Melbourne. Bolton hadn't been the only one who'd stepped up – the other assistants and development coaches had thrived on the added responsibility, and, in a way, the different voices had rejuvenated the players.

There had always been something about North Melbourne that rubbed us up the wrong way, and once again we found ourselves in a heated and spiteful affair. Things certainly erupted when Lake placed a chokehold on his opponent, Drew Petrie. It came during an undisciplined patch of play where we gave away nine free kicks in five minutes. We lost the match by 20 points, and a few days later the AFL tribunal handed Lake a four-game suspension.

Not that the coach wanted us to tone down our aggression. In fact, he wanted it to go up a notch for our Round 18 clash with Sydney. What had happened earlier in the year with Buddy getting away with physically intimidating our players had been eating away at Clarko.

He prefaced his pre-game speech by saying that he didn't want anyone to get reported, but if Buddy ran past, we were to put a forearm into his bicep, or similar. Clarko's theory was that if we all did that, if he got hit or bumped 30 or 40 times, then he would start to worry less about the ball than about us.

While Buddy still kicked three goals, we certainly regained some psychological ground by taking down the Swans, who'd replaced us at the top of the ladder.

The last couple of rounds were interesting. The top four was virtually set, with Sydney, Fremantle, Geelong and us, then a small gap to the rest. It was complicated because we played Fremantle in Round 21 and Geelong in Round 22.

After we lost to the Dockers in Perth, the debate around the Cats game was whether either side should rest players. After all, our positions on the ladder were locked and we were going to play each other in two weeks' time in the qualifying final.

In the end, both teams decided not to rest anyone, and at half-time the Cats were five goals up when we swung some changes. Youngster Will Langford was playing just his 16th game, and Clarko decided to move him onto Geelong captain Joel Selwood. It was an inspired move. The kid not only curbed the Cats' star but kicked two goals as we stormed back into the game, eventually winning by 23 points. They kicked just three goals in the second half. Their coach, Chris Scott, indicated that he would shut things down in the second half, but it was always dangerous to flirt with form.

Form was a word I would have struggled to spell at that point. I'd again struggled to get a kick, and in a couple of high-pressure situations I'd fumbled. I'd been really good over the journey at being clean at the right time and standing up when my team needed me to, but now it wasn't happening. The more I thought about it, the more I believed it was leading me to just one conclusion.

On the Monday morning, I walked into Clarko's office and revealed my decision. 'I'm happy to pass on the captaincy next year if you've got someone else like Lewy or Roughy to do the job.'

Clarko told me to sit down. 'Don't do anything yet,' he said. 'Just play footy. We'll come to a decision at the end of the year.' We agreed that I'd sit out the final home-and-away game, against Collingwood, to freshen up. Maybe a week off would recharge the batteries mentally and physically.

We'd done a good job of putting ourselves in the premiership race again. Sydney had been the best side all year but we were in with a shot, particularly as we'd finally started to get players back late in the season after what had been a horror run with injuries. We just needed a few things to go our way – like the captain getting a kick.

For the entire season the team had avoided any discussion about one particular topic. Clarko had never brought it up and the players had dodged around it, even though it was constantly brought up by the media and our supporters.

Back-to-back.

Now Clarko was putting it on the agenda. He organised for the team to get some country air at the farm of part-time assistant coach Damian Monkhorst, the former Collingwood premiership ruckman. It was part of a reset Clarko liked to do leading into a finals campaign. He looked at September as the start of a new season.

A bonfire was set up and also a large video screen, on which a special presentation from Hawthorn legend Jason Dunstall was played. He'd been responsible for getting Clarko the job as senior coach when he was acting club CEO, and he was also a long-time board member.

Dunstall played in four premierships, including back-to-back in 1988–89, and this was the topic he talked about. He had no doubt that if we could win two premierships in a row, it would be a far greater achievement than the back-to-backs he'd been involved in. His reasoning centred around how in the current era of 'football socialism', the AFL's aim was to equalise the competition. Clubs weren't supposed to stay at the top, let alone win multiple premierships. Plus there were obviously now 18 clubs trying to do the same thing, which was four more than back in his day.

'If you accomplish this, it will be the biggest thing to have happened to this footy club,' Dunstall said.

First, we had to get over the old enemy, Geelong. We tinkered with our structure from the Round 22 game, making just a slight change, with our wingers going more defensive at stoppages. This meant we were able to put more pressure on the Cats, who liked to throw it out the back and then launch forward thrusts. Our move would force them to handball more, which is what we wanted them to do.

A few wasted opportunities was the story of the opening quarter, but we still led by nine points at the first break. Both teams enjoyed a couple of purple patches in the second. We kicked three goals in three minutes midway through the second quarter to get our noses ahead, but Geelong struck back late to tie the scores up at the main break.

My trusty old right foot came to the fore midway through the third quarter when I managed to mark the ball just near the point post. I was on the wrong side for a left-footer, but my father's persistence at the Western Oval all those years ago delivered when I managed to snap the ball around my body with my right foot for a goal.

Jack Gunston then got the final two goals of the quarter to ensure we had a nice 14-point buffer at the final break. We'd learnt over the years that no lead was safe when playing Geelong, but when Breust dribbled through the opening goal of the final quarter, the momentum was ours. We always had belief that we ran out games better than the opposition and had seen stats during the week that indicated we were definitely superior to Geelong in this area.

Thankfully, this time the stats didn't lie. Roughy kicked a beautiful set shot from the boundary line with eight minutes left to give us a 22-point lead. Then Lewy came to life and kicked two goals in three minutes to finish the contest. A Langford snap in the final minute was the last score of the game and we won by a comfortable 36 points.

We'd been clinical when it mattered, and personally I'd contributed. Worrying about what was going to happen down the track was off my mind. All that mattered now was winning two more games of football.

The major talking point ahead of the preliminary final was about selection. Cyril was back training but hadn't played since Round 15 because of his hamstring strain. He was one of the best I'd played with, simply because of the impact he could have on a game with just a dozen touches. He could turn a game with a tackle or a freak goal. And the thing about him was that he did it almost every week.

It was certainly an interesting conundrum for Clarko. In the end, he elected not to go with Cyril, who would instead play in the VFL grand final with Box Hill, with an eye to being available for the AFL Grand Final if we did the right thing.

There was more controversy at the selection table, with Brad Sewell making way for defender Matt Suckling. Sewelly had been dogged by injury for much of the season, and the emergence of Langford had cost him his spot. The coach declared it was a 'team balance' selection.

Our preliminary-final opponent was Port Adelaide, who'd emerged as the hot team of September. They smashed Richmond in the elimination final and then went to Subiaco to play Fremantle, where they came back from four goals down at half-time to win by 22 points.

Sydney played North Melbourne in the Friday-night preliminary final, and it was a one-act affair. Buddy kicked five goals as the Swans won easily by 71 points. The positive I took out of it was the fact that they qualified for my 'You never want an easy preliminary final' theory.

The unusual starting time of 4.45 p.m. for our game meant a few adjustments to my preparation in terms of the morning run and whether to have a short nap, which was normally the go before a night game. I had a good distraction, though, as my old team Colac was playing in its first grand final in the Geelong Football League, against Leopold. The Tigers had left the Hampden league in 2001 and become part of the GFL as they were only an hour from Geelong. It made geographical sense.

A few of my mates were still playing down there, including Micah Buchanan and Jake Carmody, so my phone beeped every couple of minutes with updated scores. I knew how much it would mean to the town if they could win a flag against the big clubs in Geelong. The last check of my phone before I locked in to my own battle showed that after a slow start, Colac had kicked eight goals to two in the second quarter and were 20 points up at half-time. (They went on to win by 49 points.)

This put an extra spring in my step. I was going to need it – we were about to confront a team who loved speed. We'd lost our only match-up with Port during the year back in Round 10 at Adelaide Oval, but that was when we were down on troops. They liked to play a quick game, and their running power had been a feature of their rise up the ladder over the past two years under coach Ken Hinkley.

Running was exactly what they did in the first quarter. In fact, they were running away with the game and we were being blown away. They were smashing us in contested possessions and the ball lived in their forward line. The saving grace for us was that they kept missing. From 12 scoring shots they only converted three goals, and their quarter-time lead was 12 points instead of 40.

This was where experience counted. We'd been here before and knew what had to be done. The first thing was that we had to win the ball at the contest, and then the tide would turn.

For the first three goals of the second quarter, we did just that as our running game started to kick into gear. Roughead was in the zone and kicked two late goals to give us an 11-point half-time lead. We were rolling.

I got in on the act in the third quarter after Breust set me free with a nice handball that I gathered just a metre out from goal.

I slammed it through, again on my right foot. Two right-foot goals in as many games – this was becoming a trend. Roughy was having a night out and kicked three goals in the third quarter to make it six for the game, the final one an impressive soccer off the ground in the last minute of the term to give us a commanding 23-point lead at three-quarter time.

When Gunston marked and goaled at the 11-minute mark of the final quarter, our lead was 28 points and we seemed to have done enough. But sometimes things aren't what they seem. Port threw their side around, moving their wingmen to the back of the square at the centre bounce and charging forward in waves. All year their calling card had been their fitness and ability to run over teams, and now it was happening to us. They kicked four goals in quick succession, and with just over two minutes remaining, the margin was four points.

Every loose ball seemed to end up in the hands of a Port player. With 90 seconds remaining it happened again when Matthew White chipped over the top to Andrew Moore, who marked 40 metres out on the boundary line. It was a tough shot, and thankfully he pushed it across goal and we managed to punch it through for a behind.

From the kick-in, Port's Brett Ebert took the mark and then played on. Suddenly he was coming directly at me. I knew I couldn't let him past as there were free Port players ahead. Instinct is a wonderful thing on a football field. I didn't think about it. I just reacted like I'd done thousands of times before and lunged at Ebert's boot. It was the perfect smother. The ball ricocheted around and Port's Tom Jonas jumped on it, so I jumped on him. The ball was trapped underneath and my appeal to the umpire for holding was, surprisingly, rewarded. All we had to do now was control the ball.

I delivered a short pass to Mitch at centre half-back and then he went long down the wing. The problem was that Port defender Alipate Carlile marked the ball and then immediately played on. They switched into the middle of the ground and somehow had the loose man, with Jay Schulz alone on the wing. There must have been only seconds left when he kicked long to a one-on-one between Brian Lake and Angus Monfries. Brian did brilliantly to spoil it but then jumped on the ball. From where I stood, I was sure he was going to get pinged for holding the ball. It was exactly the same scenario in which I'd won my free kick 20 seconds earlier. But there was no whistle. Nothing. Zip.

Instead, there was the siren.

The relief was overwhelming and I looked to the sky. Surely there must be a preliminary-final god who had been looking after us over the past few years. Clearly he wasn't there in 2011 when Collingwood beat us by three points, but since then we'd tapped into him: Adelaide by five points in 2012, Geelong by five points in 2013, and now Port Adelaide by three points.

As I looked around at the Port players collapsing to the ground and my teammates jumping on each other, I was hit by a series of random thoughts.

Another Grand Final.

Back-to-back.

Buddy.

18

BUDDY LOVE

'He's trying to take something from you guys.'

It wasn't the first and it certainly wasn't going to be the last time Clarko referenced Buddy Franklin that week.

Emotion is the biggest thing in football, and our coach was playing on it in the lead-up to the Grand Final. Losing to Sydney two years earlier still cut deep, and Buddy defecting to them to try and win a premiership was just another wound that Clarko was pouring salt into.

'He went and jumped teams to them, and he's trying to take what you guys want,' Clarko barked.

And this was only at training. Imagine what he was going to be like on Grand Final Day. The theme for the week was clear, his message strong.

What wasn't clear was selection. Clarko had a few balls in the air and it was going to be interesting to see how they fell.

Cyril Rioli was taking up most of the attention. We'd all gone down to Docklands Stadium to watch the VFL grand final between Box Hill and Footscray. Cyril wore No.71 and did enough, gathering ten touches. He'd been on very strict orders from Andrew Russell in terms of game time and output. Part of that was sitting out the final quarter, which caused a bit of controversy as Box Hill were down on numbers, and some thought the decision effectively cost them the premiership. (They lost by 22 points.)

There was also a selection decision to be made about the ruck, with Ben McEvoy, who we'd recruited from St Kilda for the 2014 season, impressing in the VFL finals series since his return from injury. Jonathon Ceglar had done the job in his absence, but Sydney had two big units in Mike Pyke and Kurt Tippett, who could tilt the scales towards the bigger McEvoy.

And then there was Sewelly. He'd missed out because of match-ups in the preliminary final, but the issue for him was that Will Langford had again played well. Sewelly was definitely more suited against Sydney, as they were a physical team and he matched up perfectly with their big-bodied gun Josh Kennedy.

As usual, the main training session on the Thursday was open to the public, which was always a highlight. There were thousands of fans at Waverley. It was more a stretch of the legs for us, just a bit of a kick-around to keep the body ticking over. The trick at this stage of the week was to hold everything in check and not get over-hyped by the crowds at training, or find yourself doing anything different from your normal preparation.

Selection didn't fall Sewelly's way. He again missed out, while Ceglar and Simpkin were the unlucky omissions from the preliminary final team, replaced by McEvoy and Rioli.

I wasn't the only one in the Hodge household who was gearing up for a big couple of days. Cooper and Chase also had a bit on their plate, with the Grand Final parade and then, the following day, getting the chance of a lifetime to run out through the banner on Grand Final Day. One of the recent traditions in AFL football was players running onto the ground with their children for a milestone game, and the 2014 Grand Final was my 250th.

Everything had fallen beautifully into place, but it was going to come at a price later. Since 2006 I'd had a running bet with the medical staff about the number of games I would play in a year. There was a trigger number each season, and if I passed that mark they were rewarded with bottles of wine. It was my way of saying thank you. They all spent a great deal of time getting me out on the park each week, and a lot of it was above and beyond their regular hours.

It had originally started as a bet with just the doctor and physio, but now it also involved Mark McGrath, the rehabilitation staff and the strength and conditioning department. Normally if I played 18 games for the year, they'd all receive a $100 bottle of wine; if I played 22 or 23 games, it went up to a bottle of Grange. This year the trigger had been 22 games because that was how many I needed to get to 250. They'd ticked that, so I was looking at a fair-sized wine bill. I'd never been so happy about such a large debt, and the aim was obvious: we all wanted to drink the Grange to celebrate another premiership.

The parade was interesting. I was allocated a car with Clarko, which worked out perfectly because the coach got to act as baby-sitter. Two-year-old Chase sat on his lap and Cooper hung out with me. The weather couldn't have been any better and the turnout was massive, with a lot of Swans' red and white sprinkled among the Hawks fans.

Then we were off to the press conference, where a lot of the focus was on Cyril. Many of the questions from the media were about how we felt as the underdog. Sydney's impressive form throughout the year, plus their easy preliminary final and the fact that they now had Buddy, meant they were starting as overwhelming favourites. This didn't bother us in the slightest – we'd been the outsider in the minds of most for both of our recent premiership wins.

After the formalities we caught a bus back to Waverley for our final team meeting, where Clarko had a video for us to watch. And this one he nailed.

The presentation was about the 2014 NBA finals series between the San Antonio Spurs and Miami Heat. The Spurs had been one of the best teams for a long time, winning five titles in 15 years. They were recognised for being a selfless squad who relied on outstanding teamwork rather than superstars to win championships. Miami were the complete opposite, having tried to buy success by bringing the Big Three together: LeBron James, Dwyane Wade and Chris Bosh. Despite having the best player on the planet in James, the Heat were exposed, and the Spurs won the series 4–1.

The analogy was perfect. As Clarko explained it, we were the Spurs and Sydney, who were sometimes referred to as the Bondi Billionaires, were Miami. They were trying to buy success by getting Buddy, who was the LeBron James of the AFL. But success came to the selfless team. That's what we'd been for two years, and it was what we were going to be the following day.

In fact, it was already happening right in front of my eyes. Brad Sewell was simply amazing to watch in the meeting. I knew how devastated he was about not playing, yet here he was explaining to his teammates how to play against Sydney and describing the traits of their players and positioning. He was the person who'd driven the introduction of the 'selfless' team motto, and now here he was living it in the hardest of circumstances. This wasn't lost on his teammates.

The game face was on.

Normally I don't allow anything to penetrate the locked-in zone that takes over my mind in the final 30 minutes leading up to an opening bounce. But the heartstrings were fluttering as I emerged at the top of the race to go on to the MCG and found Lauren with Chase in her arms and Cooper alongside.

The sun was beaming down on what was a perfect day for football, and it was set to start perfectly as well, with my sons getting to run through the banner. We did the exchange quickly, and I gave a quick kiss to Lauren. Chase looked out of it, and I found out later he'd fallen asleep in the rooms as he waited for the big moment.

The banner was huge, and as I broke through it I made sure I grabbed some of the yellow tissue paper as a souvenir for Cooper. We jogged about 10 metres and then I started looking around for Lauren – or someone else – to take the boys. There was no one around.

I kept looking. No one. This was getting awkward. Could I leave them in the middle of the MCG? The rest of the team were already in place for the team photo and waiting for their captain to sit down in the middle next to Clarko.

Then I saw someone. One of the club's media staff was coming towards me. I quickly gave Cooper a pat on the head and basically threw Chase to her.

A nice little 15-metre sprint warmed up the hamstrings to get to the photo shoot, where I even managed to look after the sponsors by making sure their logo was beaming off the Sherrin in my hands.

There were four first-time faces in the photo. Former Swan Matt Spangher had put together his best season, and he and Taylor Duryea, who would start as the substitute, had been the emergencies the previous year. Will Langford hadn't even been in the mix 12 months ago, and Ben McEvoy had been playing for St Kilda.

Matt Suckling was there too. He wasn't a first-timer – he'd played in the 2012 Grand Final – but he was getting another opportunity after missing out on our 2013 win because of injury.

The warm-up was short and sharp and then we linked arms for the official proceedings, which started with the introduction of the two presenters of the premiership cup. There was certainly some synergy with the Hawthorn person. It was Jason Dunstall, the goal-kicking legend, who just a few weeks earlier had spoken to us about the great opportunity we had to create history by going back-to-back.

Olivia Newton-John sang the national anthem, but I barely took it in as I was thinking about other things. What was I going to say in my final address to the team? Before that there was the coin toss with Sydney's other co-captain, Jarrad McVeigh, which I won with a flicker of apprehension. I'd lost it the previous year and we'd won the game; it had been the opposite in 2012.

I jogged back to the boys and we came together in the tightest circle possible, our heads virtually touching. I felt sorry for the guys who were only centimetres away from me as I launched into a spray about being selfless and putting the team first, with a line about Buddy thrown in for good measure.

Josh Gibson was going to start on his good mate Buddy, while Brian Lake would take him if he went deep to full-forward. We had a couple of different looks in the middle of the ground to start the game. I was winding back the clock and was set to play in the midfield for the afternoon. The shock tactic was having Cyril in at the opening bounce with Mitch, while David Hale was in the ruck and McEvoy was forward.

Sydney got the first clearance through Luke Parker, but Grant Birchall got hold of it at half-back and passed it to Hale, who'd made space on the wing. I'd sprinted to half-forward and Hale sent it my way. I was in good position before Josh Kennedy interfered with me front-on. Well, that was how I saw the contest – the umpire didn't share my view.

That elusive first touch had gone begging. A minute later I got a rushed right-foot kick, but it was called back as Liam Shiels had been awarded a free kick for a good tackle on Kennedy. His shot hit the post, but you could already tell we were on. Our pressure around the ball was strong, as evidenced a couple of minutes later when Sydney had a golden opportunity to kick the first goal from their goal square but we forced them to make a couple of mistakes. The Swans did get the opening goal of the game through Kennedy, but we answered five minutes later courtesy of a nice 50-metre set shot from Paul Puopolo.

Physically, we were also imposing. Luke Breust delivered a body-slam tackle on Sydney midfielder Dan Hannebery, and we were crashing into Buddy at every opportunity. Spangher clipped him over the head in a marking contest, and then Lake spoiled aggressively and they both fell to the ground. While Buddy got up and kicked a goal, it was obvious to him and everyone watching that he had a target on his head.

Hannebery must have felt like he did too, because for the third time in the quarter he got crunched – this time by Roughy, late in the term. It was a big hit and Hannebery was still on the ground as Jack Gunston seized on the turnover to kick our fourth goal. Sydney had a reputation as the best tackling side in the competition, but we were giving them a bit of their own medicine when it mattered most.

We should have been further in front after I managed to take a slips catch on a Langford rocket pass in the forward pocket, but unfortunately I hooked the kick for a behind. Our lead was 14 points deep into time-on.

It was 20 at the first break after Langford kicked a nice goal over his head, again as a result of intense pressure that caused Sydney to make mistakes.

All week we'd spoken about how the Swans were renowned for their good starts and how we couldn't allow their run on the outside. Plus we had the recent memory of the preliminary final against Port Adelaide, when the Power had dominated the opening 30 minutes. We'd neutralised that brilliantly.

While Sydney got the first goal of the second quarter, Breust replied a minute later. Ten minutes later I got to experience the most wonderful patch of football of all time. Well, it might not have been as good as Stuart Dew's five minutes in '08 but it was up there.

Four goals in as many minutes – two of those to me – blew the Grand Final apart.

Hale nailed a set shot to start the run and then I managed to get a quick handball to Langford, who was playing an inspired game. His shot from 45 metres sailed through. We got the centre clearance again before the ball was trapped at centre half-forward. I had wandered down ahead of the play and no one came with me. Roughy managed to get a quick kick out of the stoppage and it landed in my lap in the goal square. A simple chip-shot goal meant we were now 40 points up.

From the restart the ball landed in the hands of Puopolo, who burnt off a couple of opponents and let fly from 50 metres but just missed. He then did something that embodied the selfless attitude we'd brought to the Grand Final. He saw that Sydney had a free man in the pocket, so he started sprinting almost immediately after he missed the shot. He would have run 40 metres to get to the opposite side of the ground. What that did was put doubt in the mind of Gary Rohan, who was doing the kick-in. Suddenly that easy option was cut off because of Puopolo's effort to get across, and Rohan had to find another.

I was in the zone and realised Rohan was in the motion of kicking to the man who was my responsibility, my former teammate Ben McGlynn. The kick hung in the air beautifully and gave me plenty of time to make up the 10 metres and slide in front of McGlynn for the intercept. The initial touch popped the ball up in the air and then I easily grabbed it without losing my stride. There were no Swans around me so I casually took a couple of steps and slammed home the goal from 15 metres out.

We were on.

Sydney got back a couple of the goals before Cyril showed exactly why we'd taken the punt on playing him. He brilliantly intercepted an attempted handball by Sydney big man Tippett and then executed a perfect pass to Roughy on the lead. Roughy converted from 45 metres and our lead was back out to 42 points.

In the final seconds of the term I got caught deep in defence one-on-one with Buddy. It was obvious I was in trouble, as the ball had been kicked to his side. I had one option and one option only – to pull down his arm. The question was, could I disguise it? I managed the spoil, forcing Buddy to fall over, and as I went to grab the ball I looked up at the umpire. Had I got away with it? He wasn't doing anything. I had.

Wow! It was certainly our day. The ball trickled over the boundary line and straight away I went at Buddy to let him know about his efforts. He came back at me and we chested each other. I'd forgotten how big Bud was, but after an exchange of words a smile broke out on his face. I was already smiling, not just at him but also at the scoreboard, which had Hawthorn leading by 42 points.

The stats at half-time were off the charts. The tackle count, clearances and inside 50s showed the dominance we'd had over the first hour. I'd thought we would need to play at our optimum to challenge Sydney, but I hadn't expected us to be this good.

During the break I found myself in the bathroom with Brian Lake. He was a unique person and you could never predict what you were going to get from him. This time he delivered a classic. 'We'd better not fuck this up now,' were his words of wisdom.

I wasn't big on football history, but I was tipping that not many – if any – had come back from such a big half-time margin. We just had to keep our foot on their throat, and the memory of 2012 would ensure this.

The opening two goals of the third quarter were ours, which continued the theme that it was well and truly our day. There was no doubt about it when Langford produced an extraordinary bouncing shot from the boundary line for his third goal of the day late in the third quarter, which pushed the lead out to 61 points.

Then it was kiss time. Buddy had got me a couple of times, and when we clashed again I instinctively planted one on his cheek. I regretted it instantly, and that feeling went up a level when I heard the crowd react to the replay of it on the scoreboard. Clarko was going to kill me.

He didn't, which I think was a reflection of the game. We were 54 points up.

The party for the fans started early in the final quarter, with Breust kicking his third goal and Roughy his fourth for the afternoon. But I refused to let the scoreboard creep into my mind, which, it must be said, wasn't easy to do. I managed until Shaun Burgoyne marked 35 metres out with five minutes to go. As he went back to take his shot I turned around and my gaze settled on Birchall. He was dancing in the middle of the MCG.

I started laughing. We were no longer on – we were going off, we were celebrating.

We were back-to-back premiers.

The margin was 63 points when the greatest day of my football life ended.

19

FRAUDULENT SLIP

'Hodgey, we need you to give Chip a call.'

This request made me smile. We were back at Damian Monkhorst's sitting around the fire. This time we were reflecting on our back-to-back premierships, not talking about how we were going to do it.

It was a few days since we'd won Hawthorn's 12th premiership, and already Clarko was thinking about the next one. 'Chip' was James Frawley, who'd been playing with Melbourne but was looking to move. He was an All Australian defender and was tossing up between us and Geelong.

I spoke to Frawley about why he should come to Hawthorn. There was one pretty simple reason. 'We want to win another one of these,' I said.

We'd crammed a lot in since the big day, including a trip to Tasmania, and hiding out at Monkey's farm was the perfect time to reflect. What had become apparent was that we'd played the perfect game in the Grand Final. The review system with our ratings of each other had come out with a historic mark of a minimum seven across the board for every player – obviously some had an eight or a nine, but it was the first time the whole team had received a pass mark.

There were so many good stories around the victory.

Matt Spangher was at West Coast and Sydney when they won flags but he had never got a game. He had persisted and become a cult hero with our fans and his teammates, thanks mainly to his Christ-style hair. Cyril Rioli shouldn't have played, let alone had the best nine-possession game you could ever find. His pressure and tackling had set up a number of goals, but the fact he was now a three-time premiership player was because of Andrew Russell and the medical staff. Jack had planned Cyril's every move for weeks. He hadn't been allowed to train above a certain pace, and in the VFL grand final he'd been told to stay in a certain area and control his speed. It was similar in the AFL Grand Final – he had to contain himself for small bursts and not stray from the plan, because if he did, then in all likelihood his hamstring would tear again.

The Norm Smith Medal had been a tight affair and I still couldn't believe I'd won it a second time. I'd been awarded ten votes, just one ahead of Sam Mitchell and Jordan Lewis, who collected 33 and 37 possessions respectively, while I had 35 and kicked two goals. Gibson got one vote for his epic battle with Buddy, while Langford, who had been the breakout player of the second half of the year for us, also got one vote for his 21 possessions and three goals.

The boys were still getting into me about my performance on the dais. In fact, they were still talking about the 2013 winning speech, which they said had been the longest in history. I'd followed my notes again and certainly didn't miss any of our sponsors, but my sign-off to the fans had attracted some discussion because it had a bit of Jeff Fenech's 'I love youse all' about it.

My concerns about keeping the captaincy had disappeared – it's amazing what winning a premiership can do – and after I had a quick chat with Clarko I learnt that he was keen for me to go around for one more year at least.

After we wrapped up at Monkey's there were a couple more events to get through, including the best-and-fairest. It was won by Lewy, who, it must be said, had a spectacular year. I was happy to slide into fourth place.

Hamilton Island was the venue for the family getaway and we had some company in Dan Elstone and his wife, Jewels, who were expecting their first child. Dan and I had a lot to talk about, and it had nothing to do with the premiership. We were going into business together.

It had been in the wind for a while, since I'd spoken to our former president Jeff Kennett and current president, Andrew Newbold. They were both successful businessmen and I respected their opinions. I'd started looking seriously into what my life after football might look like. My manager, Paul Connors, had got me into a few media roles, doing special comments on Channel 7 and on radio. I certainly enjoyed doing that, and it seemed more of a possibility than going into coaching.

On the business side, Kennett and Newbold gave me the same advice: if you go into business, do it with someone you trust. Dan was one of my best mates, we'd been drafted together and we'd been in each other's bridal parties. The trust box was well and truly ticked. He had a lot of experience in the finance and property industries, which had been his focus since he was forced to retire from football in 2010 because of a debilitating hip injury. Dan had been thinking about starting his own business, so it made sense that we join forces. And so Hodgestone Finance was born, with a launch planned for early 2015. The core of the business would be finding funding for clients involved in property development projects. I'd committed to improving my knowledge and had plans to study for a Certificate IV in business and finance.

My other business came calling in November – I'd been selected to play for Australia against Ireland in a one-off International Rules test match. Mark Evans, our former football boss at Hawthorn, was now the AFL's football operations manager and was keen to resurrect the series, which had fallen out of favour in recent years. His aim was to get all of the competition's best players involved. He'd started ringing around in the mid-season and we'd all said the same thing: if he could attract the best, we were in. Evans and the AFL decided that only players who'd been selected in All Australian teams during their career were eligible. Clarko was named coach, with Fremantle coach Ross Lyon and Geelong coach Chris Scott his assistants.

Evans got his wish, with the competition's best getting behind the concept. The team included Joel Selwood, Patrick Dangerfield, Nick Riewoldt, and my Hawthorn teammates Birchall, Breust and Mitch.

Players were also lured by the prospect of the following year's series, which would be in Ireland – the kicker with this was that the AFL was planning to have a training camp in New York on the way. All those who played in the 2014 game would get first choice about the 2015 overseas adventure.

The resurrection of the series was a great success. We all assembled in Sydney for a three-day training camp before flying to Perth, where the game was played in front of 38 000 people at Subiaco Oval. The importance of the match was rammed home to us by Clarko and the other coaches, and the rev-up worked. We started brilliantly and then managed to hold off a late Irish challenge to win 56–46. I was fortunate enough to be presented with the Jim Stynes Medal for best Australian player, which was a huge honour, given the legacy of the former Melbourne ruckman. Stynes had come out from Ireland to Australia not knowing anything about the local brand of football and had turned himself into a champion, playing 264 games for the Demons and winning the 1991 Brownlow Medal. He passed away in 2012 after a long battle with cancer.

After the test match, Lauren and I took the kids down to a friend's property at Margaret River. It's a beautiful part of Australia and it was great to spend time with Lauren, Cooper and Chase after a busy few months of winning a premiership, starting a business and representing Australia.

The mindset I brought to the 2015 pre-season was funny. Normally pre-season filled me with dread, but the International Rules had helped keep my body in shape and this alleviated most of my concerns.

There was an air of excitement about coming together again a couple of months after we'd climbed the mountain. I'd obviously made an impression on Frawley, as he decided to join Hawthorn, but there was a tinge of sadness about who wasn't there. Brad Sewell had decided to retire after a great career of 200 games and two premierships. He'd not only been a great player but a great friend and confidant over our long journey together.

The premiership hangover threat had dominated the previous pre-season, with our every move seemingly being monitored. The great thing about going for three in a row was that there was no manual, no template and no expectations. The most recent precedent was the Brisbane Lions back in 2001, 2002 and 2003. Motivation wasn't going to be an issue. We were all competitive beasts, and the general consensus in the group when the inevitable question was asked about the 2015 premiership was simple. 'Why can't we?'

There was something about North Melbourne. I didn't like them. In fact, as a team we didn't like them. I couldn't put a finger on why, but every time we played the Kangaroos there was an edge to the contest, lots of niggle and verbal sparring.

That was exactly how the script was running for our Round 5 encounter.

It had been an up-and-down start to the new season. A ten-goal opening-round win over Geelong – which was our fourth in the five meetings since we had broken the Kennett curse – was followed by an unacceptable two-point loss to Essendon. The Bombers led by as much as 35 points in the first half but we pegged them back. Bomber defender Cale Hooker went forward and snapped a goal with 57 seconds remaining to put them in front. We then got control from the centre bounce and Breust actually had the ball in his hands in the goal square when the siren sounded.

A 70-point thrashing of the Western Bulldogs in Launceston restored order, but then we again gave away a huge start, this time against Port Adelaide. They led by 51 points at half-time; we got back to within eight points on the siren. Clarko was fuming in the rooms afterwards, particularly at our lack of physicality in the first half, and he was still bubbling as he walked back to our hotel just across from Adelaide Oval. The players took a bus for the short journey, but Clarko and Chris Fagan always liked to walk back under the stars to discuss the evening's events.

That was a mistake.

We arrived back first and encountered a couple of lads who'd obviously had a few too many heckling us as we got off the bus. They stepped up their game when they saw Clarko, harassing him for a selfie and then blocking his path as he tried to get into the hotel. The coach didn't appreciate them invading his personal space and gave one of them a polite shove out of the way.

Naturally, in this day and age of camera phones, the incident was filmed and by the next morning Clarko was in the middle of a ridiculous scandal. The boys had hoped it would prove to be a bit of a distraction for the coach and may have tempered his reaction to what had been an ordinary performance by us.

That's why everyone was a bit on edge against North Melbourne: Clarko had demanded a response. Unfortunately it didn't work out the way everyone had planned. North forward Lindsay Thomas drew a free kick for high contact and I went into him with such momentum that I ended up straddling him. I was trying to get up when I felt someone grab me from behind. I wasn't sure who it was but I didn't appreciate being manhandled, so as I was getting to my feet I went to push them away. The plan was to push my forearm into their chest, but just as I went to make contact I tripped on Thomas's foot, which put me off balance.

That's when the trouble started. The forearm slipped up high and hit North Melbourne captain Andrew Swallow flush on the jaw. He went down and the next thing I knew I had a number of

North players trying to get at me. It had been an innocent mistake but I had a sinking feeling about how it probably looked on the replay. Thomas was awarded a 50-metre penalty, and as I jogged back to the centre I was confronted by Swallow, who bumped into me and then dragged me to the ground. I just lay there as he grabbed me around the throat. I knew I'd done the wrong thing.

That edge I mentioned? Well, it was now ramped right up. At every contest there was more and more niggle, and you got the feeling it could explode again at any minute.

From the moment he'd arrived at Hawthorn, Jordan Lewis had shown a particular liking for this type of environment. In one of the first games he played in the brown and gold, as a teenager from Warrnambool, Lewy put someone over the fence. My reaction? 'Oh, I like that.'

He'd been doing it ever since, but his timing wasn't ideal on this particular evening. Barely five minutes after my clash with Swallow, he hit North ruckman Todd Goldstein in the head with a round-arm spoil. And I just happened to be standing right there when it happened.

Another melee broke out as North players came from every-where. It wasn't the first time Lewy and I had been reported in the same game against the Kangaroos. Thankfully, when the focus went back to football we were able to exert our influence in the proper way and won easily, by ten goals.

I approached Swallow afterwards to offer an apology, but he was still pretty flat and didn't want to engage. The next day I rang him and also contacted North coach Brad Scott to explain my actions. 'I just wanted to let you know that I had no intention of getting him on the chin. Yes, I was trying to be physical, but more in the chest area.'

Scott was appreciative of the call. 'You didn't have to ring, but thanks for apologising,' he said. 'I understand where you're coming from.'

I just hoped the AFL tribunal did too. The match review panel (MRP) had referred it straight to the tribunal, which wasn't a good sign, indicating that I was looking at a three-week penalty at least, possibly more. Lewy was dealt with by the MRP and copped a two-week ban.

My hearing was on the Tuesday night, so my fate was debated on radio and TV for three days. If you went by the MRP's criteria, it was likely that my two weeks would be reduced to one because there had been no injury from the incident. It was high contact, but you could debate the impact as Swallow had played out the rest of the game and wasn't going to miss any matches. The problem for me was the image of the game and how there had been potential for serious injury. I didn't really understand that – there was the potential for injury with every report.

Initially I wasn't going to address the tribunal, but then it was decided that if I pleaded guilty, it would probably be a good idea to explain the incident in my own words. Just before the hearing started, we got word that the AFL was looking for a four-week ban, which made me decidedly uneasy. So did watching the replay over and over as the AFL launched its case, although on the slow-mo you could see the shock on my face when I realised I'd struck him in the face.

'It was a genuine mistake,' I told the three-member panel. The small room was packed with media, and I was feeling more and more uncomfortable on the witness stand. 'I didn't mean to make contact where I did. It was meant to be the chest. I was trying to go to him during the match and explain I didn't mean to get him where I did . . . I was falling off balance.'

I'd been suspended four times before but I'd kept my nose clean for a while, the last indiscretion being in 2008, and we hoped that would be looked upon favourably. I'm not sure if it was that or my speech that did the trick, but we managed to keep the damage to a three-week suspension.

What shocked me throughout the whole incident was the vitriol on social media. I was branded a thug, which was probably the most polite description for what was being said. I had a pretty thick skin, but it did make me stop and think about what motivates people to be anonymous keyboard warriors who hurl abuse. Like most people, I'd come to enjoy Twitter and Instagram, but after the Swallow incident I had to turn them both off. It all became too much, even for me.

Clearly I knew I'd crossed the line and that from time to time I was capable of doing so. I usually got the best out of myself when I was angry, when I was being physical and ruthless towards the opposition. Clarko knew that, which was why he didn't make a big song and dance about my suspension (or maybe he was still recovering from the Port fan incident).

That certainly wasn't the case for several media commentators, who didn't take long to start questioning my leadership. Again I tried not to listen, but when they continued to disregard everything I'd done previously, including captaining two premiership sides, and questioned my character over this one incident, it certainly got my back up.

The suspension controversy kept bubbling along. We lost two of the three games when I was out, and at four wins and four losses we'd hit a crossroads in our season. We were sitting seventh after losing to Sydney in Round 8, and Clarko was concerned.

'We're too inconsistent,' he told us. 'One week we're keen to play, the next we're not. Our target is top four, but if we keep going along like this, we're not going to get that. We can't go deep in the finals if we're not in the top four. It's up to you from this point on what happens. You decide.'

A picture had been hung on the wall in the change rooms at Waverley Park. It was a group shot of the premiership team from 2014, but we'd all been shaded out so it was just an outline. Above the picture were two words: YOU DECIDE.

Clarko was putting the pressure on the leadership group and we were doing the same to those on the rung below us. A new batch of leaders had to start to motivate the group if we were to avoid stagnating. To lift improvement we looked at the players in the 25 to 28 age bracket, and guys like Gunston, Shiels, Stratton, Breust and Birchall needed to push the standards.

Clarko had made his stand and he was sticking to it. 'I'm not angry,' he said. 'It's your decision. I'm doing what I can – it's up to your mindset. I could come up with the best game plan but if you don't have the intensity, if you don't have the desire to do it, then hang it up now, boys, and we'll go on holidays.'

The penny certainly dropped – we won the next eight games in a row. However, it wasn't all plain sailing during that period, with two events that put playing football into perspective.

I had a phone call from Clarko on the Tuesday leading into the Collingwood game in Round 14. 'We've had a scare with Roughy,' he said. A small scar on Roughy's lip, which had been there for ages, had been tested and come back positive for a melanoma. He needed surgery and wouldn't know if the cancer had spread until afterwards.

The news hit the playing group like a ton of bricks, despite Roughy telling us he wanted to deal with it quietly and urging us to get on with things. With his red hair and fair complexion,

Roughy had always been fanatical about being sun-smart, and the boys were always hanging it on him about his zinc-cream usage.

That wasn't the only shock for the week, with the horrible news of the death of Adelaide coach Phil Walsh on the Friday morning. Everyone was in shock and it cast a shadow over the lead-up to the match.

It ended up being an enthralling game, with Collingwood's inaccurate kicking helping us to get home by ten points. Afterwards, players from both clubs linked arms in a large circle in the middle of the MCG and paid tribute to Walsh. It was one of the most moving moments I'd ever been involved in.

Thankfully the following week was a lot brighter, with news that Roughy had been given the all-clear and would be back playing in a couple of weeks. He actually travelled down to Launceston with the team for the Round 15 clash against Fremantle, who were sitting on top of the ladder thanks to an impressive record of 12 wins and one loss. We'd obviously started to click during our winning streak and all cylinders were firing against the Dockers, who we kept to one goal in the opening half. By the end of the game the margin was 72 points and a message had been sent to the rest of the competition.

If the other teams hadn't received the message after that victory, we sent another one the following week against Sydney, with Roughy back in the team. Our second clash for the year against our arch rival became a one-act affair. Roughy led the way with five goals as we kicked 14 goals to three in the second half to win by 89 points.

More tragedy hit after our Round 20 victory over Geelong, when the 16-year-old son of our assistant coach, Brett Ratten, was killed in a car accident. It was so sad and, as a parent myself, I couldn't fathom what Ratts would be going through. These were the times when the strength of a football club shone through, and we all rallied around him as best we could. Ratts and his family were on our minds the whole week and I think you could see it against Port Adelaide the following Friday night at Docklands Stadium. We just weren't there. The Power were almost out of contention for the finals but played an inspired last quarter to come over the top of us to win easily by 22 points. I had a dirty night and my mood wasn't going to get better in a hurry – I'd put myself in the hands of the MRP again after an incident in the third quarter involving Port's Chad Wingard.

Again it was an accident, but again it didn't look great on the slow-motion replay. Wingard had grabbed the ball in one hand just near the point post and I was coming in at full speed to bump him. I slowed down for a stride as I thought he was going to keep going through for a behind, but he didn't. Instead he stopped, put his head down and tried to come back into play. It was too late for me to change direction, and the end result was my hip sandwiching his head against the point post. It looked horrible, and given what had happened with Swallow earlier in the year, I knew I was in trouble. I had the weekend to stew on it as the MRP didn't meet until the Monday morning. Once again, this meant that the media spent most of the weekend discussing my penalty. Some even predicted three weeks, which would mean I'd miss the first final.

Three weeks was the eventual figure, but I took an early guilty plea and it was reduced to two matches. It was a disastrous lead-in to a finals campaign, but I tried to look for positives and figured my run of misfortune in season 2015 must be over.

I was wrong.

20

POKER NIGHT

The message got me thinking. It was from Tony Hachem, the brother of poker professional Joe Hachem, who I'd got to know through my former premiership teammate Campbell Brown. We shared an enjoyment of playing the odd game of cards.

The message had been sent to a large group, probably around 20; I knew about half of the names. Hachem was organising a poker night in the city, a low-key event with a few guys sitting around having some fun. I'd knocked back a couple of previous invitations from him because they'd been during the season, and with my dodgy back there was no way I could sit down for four or five hours to play cards in the lead-up to a game.

But now my diary was free of football for a couple of weeks courtesy of the MRP. I spoke to Browny and he was keen, so

I confirmed my attendance. It was on the Thursday night before the last game of the season and I thought it would be a perfect opportunity to catch up with a few guys I hadn't seen for a while.

I decided to drive – I had no intention of drinking. Browny had been stirring me up about getting on it with him like in the good old days, but I had no interest in doing so.

As soon as I got there, some of the guys ordered food from the restaurant next door. I'd eaten at home, so I declined to join them. They also ordered some beers, which suddenly looked very appealing. Hmm. I wasn't playing on Saturday so there would be no issue if I just had a couple.

What the hell! 'Yep, I'll have one,' I said.

The atmosphere was great, with funny stories and lots of laughter. The cricket was on TV in the background. It was the first game of the one-day series in England, following on from what had been an amazing Ashes series that the Aussies had lost 2-3. Shane Warne was commentating. He was a regular at Tony's poker nights so the boys thought they'd put a picture on Instagram and tag Warnie in it.

I was so enthralled in the card game that I lost track of time and suddenly it was 11 p.m. I finished my fourth drink and decided that was it. I had to drive home, so I'd certainly had enough. Lauren texted me to see what was happening. She'd woken up after crashing earlier – she was more tired than usual as she was pregnant again. Baby number three was due in January, which we were all very excited about. I told her not to worry and that I'd be home soon.

The poker game finished at 12.30 a.m. Browny and a few of the boys were going to get something to eat. I felt a bit peckish but had my weekly radio gig with KIIS FM at 7.40 in the morning so figured I should head home.

When I got in the car, the clock read 12.45 a.m. It wouldn't take me long to get home, particularly at this time of night – all I had to do was go down the Monash Freeway, turn left into High Street and then drive a few blocks up the hill. I'd done the drive thousands of times, so I wasn't really paying attention as I turned off the freeway.

Then I saw them. Flashing lights. Blue and red.

The police were stopping drivers for random breath tests. I'd never seen them on this side of the road before – they were usually on the opposite side. I'd done the right thing and stopped drinking a couple of hours earlier, so I shouldn't have a problem.

I exchanged pleasantries with the policeman, who asked me to blow slowly into the device until he said stop. Then something happened. He looked up from the device and turned to his colleague before leaning back down to the open window and saying, 'Have you had anything to drink tonight?'

'Ahhhh yeah, I had three or four drinks a while ago,' I replied.

The policeman explained that the device had detected alcohol. 'What did I blow?' I asked, as my heart started racing.

'It doesn't give a reading – it just detects alcohol on your breath.'

I got the distinct impression that things were turning very bad very quickly. To get a proper reading I was required to go to Box Hill Police Station – in the back of a divvy van.

As I climbed out of my car, panic well and truly set in. I looked around to see if there was anyone watching. In this era of smart phones it's pretty easy to get a quick photo, and I was tipping that a shot of Hawthorn's premiership captain getting in the back of a divvy van would be worth a bit of cash.

I started to run over the entire evening in my head. I definitely didn't feel drunk – four drinks in five hours surely wasn't enough to put me over the legal .05 limit. But then I remembered that I'd hardly eaten anything all night. I'd had a light meal before I left home, but that was it. I should have gone out for that late dinner with the boys before driving home.

At the station I was ushered into a room where I had to fill out some paperwork before doing the proper breath test. Surely now that another 15 minutes or so had passed I'd be under.

Surely.

I was praying for a miracle that didn't come. The reading was .068. I was in trouble.

One of the policemen explained that because it was only just above the limit there would be no loss of licence. I'd have to pay a $450 fine and cop ten demerit points.

I had a sinking feeling that I'd lost a few points previously, which would complicate the equation. My mind moved into damage control. 'Will this get out if I don't lose my licence?' I asked.

The main policeman knew where I was coming from. 'We take our job seriously – we're professionals,' he said. 'It will stay between the five policemen here and whoever you tell.'

I wanted to feel confident that was true, but I had my doubts. These things always seemed to get out.

They gave me a lift home and I tried to gather my thoughts. What the fuck had I done? This was a disaster in so many ways. What was I going to tell Lauren and Cooper? What about my teammates? And then there was Clarko. It was one big mess.

I paused at the front door for a few moments before quietly sneaking in. Lauren's parents were staying the night, which wasn't ideal. I crept into the bedroom. Lauren was sound asleep, looking peaceful. What was she going to think?

I turned the light on, and as she was adjusting to it I told her the full story. She was shocked initially and didn't know what to say. And then she was worried. I'd already sailed past that point, and instinct was telling me I needed to tell the club right now.

It was 2.30 a.m. when I rang Chris Fagan. 'Hodgey, what's wrong?' he said quickly.

'Fages, I've fucked up, mate.'

'What did you do?'

I explained how my innocent card night had turned into travelling in the back of a divvy van.

'So it was .068? Gee, that's just over. Why didn't they let you go?' Fagan joked, trying to ease my stress levels. He asked a few more questions and said he'd break the news to Clarko. 'It's done now – we've just got to deal with it and move on.'

I tried to go to sleep but my mind was racing at a hundred miles an hour. I ended up barely getting 30 minutes rest.

The first thing I did in the morning was walk the 1 kilometre to pick up my car. I then drove to Waverley and was there by 7 a.m. I was training in the rehab group while I was suspended. I was having a shot of basketball when Clarko arrived. 'Oi! Come in here!' he yelled as he strolled into his office. I followed him in and he shut the door behind me.

'What were you thinking, you deadshit?' It was hard to argue with his opening statement. 'Having said that, plenty have made the same error you have made. As captain of the club, however, it's just not acceptable. The position you're in, you've got to be smarter.'

The biggest issue for the coach was the impact it could have on the team. 'Don't let it affect the way you are around here. Still be upbeat, still play basketball with the young guys,' he said. 'Don't be a sook and bring down the mood of the group.'

Clarko was really good about the whole thing. Next on my list was chief executive Stuart Fox. He said straight away that it would leak within 24 hours and we needed to prepare ourselves for it to happen at any time. Media manager Leah Mirabella was brought into the discussion, which turned towards breaking the news ourselves. 'That way we can control the story,' Fox said.

After training I was scheduled to do some filming for Hodgestone Finance. All the way there I was exchanging phone calls with Leah, Fages and my managers, Paul Connors and Mel Oberhofer. The filming was pretty basic stuff but I kept stuffing up my lines. My head was clearly elsewhere, and it took a lot longer than it should have. I was there for over an hour, and as I was walking back to the car I got a text from Foxy. It said he'd just had a message from a *Herald Sun* journalist, Jon Ralph, saying something along the lines of 'We've got him.'

That was the moment everything hit. It felt like a sledgehammer had knocked me over. I sat in the car for a couple of moments and tried to get my head around everything. So much for the police keeping it in-house. I should have known.

My phone was going berserk.

More discussions followed with Leah, Foxy and Fages about the next move. We had planned to release it ourselves on Saturday morning, but that was now out. They were pushing the strategy of getting on the front foot and doing an interview with Channel 7 during the Friday-night football coverage. I wasn't so sure. The thought of sitting in front of a camera on live TV made me very uneasy.

They were also trying to work out who should interview me. Former Geelong captain Cameron Ling was working the game and I got along well with him, but there was a thought that we needed someone more serious. A few other names were thrown up before we settled on host Hamish McLachlan. I knew him pretty well, he was easy to talk to and, importantly, I trusted him.

I went home to get changed and then waited for Leah and Clare Pettyfor (who also worked in the media department) to pick me up for the Channel 7 interview. While I was waiting I deleted my Twitter, Instagram and Facebook accounts – that was the one good lesson I'd learnt from the Andrew Swallow debacle.

Then someone rang the doorbell. I froze. Had the media found out where we lived? I went to the window and tried to see who it was but there was nobody to be found. Lauren, Chase and her parents had been at Cooper's futsal game and as I heard the garage door go up I went out to meet them.

That's when I saw her. A photographer got out of a car across the street and was heading towards the house. 'Shut the door. Quick, shut it!' I yelled to Lauren.

It seemed like the door was in slow motion. It took forever to close but thankfully it was quick enough to block the photographer. I tried to pretend everything was normal because I didn't want Cooper to get spooked. Chase was too young to understand what was going on, but my older son was switched on. Leah and Claire arrived and I decided I'd sit him down when I came back from Docklands.

We managed to sneak into the stadium through a back door, which was at least something. I was more nervous than I'd been for any of the grand finals. I was starting to sweat and had an overwhelming urge to get the hell out of there.

'I obviously made a stupid error,' I told McLachlan when the cameras started rolling. 'I thought I was okay. It was a silly call, an error of judgement, and I feel like an idiot. I had three or four (drinks). I thought I was okay to drive, otherwise I wouldn't have jumped in the car.'

Once it was done, I shook McLachlan's hand and got out as fast as I could. I needed to see my family.

Cooper was now seven – old enough to understand what had happened. My biggest fear was what other kids would say to him at school. I was petrified he'd get teased because of what his stupid father had done. He was a good kid who didn't deserve that.

'Dad has been silly,' I told him. I explained how I'd had one beer too many and broken the law. 'You might see something in the paper or on TV and they will say some things about me, but I don't want you to worry about it. I made a mistake and everything is going to be okay.'

I had been planning on taking him to the game against Carlton the next day, but I was now worried that people in the crowd might yell out something that could upset him. Instead, Lauren's parents were taking him and Chase to Geelong to stay with them for a few days. I told him, 'If you want to ask me any questions about it, you just grab Pa's phone and call me.'

I finally collapsed on the couch at 8.30 p.m. I was exhausted but relieved that everything was out. Hopefully people would move on soon.

After not sleeping the night before, I was out like a light the moment my head hit the pillow and didn't stir until my alarm went off. I'd hardly eaten the previous day, and a check of the scales showed the toll the stress had taken on me – I'd dropped nearly 3 kilos in 24 hours.

While I'd received a few messages from my teammates, I hadn't seen them since it all came out. So I was a bit nervous when I entered the rooms at the MCG before the game. Any concerns were washed away almost immediately when a few of the boys came up and gave me a hug. Instantly, I felt better.

I had to speak at the President's Function before the game and in a weird way it helped. I was finding that the more I spoke about it, the better I felt.

What I didn't feel good about was the timing of my indiscretion. Brett Ratten had lost his son Cooper in a car accident that involved drink-driving, and here I was, three weeks later, making this dumb decision. Given Brett was a former player and coach at Carlton, the two clubs decided to run out together through the same banner at the start of the game to honour Cooper.

We ended up playing pretty well, cruising home by 57 points. Afterwards we had a leadership meeting in the coach's room, where I went through everything that had happened over the previous 48 hours. I didn't leave anything out – I was completely honest.

They were understandably not happy and had questions, but they weren't filthy, which was at least something I could take away. It was agreed that I'd make a $5000 donation to a charity, most likely one linked to road trauma, as part of my sanction from the club.

I'd been in contact with a few of the boys during the saga. Mitch had called on Friday and his first words were, 'What the fuck?' Lewy had called me 'bloody stupid' but wasn't angry – he understood I'd made a genuine mistake, while Josh Gibson grabbed me after the meeting and said, 'Mate, I know you don't do it all the time. I trust you.'

Andrew Russell was filthy. He said he wanted to hit me – but I'd heard that a few times from the fitness boss. What was upsetting was that he asked me if I did this sort of thing all the time. He and everyone else had every reason to ask the question. I was front-page news in the Saturday papers, with the *Herald Sun* running the photo Tony Hachem had taken and posted on Instagram.

When I got home from the MCG, I was grateful to find some friendly faces in my living room. Brent and Rachel Guerra and their little boy, Jack, were hanging out with Lauren. It was times like these that you treasured your friends.

That night I caught a replay of Clarko's press conference after the match. He'd been sensational in dealing with the media and had thrown his full support behind me. 'He's been a ripper for our footy club,' Clarko said. 'If there's a bloke who I will have his back and he'll have mine, it's Luke Hodge.'

You can say whatever you like about Clarko, but one thing he does is back his players through anything. And that's a great trait to have. The following morning I messaged him, saying, 'Hey mate. Thanks for what you said in your press conference after the game.'

His reply lifted my spirits instantly and put a smile on my face for the first time in three days. 'It will take much, much more than that for me to lose faith.'

21

WHY CAN'T WE?

'We're not going to play you in the middle because we know what you're like.'

Clarko was explaining my role for the qualifying final against West Coast at Subiaco, and I was confused. He felt that for my 'composure' it would be better if I played across half-back, because after the suspension and drink-driving incident I'd be 'over the top'.

'I'm worried you'll try too hard, be physical and get reported again,' he said.

I could see where my coach was coming from, but I didn't agree with his theory. There was no doubt I was motivated to prove a lot of people wrong, but I was also confident I could control myself. Hiding me away on the half-back flank wasn't going to lessen my attack on the ball and the man.

But I wasn't really in a position to argue given the events of the previous couple of weeks, so I just focused on getting ready for the Eagles on Friday night. They'd finished second on the ladder, with Fremantle finishing on top. The Dockers were playing Sydney in the other preliminary final, also at Subiaco but on Saturday afternoon.

I addressed the whole playing list on Monday and explained that I felt I had let the team down and was determined to make up for it. From there, my teammates and the club moved on.

Unfortunately, the media didn't. A few reporters continued to question my character and my captaincy, and suggested that I'd derailed Hawthorn's premiership campaign. The interesting thing about the media coverage was that just a couple of weeks earlier, Adelaide's Matthew Jaensch had been caught drink-driving and had blown 0.137. It had resulted in just a few paragraphs tucked away in the back of the sports pages, while I'd been front-page news for a couple of days and the commentary just kept rolling.

It was hard to cop, but it added fuel to the fire that was smouldering inside me. Getting out of Melbourne was probably a good thing, even though West Coast's record at its home ground was formidable. I was certainly on edge. The week had seemed to drag on and on. I just wanted the sanctuary of the football field.

Taking the crowd out of the equation early was always the first aim of a visiting team at Subiaco, and we seemed to do that, with the tally two goals each at quarter-time. The tackling and pressure were intense, but I was having one of those nights when the ball seemed to go everywhere I wasn't.

Things got worse in the second quarter as the Eagles charged and key forward Josh Kennedy became dangerous. They kicked five goals while we could manage just one point. The margin was 32 points at half-time, and we were in trouble.

I'd been shit. Nine touches was the sum of my work and I think the coach could sense my frustration. At half-time I was one of a number of changes, being moved into the midfield to play alongside Mitch, who was virtually playing a lone hand.

A good mark and goal from Roughy were the perfect start to the third quarter, but there would be no miracle comeback. The Eagles had their tails up and were the type of team that when they got rolling, particularly on their home deck, they were almost impossible to stop. At three-quarter time the margin was out to 50, and while we got some late 'junk time' goals, our premiership hopes took a big hit with the 32-point defeat.

I ended up with 29 possessions and a goal, but had nowhere near the impact I wanted. And I'd copped it from the West Coast supporters, who had even taunted me by hanging over the fence and offering me beers. It would have been amusing normally, but I wasn't seeing the funny side of anything.

We were a pretty dejected lot on the plane home, in particular Jack Gunston, who'd suffered a nasty ankle injury that was going to put him out for at least a week.

I wasn't great company over the weekend. We were embarrassed by our performance against the Eagles, and as captain I took it particularly hard. But the beauty of finishing in the top four was that we got to fight another day.

Motivation clearly wasn't an issue ahead of the semi-final against Adelaide, but I got extra from an unlikely source. On the Wednesday morning, word reached me that I should have a look at the *Herald Sun*, as there was an article I might want to read. I flicked inside from the back page and saw a photo of Clarko and me in conversation at training the previous day. The headline was 'Wake up, Hodgey.'

The article was by Mark Robinson, the paper's chief football writer, and started, 'Snap out of it, Luke Hodge.'

My blood started to boil. I read on.

'You're feeling sorry for yourself and it affected your football last week and, as captain, it affected your team.' The piece went on to talk about how the drink-driving charge had weighed heavily on me and that I'd been 'sheepish' against the Eagles and played like a 'scolded child'.

I wasn't the only one to cop it, in what was a scathing assessment of our qualifying-final performance. 'Hodge was mild. Breust flew one-handed, Roughy stunk, Hale looked 40, Frawley looked lost, Smith couldn't run, Birchall was fiddly, and Puopolo and Suckling looked like they were chasing bubbles from a kid's gun and kept clutching at and missing the bubbles.'

It then went back to criticising me again.

I was shocked after finishing it, and my first instinct was to dial Robbo's number and give him a piece of my mind. But I refrained, instead saving the article in my phone as I'd done with Mike Sheahan's comments a few years earlier.

I was furious. I couldn't get the article out of my mind. No matter what I tried, it was there, repeating, over and over. That was pretty much what happened for the next two days leading up to the game.

Clarko apologised to me before our team meeting on Thursday. 'I stuffed up,' he said. 'I'm never going to say to you again to pull back and be composed – I softened your mind by telling you that.'

He'd done a complete 180 for what he was expecting against Adelaide: I would be starting in the centre bounce and playing midfield, not half-back. 'You are a bull. Go and crash and bash packs,' he said. 'Play your way.'

Sometimes Clarko can deliver a speech that has you wanting to go out and play right there and then, and that's what he delivered at that team meeting. He spoke about how he felt he'd let the team down with his own preparation before the first final, and then stoked the fire of a few players by reminding them that they owed us an improved performance. There was one clear feeling when I drove home from Waverley afterwards: Adelaide were in trouble.

My hunch was right. Within two minutes of the game starting, I'd drilled the opening goal from a set shot 40 metres out after intercepting a kick-in. Every Hawthorn player converged on me after the goal, in what was a great moment. They understood what I'd been through and were pumped to see me impact the game so early.

It was the start of something special. Thirty minutes later, when the siren sounded for quarter-time, we'd kicked eight goals – three of them from Breust – and our lead was 38 points. All the built-up tension and anxiety of the past few weeks flooded out of me, almost like a valve had been released.

Everything clicked. By three-quarter time our lead was ten goals, and it finished at 74 points. We kicked 21 goals for the match, six of which were by Breust, and I enjoyed a night out, with four goals from 24 disposals. It had been one of the most satisfying games of my career.

Thanks, Robbo.

It seemed like a good idea at the time. Getting to Perth a day earlier than usual to prepare for the preliminary final against Fremantle made sense on a number of fronts. I often did it because it helped loosen up my back and gave me extra time to prepare before the final training session.

Six of us were at the airport at midday on Wednesday; we'd decided to go a day early. The rest of the team were coming on Thursday ahead of the Friday-night game. Five hours later we were still there. The flight had been cancelled and its replacement wasn't until 5.30 p.m.

Fremantle had finished a game clear on top of the ladder and had just managed to get over Sydney in the qualifying final to earn the week off. Our only meeting with them during the season had been in Round 15, when we'd played one of our best games and won by 12 goals.

If anything good had come from the Eagles debacle two weeks earlier, it was that talk of the 'three-peat' had been put on the back-burner. We certainly hadn't addressed it as a group like we had the previous season when we were chasing back-to-back premierships. But to us, there was a sense about this finals campaign that was best summed up by the question, 'Why can't we?'

Why couldn't we win a third premiership in succession? We'd put together an impressive season, particularly in its second half, and had put ourselves in the frame. There was nothing about the teams who remained – Fremantle, North Melbourne and West Coast – that we feared. We were in form, and if we needed a prod, the Eagles loss had certainly provided one.

So why couldn't we?

When Fremantle kicked the first two goals of the game, the stadium went bananas and there were flickers of deja vu from a couple of weeks earlier. But this time, we settled. By the 18-minute mark of the opening term we were in front, and from there we never looked back.

Our lead was 17 points at three-quarter time after Matthew Suckling nailed a set shot on the siren, but two minutes into the last quarter, things changed. I ran sideways into a pack at centre half-back to try to orchestrate a spoil, but it all went pear-shaped. My legs were taken out from under me and I crashed heavily, with the back of my head smashing into the turf. I was away with the fairies for a few seconds and took a while to gather myself before slowly getting up. The medical staff suggested I get off the ground, and as I slowly made my way to the bench it wasn't my head that was causing concern.

My right hamstring felt off. I'd obviously tweaked it when I'd been flung backwards in the marking contest.

The physios did a bit of work on it as I lay in front of the bench. It felt like a cramp, so the massage would hopefully help get it going again. There was a discussion about whether I should go back on – the doctors were more concerned about the head knock initially, but then the topic of the conversation turned to the hamstring. They were worried that if I went back on, there was a chance I would do more damage, which would rule me out of the Grand Final. I pointed out that with ten minutes to go in the preliminary final there was only one option in my mind. 'What if we lose and I'm sitting down here feeling okay?' I said.

While I gathered my thoughts, the Dockers enjoyed a good patch. Michael Walters kicked a goal to get them within 11 points, and then a minute later Michael Barlow missed a relatively easy set shot to reduce the margin to ten. Another miss from Walters helped, but while I could feel my hamstring when I ran, if we lost the preliminary final, it wouldn't matter.

The Dockers were coming hard – but then they gave an opening to the wrong person. They were switching the ball across half-back when Tom Sheridan dropped a simple mark that opened the door for Cyril Rioli. Sheridan had been under no pressure but he certainly was now, with Cyril swooping in and gathering the ball. Off one step, he snapped a goal from 50 metres out.

It broke the locals' hearts.

When the siren sounded to announce that we were through to our fourth consecutive Grand Final, the margin was 27 points – we'd kicked the final three goals of the game.

Relief was always the first emotion, and then the mind flicked forward. I reached down and felt my hamstring. It would be interesting to see how it pulled up after I'd cooled down and endured the four-hour plane ride home. I wasn't going to miss the Grand Final because of a little twinge, but I had to make sure I prepared well enough to not let down my teammates on the big day.

The song was sung with gusto, and we were certainly in a better mood than the last time we'd left Subiaco. I was careful not to show any signs of an issue with the leg, especially near the coaches or at the airport, where the cameras were waiting for us.

That question kept coming back to me as I used the downtime on the plane to think about what was ahead. Why can't we?

22

FOUR TIME

It didn't feel like Grand Final week. Maybe it was because my focus was on treatment, or maybe we were just getting used to how the best week of the season worked.

I received non-stop massage on my back and hamstring, with every minute of Sunday, Monday and Tuesday focused on recovery. We took a conservative approach to the first training session of the week on Tuesday, and I watched it from the upstairs gym behind the glass.

I wasn't the only player feeling aches and pains ahead of the biggest game of the year. Jack Gunston had been fighting for two weeks to recover from his bad ankle injury. There was no issue about me playing, even though I hadn't fully tested it out yet. We didn't bother with scans. In my mind it had just been a cramp, and that was the story I was selling to everyone – including myself.

By Wednesday it was starting to feel more like Grand Final week. That certainly hadn't been the case over in Perth, with TV footage showing thousands of people watching the West Coast Eagles' every move. It reminded me of 2013 and the hype that had surrounded Fremantle. We were going to get the chance for some qualifying-final revenge – the Eagles had been too good for North Melbourne, recovering from a slow start to win by 25 points.

And once again we were being portrayed as the underdog. It was a title that had worked beautifully for us in the past. In 2008 Geelong had clearly been the superior team all season and started the Grand Final as red-hot favourites; Fremantle's much-hyped defensive systems had sent a groundswell of positive opinion their way in 2013; Sydney had Buddy and favouritism in 2014; and now the Eagles' mysterious 'web' had the football world transfixed.

Questions were being asked. How were Hawthorn going to get through West Coast's defensive press? Who was going to stop Josh Kennedy?

The main point about the Eagles' web, which is what they were calling the defensive press, was the fact that the game was to be played at the MCG. It would be a whole different story enforcing the press at the MCG compared to the Eagles' home ground at Subiaco, simply because of the different measurements of the ground. Subiaco was considerably narrower, which made it easier to trap the ball in certain areas.

The official measurement had the Perth ground 15 metres longer than the MCG, but 20 metres less in width. This was the reason that, when visiting teams played there, they often kicked the ball out on the full from full-back. What worked at other grounds simply didn't at Subiaco, because you didn't have the room. The narrowness made it easier to execute a press as you were guarding less space, with the boundary line acting as a fence to keep the opposition trapped in.

This is a lot harder to do at the MCG, where you have an extra 10 metres of space on each side. And the beauty of our team was that if you gave an extra 10 metres to Sam Mitchell, Shaun Burgoyne, Grant Birchall or Matt Suckling, who are all beautiful kicks, they would slice through it with their foot skills.

The Kennedy dilemma was a major one, given he'd kicked 75 goals to win the Coleman Medal and had caused problems for us in the qualifying final. But we'd got the match-up wrong from the start that night. James 'Chip' Frawley had started forward because Clarko was concerned we were too big down back, with Brian Lake and Josh Gibson also there. The fear had been that we wouldn't have enough run being generated from defence. Poor old Chip hardly got a kick that night.

He rebounded brilliantly the following week against Adelaide, when he played on Tex Walker and Lakey took Josh Jenkins. Then, against the Dockers, Chip played on Fremantle captain Matthew Pavlich and Lakey took care of the resting ruckman. Gibbo could play on bigs and smalls, which helped considerably.

Kennedy was the perfect match-up for Chip because Chip equalled him in strength and speed. The Eagles full-forward liked to operate in the centre corridor, and this also played into Chip's hands as his pace off the mark was better than a lot of other defenders. Chip was as confident as anyone throughout the week about their Grand Final match-up. He was also pretty happy about his decision to come to Hawthorn.

Chip was one of two new faces in the team. Ryan Schoenmakers, who'd come in to replace Gunston in the semi-final against Adelaide, had done his job and then been impressive in the preliminary final, kicking two goals, so that although he'd missed the previous two flags he wasn't going to be left out of the team this time. With Gunston fully recovered from his ankle injury and coming in, the straight swap for Schoenmakers was no longer the obvious call. The unlucky one to miss out was youngster Billy Hartung, who'd really come on during the season and had played as the substitute in the first two finals.

That lack of Grand Final feeling certainly disappeared on Thursday, when our main training session at Waverley was conducted in front of thousands of fans cheering our every move. Players can often take for granted the support they receive. We live in a bubble a lot of the time, just worrying about getting up for games each week and shutting out the outside world. Seeing the smiles on the faces of the boys as they looked around at the sea of brown and gold was a highlight, as was the fact that my hamstring didn't even register in my mind as I cruised through training.

That night I sent Clarko a text. I wasn't sure what tricks he had planned for the final team meeting or whether he'd settled on a theme, but I thought I'd offer a suggestion. Accompanying my text was Mark Robinson's article. 'Hey mate, before the game, to get pumped up, I go through articles that piss me off, dent the ego and put me in the mood,' I wrote. 'I was reading Robbo's article from two weeks ago – not sure if you want to use it, but plenty of motivation for players considering how we normally respond after a bake.'

I was still hurting from it. I still felt like I had something to prove after the last month.

And I felt like the Eagles were going to pay.

*

One of the biggest changes to this Grand Final week came in Friday's parade, which took a new route. It started at the Old Treasury Building, where in previous years it had ended, and then went along Wellington Parade to finish, fittingly, at the MCG. It was also a public holiday for the first time. These factors certainly didn't impact on the crowd, who turned out in droves under perfect sunny skies. Cooper and Chase were again along for the ride. Chase had been asking the same question all week: 'When do we get to go in the back of the ute?'

It was a big couple of days for my younger son. The later start to the season, combined with the mid-year break, meant the Grand Final had ticked over into October and landed on his third birthday. Lauren and I took the punt that the little man wouldn't be across everything and wouldn't notice that we weren't having a family get-together to celebrate this milestone.

Not that he was going to miss out – Lauren made plans to have his birthday cake presented at the footy creche in Richmond on the morning of the game. All his friends would be there, including his bestie, Leni, the daughter of Shaun Burgoyne. The creche was situated just near the MCG, and Chase enjoyed hanging out there during games while Lauren went across the road to the stadium.

Chase loved his ride on the back of the ute, as did Cooper, who was becoming an old hand at it. The change of route meant that there were thousands of people waiting for us at the MCG. I got my hands on the premiership cup again, this time with Eagles captain Shannon Hurn, and then sat next to Clarko for the traditional media conference.

A variety of topics were thrown up, including the weather – the temperature was expected to hit 30 degrees on Grand Final Day.

I played a straight bat to questions about my hamstring and limited training in the lead-up. 'Everyone has a different post-game routine, and mine was a bit more low-key during the week,' I said. Pressed further on the hamstring injury, I offered little. 'It was more of a jolt to the back. I trained yesterday and there's no problems.'

After the media conference, it was back to Waverley for a light training session, which was essentially a kick and catch, followed by a team meeting. It started with a focus on what the Eagles had done well against us in the qualifying final, and how we weren't going to let that happen again. At the end, Clarko handed out copies of Robbo's article. 'Take one of these and do what you want with it,' Clarko said. 'It might help.'

Reading it was the last thing I did on Grand Final Eve, and it got the same reaction as before – my blood started to boil. I've always been the same. Tell me I can't do something, or doubt my ability, and I will do everything in my power to prove you wrong. That would be my mindset the next day.

It arrived earlier than I wanted it to. The clock said 4.30 a.m., and I was wide awake thinking about what lay ahead. While it could certainly be classified as a change of routine, I was wise enough not to let this sort of unexpected development rattle me.

We had a bit on in the morning, given it was Chase's birthday, and he was certainly not going to celebrate it with a sleep-in. While we kept things low-key, there were still presents to unwrap, which put a smile on everyone's face.

Cooper came along for my pre-game jog and we had a kick in the park. The most telling thing about that was the weather: it was already warm and windy. The forecasters were on the money – it was going to be a hot one. This would add another dimension to the game. According to Andrew Russell we were prepared for it. We'd been doing steam room sessions for months and had also done them in the lead-up to the previous three grand finals. Did it really prepare us for a 30-degree Grand Final day? I didn't think so but what Jack was great at was selling a message and preparing players so they wouldn't be shocked on the big occasion. It was classic mind games and, like Clarko, our fitness boss was a genius at it.

The trip to the ground went without a hitch, and as usual the Wiggles soundtrack was the background music. I actually liked it, but it had certainly raised some eyebrows over the years. Recently Dan Elstone had accompanied me to a match and commented that I was probably the only AFL footballer who listened to kids' music as part of his pre-game preparation. It worked for me, and once again it did the trick. I felt good when I arrived in the rooms, and from there the process started. I knew what I had to do in the next two hours to be ready, and the beauty of this team was that everyone had exactly the same attitude as I did.

Just before we were scheduled to run out, Clarko called us all together. It was a tight circle, with Clarko's head buried down low and everyone leaning in to get as close as possible.

I'm never entirely sure what is said in these situations most of the time – you either can't hear properly, or your mind is already thinking about the opening bounce – but this time we were going to footy war. That had been the theme of the build-up. Clarko wanted us to be brutal and fierce – to win the hard ball on the inside but also have the courage to run on the outside. With the warm conditions, it was going to be the team who were the toughest mentally who'd survive. The coach again referred back to our Kokoda experience, and his war cry hit the spot.

Then I got to do one of the best walks in Australian sport.

With a Sherrin in my hand, I paused at the doorway of the rooms to make sure everyone was ready. Then it started. There is a short walk out of the rooms to a small doorway. Once through there, you take a left-hand turn to the ramp that leads up onto the ground. This is the gladiator's moment, and it's exactly like in the movie but without Russell Crowe. The cauldron is only a few metres away and the noise gets louder with every step, then the light hits half-way up and momentarily blinds you. This is the moment when your senses are on overload.

Once I got near the top, I broke into a jog, had a bounce of the ball, and then looked up at the banner. There was a giant team photo on it with three words: WHAT'S IMPORTANT NOW.

The team.

The first passage of play was exactly the opposite of what we'd planned. At the opening bounce, West Coast's athletic Nic Naitanui, who was not only an excellent tap ruckman but a very good clearance player, sidestepped David Hale, grabbed the ball and slammed it forward. It bounced dangerously towards goal but we managed to rush it through for a behind.

From the kick-in, Jordan Lewis marked near the boundary line and then went long in my direction. Gunston had pushed forward and was in the marking contest, while I stayed down front and square in a perfect position. The ball was spoiled and fell beautifully for my all-important first touch in the Grand Final . . . or so I thought.

It went sideways. Nine times out of ten it would have sat up perfectly. Instead, it bounced out of my reach.

I had to wait a few more minutes to get my hands on the Sherrin, and in that time Luke Shuey kicked the Eagles' first goal. We responded quickly, with Roughy getting a slick handbill to Cyril, who snapped truly. A quick handball as I was getting crunched got my day moving.

Shortly after that, West Coast had another golden opportunity but Shuey decided to attempt a difficult dribble goal instead of handballing over the top to his teammate Jamie Cripps, who would have strolled in for an easy goal. Selfish acts like that one are something players look back on, as we did in 2012, and regret.

We transferred the ball down the outer wing before setting up a mismatch between our ruckman, Ben McEvoy, and a smaller Eagles defender. McEvoy marked strongly. For a big man he'd always been a good shot at goal, and there were no problems with his execution.

For myself, I was still having a few. With my next possession I went to kick long into the forward line but it was smothered. Then, as I went to recover, I was wide open and West Coast's Sharrod Wellingham ran through me. It was a solid bump that sat me on my backside.

Things certainly weren't falling for me, but at least they were for Cyril. He was everywhere in the opening quarter, kicking two of our five goals and providing Brad Hill with the last of the term, inside the final 40 seconds, to give us a handy 19-point lead.

It was almost the perfect start. The Eagles' web had been non-existent – in fact, we'd created our own version of it, trapping the ball in our forward half for the majority of the quarter.

While there may have been a lack of personal highlights in the first term, I quickly made up for it inside the first minute and a half of the second when Cyril sent a pass my way. I was tucked up against the boundary line and the ball hung in the air, allowing Eagles defender Will Schofield to spoil. The ball stayed in and dribbled towards my teammate Paul Puopolo, who picked it up and handballed it back to me.

I had nowhere to go with an Eagles defender right there, so instinct took over and I turned the ball in my hand to execute a banana kick. The breeze was blowing towards our goal and, in that split second, I thought if I floated it up high the elements might help push it through.

As soon as I struck it I knew. It's the same feeling golfers have off the tee when they nail a drive. I'd hit the Sherrin in the perfect spot and it was never going to miss. The goal also probably saved me from a bake from the coach – normally in that situation you'd look to centre the ball. But I simply didn't have the time.

Even before the ball had crossed the goal line, I turned to the crowd in the pocket with my arms raised. It was a sea of brown and gold and I gave them a good old-fashioned fist pump. Maybe it was going to be my day after all.

It was certainly Cyril's. He was inspiring us and we were dominating the Eagles. A handball over the top from him handed Gunston his first goal, and then a minute later he produced an inspirational act of play that was typical Cyril. If the Eagles weren't already rattled, they were now. West Coast's Mark Hutchings received the ball at half-back and had time to take a bounce, with no-one near him – or so he thought. Cyril sprinted 30 metres to drag Hutchings down and earn a free kick due to illegal disposal. It was brilliant to watch and the crowd went berserk. They were still cheering as Cyril played on, kicking long to the forward pocket, where it went over the back to Luke Breust. Breust then produced his own piece of magic, tapping the ball over his head and into the path of Gunston, who kicked his second goal with a nice left-foot snap.

The score was 49 to 12.

A couple of minutes later we got our ninth consecutive goal when Isaac Smith nailed a long bomb from 55 metres. I almost joined in on the act, with my trusty right foot getting an opportunity. I got good contact and it carried the 45-metres easily, but drifted late for a behind.

We were all over them. They eventually got their second goal for the day through Josh Hill midway through the second quarter, and a goal to Elliot Yeo after the half-time siren meant the lead was reduced to 31 points.

It was a good buffer, but as soon as I got into the rooms I realised we were going to need it. The boys looked stuffed. The warm conditions were clearly taking a toll, and as a group we were collectively spent. The room resembled a casualty ward. Jumpers were off and bodies were lying all over the place, with training staff buzzing around providing fluid and towels, and every player getting his legs massaged. I had a sickening feeling about it all. We were in trouble.

Clarko's message focused on playing smart football at the start of the third term. We needed to be composed because, given our physical state, we didn't want a high-octane quarter. If that happened, we would be vulnerable.

As expected, West Coast brought a renewed intensity to the start of the third quarter. We were instantly on the backfoot, and for the first ten minutes the ball seemed to live in their forward half. Jack Darling got the first goal of the quarter at the four-minute mark.

It was obvious they were running harder and spreading better across the ground.

What they weren't doing was converting their chances. Shuey blew another golden opportunity, which saved our bacon. The Eagles had caused a turnover at half-forward and when Shuey burst clear he had two options, one on each side of him – but his kick went in between them to Taylor Duryea, the only Hawthorn player in the vicinity. Then a minute later we got some divine intervention when the sun got in Darling's eyes, causing him to drop a simple chest mark 30 metres out, directly in front.

We just needed to score. That was always the best way to stop the other team's momentum. Enter Cyril.

On one of our rare ventures forward, he took a nice contested mark in the forward pocket and played on immediately, seeing a two-on-one back across the other side of the goal. The Eagles managed to make the spoil, but we had numbers. Brad Hill flicked it to Gunston, who handballed back over the top to Schoenmakers for the crucial goal.

Any sighs of relief were brief – Hutchings got the reply for West Coast almost immediately. We were just hanging in there, and the noise was getting louder as Eagles fans sensed that if the comeback was on, now was the time.

But the reason we'd become a good side was the little things – we were so well trained now that they'd become second nature.

While Chip Frawley had been played out of position and had no impact against the Eagles three weeks earlier, today he was playing the game of his life. He'd had the better of Kennedy, but it was his ability now to win a one-on-one contest that changed everything. He managed to get his hand in to spoil, and then followed it up by brushing Kennedy aside, picking up the ball and kicking it long into the forward line. A couple of Eagles misjudged the flight and this allowed Gunston, who was playing in front, to float in and mark on his chest.

The little things.

Gunston is one of the best set shots for goal in the competition, and he didn't miss. It meant that for all the Eagles' effort and momentum, the margin was back to what it had been at half-time.

We kicked the next three goals of the game. It's amazing what a few goals will do for the energy levels. We were suddenly a different unit. Gunston got his fourth goal after another magical Cyril intercept; Isaac Smith produced a freaky dribble goal from the pocket; and Matt Suckling, who'd started as the substitute and had only been on the ground for about a minute, snapped truly on his left foot after being set free by Mitch.

Right on the three-quarter-time siren, I was crunched by West Coast's Jeremy McGovern. It was a fair bump and knocked a bit of the wind out of me. To my surprise, as I went to get up, it was McGovern who offered his hand and helped me to my feet. It was a nice gesture, but grand finals aren't the place for nice gestures. There's no way if I was 50 points behind that I'd be helping my opponent up off the ground. We'd been more ruthless than them for the whole day, and McGovern had innocently reaffirmed that fact.

It was business as usual during the three-quarter-time break. Even though the scoreboard suggested otherwise, I was always more of a pessimist than an optimist in these scenarios. While every player was thinking the same thing – that we were about to win our third flag in a row – none of us was game enough, or silly enough, to say it out loud yet. Clarko was particularly fired up about not taking the foot off the gas. As far as he was concerned the job wasn't complete until the siren sounded. I felt that we probably needed to put together another ten minutes of serious football and then we could sit back and enjoy the ride.

Flicking onto autopilot is probably the best way to describe how it felt at the start of the last quarter. You were doing everything possible to trick your mind into thinking it was the first quarter and every touch mattered.

This serious focus lasted about two minutes, thanks to Roughy. After the Eagles missed another set shot, we quickly moved the ball from the kick-in to half-forward, where Cyril again got out the back and marked. He wheeled around on his left foot and went long to the goal square. Roughy was running back to the square and had metres on his opponent. Cyril saw that, so he gave the kick everything, hitting it so well that it looked like the ball was going to sail over the line for a goal.

The benefit of the doubt would say Roughy did the safe thing and marked it on the line. That, or he wanted to get his name on the score sheet in the Grand Final. Regardless, it was very funny and Roughy was a bit sheepish as he went back for the simple shot. All the boys had a bit of a laugh and Mitch gave me a look that said, 'We're going to hang shit on him for that afterwards.'

As I made my way back to the middle of the ground I saw Frawley gazing into the stands. The realisation that he was now a premiership player had clearly just hit the former Demon.

And I was now a four-time premiership player. FOUR TIMES.

A handball from Mitch set up the next centre clearance for me and I went long to Brad Hill, who was leading into the pocket. He gathered on the bounce and then handballed to Roughy, who was somehow by himself. No Eagles even ran at him, but clearly stealing Cyril's goal was still on his mind. Instead of taking the shot, he tried to get a 10-metre pass to Gunston at the top of the square.

It went pear-shaped, but Roughy made up for it by producing a big smother to keep the ball in a very dangerous spot. Breust eventually won a free kick for too high, but Smith had taken the advantage and kicked his third goal of the day.

It was party time.

And then Brian Lake got us smiling even more. You never really knew what you'd get with Brian, but he'd again been significant down back and produced a piece of defensive wizardry that summed up a magical day. Josh Hill looked set to get an easy goal after taking two bounces from half-forward. Brian was the only Hawthorn player in the vicinity, but instead of charging at him, he waited in the goal square. This put Hill in two minds. Should he take the shot from the angle? Or should he handball to a teammate? In the end, the Eagles forward took the shot and Brian timed his leap at full stretch to perfection, getting a finger on the ball to save the goal.

Things were just getting silly now.

Brian got up and gave his former Western Bulldogs teammate a look that said, 'Not on my watch today.'

Every time I caught a teammate's eye it was followed by a wink and a nod. We were premiership players . . . again. The game went through the motions for the last ten minutes. It was such a great time, running around the middle of the MCG without a care in the world and a smile on my face.

West Coast kicked a few goals in the end, but they were irrelevant. We were all waiting for that sound. My final act of the Grand Final was a big tackle on Eagles midfielder Andrew Gaff at half-back. I'd just got myself back on my feet when I heard it.

A double fist pump and a roar that came from deep within was my immediate reaction. Then I realised I had no teammates around me, so I went looking. Breust was the first to get a bear hug.

It was a weird feeling. The previous three all had a specific feel: excitement, relief and pure joy summed them up. Winning a fourth was just unbelievable. Channel 7's Tim Watson grabbed me away from the group for a quick interview, but I wasn't much use to him.

'Mate, I'm lost for words,' I said.

It was true. I didn't know how to describe my emotions. There was a satisfaction about proving everyone wrong – I think that was the case both personally and as a team. The past five weeks had been the toughest of my life.

I went and grabbed Cooper and Chase out of the crowd and brought them over to the presentations, where there were players' kids running around everywhere. We were certainly the family club.

In what must have been a tight call, Cyril won the Norm Smith Medal. This sent the crowd into hysterics again. He was one of the most popular players at Hawthorn and had played an amazing game.

The presentations flew past and my speech was a bit shorter than previous ones. I was obviously getting the hang of it. 'Football is an up-and-down sport, and you guys ride the rollercoaster with us, so thank you for your support,' I said about the players' partners and families.

Then came the big moment. Former Hawthorn champion Peter Knights had been given the honour of handing over the cup to Clarko and me, and the roar from the crowd was the loudest of the day as we lifted it into the air. In a flash, the boys were up on stage for the money-shot photos. Confetti rained down on us and once again it all felt a bit surreal. Another few team photos were taken before I quietly grabbed the other five players who'd played in all four flags. I held the cup in one hand and gave a four-finger salute to the camera, with Roughy, Mitch, Cyril, Birch and Lewy doing the same. That was certainly one for the pool room.

For the next little while we basically just hung out in the middle of the MCG. Cooper and Chase had a great time playing with the confetti, and on the victory lap I found Dylan in the crowd with a few relations and mates. There were more photos and selfies there.

Eventually we retreated to the change rooms, where beers were waiting. Clarko took us straight into the meeting room and closed the door. He walked over to the corner, where there was a CD player, and pressed play. A very familiar song started, and the boys went nuts. Daryl Braithwaite's power ballad 'The Horses' had been our song in the three previous premiership years. We only sang it after significant wins – maybe once or twice during the regular season.

After the 2013 victory, the club had actually organised Braithwaite to play at the celebration dinner at Crown Melbourne, with Brent Guerra getting up to assist on vocals. Gooey was the one who had started the tradition – it was his favourite song. Now it was everyone's favourite song, and there had never been a more emotional rendition than this one.

After a few words from Clarko, the boys started to drift out of the meeting room to catch up with their families and friends, who'd spilled into the change rooms along with the media. It was always mayhem out there in the hour or so after a game.

I decided to stay put. I was emotionally spent and just wanted to shut out the world. I'd hidden a lot of the pain that I felt after the drink-driving incident and the qualifying-final performance. The only people I wanted to see were my family.

I asked one of the staff members to let Lauren know where I was, and she soon arrived with the boys, Mum, Dad, Bianca and Dylan. We went into a small trainer's room off to the side, grabbed a few beers and sat together, soaking up everything that had happened. It was perfect.

I then grabbed the three premiership cups from 2013, 2014 and 2015 and placed them in the middle of us all, and we posed for the best photo in Hodge family history.

The fat kid from Colac had come good.

23

WHAT IF?

'How does it feel to be in the twilight of your career?'

I looked at the journalist and bit my tongue. This felt like the 20th time I'd been quizzed about being an old fart in the past half an hour. The AFL captains-day media session ahead of the 2016 season launch was, thankfully, coming to an end.

'Who says I am?' I replied, with a bit of sting at the end.

Clearly the media had decided the topic of the day was the fact that I was 31, rather than Hawthorn's chances of winning a fourth-straight flag. While I may have been a bit tired of the conversation, I understood how the two things were linked. I'd already had the birthdate discussion with the club.

At the start of the year, the hierarchy had called all the 30-somethings together: Mitch, Gibbo, Shaun Burgoyne and myself.

The tale of the tape had Shauny and Mitch turning 34 later in the year, Gibbo hitting 32 just before the start of the season, and me clicking over to 32 in June. A couple of other 30-somethings from the 2015 premiership team had moved on, with David Hale and Brian Lake retiring. Chief executive Stuart Fox, recruiting manager Graham Wright, football boss Chris Fagan and Clarko were all in the meeting. Their message was clear: 'We want you guys to go on if your footy is going well, if the club is in a good position and if your bodies are still up to it.' It was good to put it on the table this early, as we all knew it was going to be an issue throughout the season.

Mitch then made a good point, saying, 'Don't put us all in together.' He was referring to a few teams who'd recently transitioned players, and how it seemed as if the club had made a call on the need to refresh their list, requiring a certain number of veterans to leave. From the outside it appeared not to be a purely form-based decision – more a philosophy of change, which meant a player's birthday had them in the gun. Mitch wanted each of our cases treated individually, and the hierarchy understood where he was coming from.

The problem was that I was feeling more like 41 than 31.

It had been a big six months. Following the premiership celebrations, I'd taken off the morning after the best-and-fairest count (where I'd finished fourth behind Gibbo) to Kokoda with a group of Hawthorn's corporate supporters. Once again it was an amazing experience. I met some great blokes on the trip, all passionate Hawthorn members. I was the youngest of the group, with a couple of 60-year-olds involved. They were right into the history of the trail, and we also spoke a lot of footy over the ten days. They were intrigued about how we'd won three flags in a row.

I actually really enjoyed talking about it, which I didn't expect – usually at the end of the season the last thing you want to think about is football. It's obviously a bit different when you're talking about winning grand finals.

After Kokoda there was a brief stopover at home before I was off again, this time to New York and Ireland for the International Rules Series. My little brother, Dylan, came with me, which was great for the two of us. We'd never really had a lot of time to hang out with each other due to the 12-year age gap and the fact that when I'd left home he was just getting out of kindergarten. He'd turned into a very handy sportsman and been awarded a cricket scholarship to the prestigious Geelong Grammar School, where he boarded and finished his secondary education.

The trip was a good way to make up for lost time, and it certainly played to Dylan's love of sport. The AFL had been true to its word about making the International Rules games worthwhile for the players who'd helped to resurrect the series the previous year. Having the training camp in New York was a masterstroke. We got the opportunity to see three NBA games, which included Le Bron James and Australia's Matthew Dellavedova with the Cleveland Cavaliers, plus the Los Angeles Lakers and legend Kobe Bryant. We also saw two NFL games, the second involving legendary quarterback Tom Brady and the New England Patriots, who won with a field goal in the dying seconds over the New York Giants.

The social side of the trip was also a great experience. Dylan and I were soon dubbed 'The Twins', as my little brother – who was anything but 'little', given he already had me for height. He also really enjoyed hanging out with the boys. One of the best things about these trips is the opportunity to mix with guys whose path you've crossed but you've never really got to know. Western Bulldogs captain Robert Murphy was a perfect example, and proved to be great company on the trip.

The actual test match was one to remember. We launched a stunning fourth-quarter comeback to just fall short, with the final score 56 to 52. It was a significant night for the locals, being the 95th anniversary of Bloody Sunday – a day of tragedy in Dublin, 21 November 1920, when 32 people died, 14 of those at Croke Park. The Irish lads certainly played with a lot of emotion early. We were on the backfoot for most of the first half but then managed to get our running game going – although we struggled for accuracy with the round ball in front of goal.

The most exciting part about returning home from my time away with Dylan had nothing to do with the trip. Lauren had been unable to come because we were expecting our third child, and on 22 January 2016 Leo Clifford Hodge was born. His two brothers were very pumped to have another boy join the clan. I stayed with Lauren and Leo in the hotel suite provided by the hospital after the birth, and it was a busy time.

There was one unhappy event around this time, which I found out about a few days later when I returned to training. My dodgy back, which all through my career had been the biggest challenge to keep under control, flared again, most likely because of my different sleeping arrangements. When the back goes, it generally means problems start to pop up elsewhere, and sure enough my groins went, which stopped my pre-season in its tracks. They didn't improve quickly, and my lead-up to the opening round was far from ideal. Instead of jumping out of my skin about the premiership defence, I was hobbling around like an old man, with a crook back and constant groin pain.

Unfortunately that was only the entree – the main course came during the game itself.

Easter was early in 2016, which meant that the traditional holiday Monday fixture against Geelong fell in Round 1. It was the first game with their prized recruit Patrick Dangerfield, who'd returned home after eight years in Adelaide. He certainly started with a bang, and at half-time had led the Cats to a 30-point lead. Thankfully we woke from our premiership slumber in the third quarter, holding them goalless while we kicked five goals. We led by two points at three-quarter time.

The last quarter was yet another epic between the two sides, but I didn't see the end of it. With five minutes remaining I ran back with the flight and was collected by Geelong's Mitch Duncan. It wasn't a classic shirtfront because he actually missed most of me, only really catching my right arm with his hip and shoulder. The problem was that the force was extreme. I knew the moment I hit the deck that my arm was broken. I took the free kick I'd been paid for the incident, but then signalled to the doctors, who ushered me off the ground. When the siren sounded to declare Geelong's 30-point victory, I was still on the bench with ice wrapped around my forearm.

An hour later I drove myself to the Epworth Hospital for scans, much to the annoyance of my wife. She wasn't upset about the injury, more the fact that I wouldn't let her drive.

The best part of the footy for Lauren was catching up and having a couple of drinks with other players' wives. Watching the actual game was a fair way down the list of priorities. Lauren certainly wasn't a football groupie. In fact, she didn't know what position

I played, which was always good for a laugh when she explained this to people. The look of shock and horror on their faces was priceless.

A couple of years earlier, we'd had a conversation about how it probably wasn't a good idea for her to drink too much in case she had to drive the car home from a game if anything happened to me. Since then she'd been sticking to one or two drinks.

My wife understandably thought that a broken arm would be classified as an emergency situation. 'You're not driving. I hate it when you drive,' I said. Poor old Loz was shocked and then not happy. By her calculation, she'd wasted three years of her social life by limiting her drinking at the footy!

The broken arm required a plate being inserted, but it only kept me out of action for two weeks and I returned in Round 4 against St Kilda.

They say things happen in threes. Well, I completed the trifecta three weeks later: groins, arm . . . knee.

It happened in the first few minutes against GWS up in Sydney – I hyperextended my knee. As soon as I did it there was pain, but I figured it was just one of those hits that you can run out. I managed to get through the game but it was a forgettable one for us, with the much-hyped Giants getting hold of us and winning by 75 points.

The knee was sore when it cooled down, and by the time I got back to Melbourne it had stiffened up. The doctors were keen for me to go in for a scan. That didn't go how we wanted – the diagnosis was a lateral meniscus tear, which meant at least six weeks on the sidelines.

One phone call a couple of weeks later quickly put everything into perspective. I was at home when Clarko rang and delivered news that rocked not only me but the entire football world. 'Mate, we've got some bad news about Roughy,' he said. 'It's spread.'

I stopped still and nearly dropped the phone.

Clarko explained that during one of Roughy's regular body scans they'd detected spots on his lungs. Further tests revealed that the melanoma had returned. I thanked him for the call and went over to the couch, where Lauren was watching TV. I told her what the phone call was about and she broke into tears.

'What do we do?' I asked her. We debated the best way to reach out to Roughy and his wife, Sarah. They were a great couple who'd recently got married, in January. The wedding had actually been Leo's first public outing – it was only about a week after he was born.

'Do we send a text? Do I call him? Or do I get in the car and go around there?'

We were trying to think what Roughy would want, and decided he probably wanted to be left alone, and that even talking about it on the phone would probably be too difficult for him. I settled on a text, saying that Lauren and I and the boys were sending our love. Words had never really been my thing, and at times like this they certainly didn't come easy.

The following day Roughy addressed the playing group, explaining what had happened. It was very emotional. I'd never seen the group so silent as they tried to comprehend what one of their mates was going through. Roughy's message was clear: he was going to fight.

'I want you to still treat me the same,' he said. 'If you see me out there, hang some shit on me, kick the ball at me. Don't treat me any differently.'

After the meeting I started doing a circuit as part of my rehab and Roughy came and joined in. He actually hadn't played since having a posterior cruciate ligament reconstruction in February, and had been only a few weeks away from returning. Nothing had to be said between us. We just put our heads down and completed the circuit. That's how Roughy wanted it.

Shortly afterwards it was announced that he would be having immunotherapy treatment, which involved a series of injections over the next couple of months. It says a lot about Roughy that how he reacted and the attitude he adopted actually made it easier for his teammates to deal with it. That sounds selfish, but he wanted everyone to get on with their lives because that was his own plan.

'I'm the same bloke,' he said. 'I've got shit to deal with, but around here I'm still the same person.'

He was an inspiration. Roughy was adamant he wasn't retiring and would be playing football again the following year.

The same couldn't be said about my career.

Former Essendon full-forward Matthew Lloyd put it on the agenda on Channel 9's *Footy Classified* program. I was on the couch watching when he did an assessment of Hawthorn's list and declared I was a 'banged-up warrior', saying, 'I think Hodge is one of the most vulnerable at the end of the year.'

There was no throwing of the remote at the TV, but I bristled. Of course I was the vulnerable one out of all the veterans, for one simple reason: I wasn't playing at the moment. It was logical that the one who was currently missing was deemed the one in the most trouble. What I didn't like was Lloyd's theory that Hawthorn wouldn't have a spot for me if I played on in 2017. Given that I'd played back, forward and in the midfield during my career, and not just in one position like he had in his, I was pretty sure they'd fit me in.

On my regular Friday-morning slot on KIIS FM later that week, the topic of Lloyd was brought up. I said, 'The four blokes he mentioned came four out of our top five in the best-and-fairest award last year, and have been consistent for the last three years throughout the premierships. The three other blokes haven't missed a game, or have played a majority of games for the last three years, and they're playing sensational football. That might have been the conversation [Lloyd] had at the end of his career because he only had one role [up forward]. But that's the best part about our sport – everyone has an opinion about it. Some people agree, some people don't. And it's my job to prove him wrong.'

The media grabbed onto my comments and suddenly started saying I was in a feud with Lloyd. I actually didn't give it any more thought. It was a storm in a teacup as far as I was concerned.

But then the following week I was a guest on radio station 3AW before our game, and Lloyd was working on special comments. The producer wanted me to play along, so we had another debate, where I again explained that I agreed with parts of what he'd said, but saying they couldn't find a spot for me was just wrong.

In reality, Lloyd hadn't been the only one to question where I was at. My main confidant at the club, Andrew Russell, had also expressed his concern.

He'd been more worried about the back and groin issues pre-season than the broken arm and knee, because they were impact injuries. 'Mate, your body has copped a pasting,' he said.

When I pushed him, he declared his hand. 'I think you're done at the end of the season,' he said. 'And that's what the guys upstairs think as well.'

I always enjoyed a challenge, and now I was facing one of my biggest. My gut feeling was that I wanted to continue playing.

Rather than rush back from the knee, Jack and the medical staff decided to give me a mini pre-season to ensure I would have kilometres in my body when I came back. This was my window. If I could get my body right and prove to them that I wasn't a spent force in the second half of the year, I might just stave off retirement.

As part of my training block, I started a new program to stabilise my groin issues. It worked, and by the time I got the green light to return in Round 14 against the Gold Coast Suns in Launceston, I was a different player from two months earlier – and Jack knew it. He had an amazing ability to look at a player out on the training track and know instantly if there was something wrong, or if they'd added a couple of kilos or weren't going 100 per cent. There were plenty of times when he'd wandered up and said, 'You're carrying a bit' or 'How's your diet?' He would often fire little bullets like that, but they always worked. Thankfully, on this occasion he was full of praise.

'I've done a one-eighty,' Jack said. 'I think you can go on.'

I managed to find a bit of it against the Suns as we won our fifth straight game, which moved us to the top of the ladder. We then won our next four games, which meant that, coming into Round 20, we were two games clear on top. It was strange because with the footy we were playing, we never thought we should be in that position. Talk of four-in-a-row was starting to get serious mileage in the media, but we'd learnt a long time ago not to start thinking about finals in any way, shape or form until they were on our doorstep.

What was more pressing was a decision about 2017. As the deadline approached, my former captain Shane Crawford wrote an interesting column in the *Sunday Herald Sun* in which he revealed that he'd twice almost come out of retirement, and that he'd often run past Clarko's house and wanted to knock on the door to say he was ready for another shot, but each time kept jogging.

Crawf made the point that you're a long time retired, and that while his body wasn't in great shape when he made his call following the 2008 premiership win, it improved dramatically with some time off. Even two years later he was still thinking about it, and the scary thing was that if anyone would have backed him to make a comeback, it was Clarko.

I enjoyed a good second half of the season and was confident that physically and mentally I could play again. My manager, Paul Connors, was adamant that 2017 should be my last year, as opportunities in the media could become available, and if I went on for another season in 2018, that door might close. I was heading more towards a media role than a coaching one, even though I'd really enjoyed working with the guys at Xavier College for a couple of years. Considering the amount of work assistant coaches do in the AFL system, I was pretty certain I would need a break and some serious family time before considering jumping back into that environment.

What I was sure about was giving up the captaincy. I'd spoken to Clarko a couple of times throughout the year about a succession plan, and how it would be perfect if I handed it over in 2017 and was able to help whoever it was for a season before I left. Jordan Lewis and Roughy were the designated next two in line, but the coach said he wanted any further discussion to wait until the end of the season.

We had a bigger concern: our form.

We lost two of the last three games of the year and slipped to fourth coming into the final game against Collingwood, who were already out of the finals race. Positions inside the top four were at stake, yet once again we were inconsistent across the afternoon and pretty unconvincing. It took a miracle goal from 70 metres by former Melbourne big man Jack Fitzpatrick, who was appearing in his first game as a Hawk, to level the scores at the 27-minute mark of the final term. Then Paul Puopolo managed to score a point right at the death to give us a one-point victory. It ensured that instead of finishing sixth, we finished third and got the double chance.

But something wasn't right.

All year it had been the same story. We'd won six games by single-digit margins, including three games in a row that we'd won by just three points. There wasn't the excitement after wins that there had been in the past. It felt like we were going through the motions, probably because we all knew that we weren't playing the right way.

What we all had was hope that it would click. Given we'd won the previous three flags – a pretty good block of work – it was believable that if anyone could flick the switch in finals, it was this group of players. And who better to do it against than our arch rival, Geelong?

In keeping with tradition, the game was an arm wrestle played at high intensity, with the two sides taking turns to have the momentum. We had our noses in front at half-time, and early in the third quarter it felt like that switch had been flicked, but the Cats ground their way back into it and led by two points at the final break.

You could almost watch a replay of any game from the previous eight years, since our famous Grand Final win over them, to describe the last quarter. Bodies were flying everywhere, the pressure was off the charts, and any slight mistake was seized upon by your opponent. In no surprise to anyone, the game came down to the final two minutes.

Geelong were two points up and had managed to keep the ball in their forward line. I was playing the sweeping role at the back of the pack when suddenly it was squirted out in my direction. I went to grab it but Cats forward Steven Motlop was right there and it spilled towards the boundary line. He got to it first and attempted an impossible dribble goal from next to the behind post. I knew that if anyone could make that shot, it was Motlop, and there were a few anxious seconds as it bounced towards the goal before, thankfully, it veered off for a behind.

A behind was perfect for us as it gave us a kick-in, and with less than a minute remaining we knew how to approach it. Birch quickly grabbed the ball and I thought he was going to go long but instead he went short to Lewy at centre half-back. Lewy turned around straight away and attempted to unleash a torpedo, but instead kicked a mongrel punt that somehow ended up in the arms of Shaun Burgoyne in the middle of the ground. He had Taylor Duryea running out wide on the wing. We had loose men everywhere, and Duryea found Luke Breust out on the half-forward flank.

There must have been only about 20 seconds left.

Breust was called to play on, which let Cats defender Corey Enright in to execute a brilliant smother. Luckily, the ball bounced kindly for Breust, who gathered again, brushed off a tackle and had the presence of mind to find Isaac Smith, who was alone 30 metres out, directly in front of goal.

I couldn't believe it. Geelong had done this sort of thing to us so many times in the past, and now we'd done it when it mattered most – to get through to a preliminary final. Then the siren sounded. I was in the middle of the ground when it happened and was more than happy the ball was in Isaac's hands. He didn't lack confidence. I expected him to take time over the kick, given that he could sit there for a minute if he wanted to.

Suddenly I was anxious about him rushing the shot – and my gut was right. The kick never looked good at any stage. From the moment it left his left foot, the ball started swinging to the right.

We'd lost.

Our luck had finally run out.

We quickly got around Isaac, with the message from the senior players to the group being a simple one: 'We've got a second chance.' We'd done it the hard way the previous year, so there was a precedent.

The night before, we'd watched our next opponent, the Western Bulldogs, destroy West Coast in Perth in the elimination final. They were a good young team, who we'd only just got over earlier in the season by three points, courtesy of a late James Sicily goal, and there was something about the way they'd dismantled the Eagles that had me on edge.

The opposition analysis during the week confirmed that the Bulldogs were the best pressure team in the competition. Their contested-ball and clearance stats were off the charts. But they were the new kids on the block, and finals experience is invaluable when there are 87 000 people inside the MCG on a Friday night.

Clarko spoke about capitalising at the start of the game, and we certainly followed instructions. We were helped by the Dogs' inaccuracy in front of goal, and by midway through the second quarter our lead was 23 points. I got involved with a goal early in the term, once again using my trusty right foot, which in recent times had begun to see more goal kicking than my left.

However, in the ten minutes leading into half-time, the game changed. The Dogs started to settle, and their work around the contest and spread began to stretch us. They had eight of the last nine scoring shots to cut our lead to just one point at the break.

We steadied, with Breust getting the first goal of the third quarter, but then that nagging doubt I'd had about the match-up a week earlier became a stark reality. It was like the floodgates opened. Suddenly we couldn't get our hands on the ball, and they kicked six consecutive goals to lead by 26 points at three-quarter time. Now it was our turn to miss chances, which didn't help the situation.

A piece of magic early in the last quarter from their best young player, Marcus Bontempelli, resulted in another goal, which almost put the game out of our reach. We rallied because we're a proud team, but it was quickly becoming apparent that the dream run was over. There would be no four-in-a-row.

The final act was the Dogs' smallest player, Caleb Daniel, kicking a goal after the siren, which ignited a stampede of his teammates.

It was an odd feeling. I couldn't put my finger on it until we assembled as a group at the Royal Oak in Richmond after the game. We'd all gone home, got changed and come back in to drown our sorrows. The more we sat and talked, the more clear it became: we were almost relieved it was over.

That sounds bizarre, but as a team we knew deep down that we hadn't been playing at a standard capable of winning the premiership.

We obviously hadn't had that feeling for a long time. Whether teams had caught up to us or we'd dropped a couple of per cent was up for debate. Rather than find another gear over the past six weeks, as we had in previous years, we'd gone backward and got what we deserved in the end.

But what if Isaac Smith had kicked the goal against Geelong? We wouldn't have played the Bulldogs and we wouldn't be sitting in a Richmond pub having a quiet beer. What if? What if? What if? That was how the whole season had felt to us. We'd never really been convincing.

The relief on the faces of the boys around that bar was something I hadn't witnessed for a long time. They were cooked, and it seemed like they wanted to get as far away from footy as possible.

For a couple of days there were mixed emotions. It was foreign territory – I'd played in the previous five preliminary finals. At the post-season review, I mentioned to Clarko that I'd been working on a speech for the best-and-fairest night about giving up the captaincy. It was the perfect forum to thank everyone at the club, thank the players and signal the start of a new era.

For some reason Clarko was cold on the idea. I soon found out why.

24

PARK OR EXPLORE

It was a typically beautiful Noosa morning. The sun was shining and the town was living up to its reputation as being a slice of paradise. Lauren and I were there for a wedding and had been out for dinner the previous evening with my teammate Jonathon Ceglar and his partner, Charlotte.

When I checked my phone first thing, there was a text message from Lehmo – his real name is Anthony Lehmann but everyone knows him as Lehmo, the comedian and breakfast radio host who is a mad Hawks fan.

'Mate, is Mitch really leaving?' the text read.

The official AFL trade period was about to start and rumours were flying thick and fast. I wrote back, 'Him and Simmo [former Hawthorn player Adam Simpson, now West Coast Eagles coach] are great mates. I think when he finishes playing he will go over there as an assistant. Can't see him leaving as a player.'

He replied, 'Thanks, mate.'

Lehmo's message got me thinking, and I decided to fire off a few texts to people at the club who would know if anything was happening. Nine minutes later I texted Lehmo again. 'But I could be wrong!'

Then I rang Mitch. As soon as he picked up, I said, 'What's going on?'

'Clarko came around and sort of said, "Are you interested in going to West Coast and playing there next year?"'

Mitch went on to explain that he was initially shocked but then spoke to his wife, Lyndall, about it and, given the stage their kids were at with schooling, it wasn't a bad idea to go over 12 months earlier.

He was making sense but my head was spinning. What was happening to my football team?

'How far along is the conversation?' I asked. 'Is it done? Are you 50-50?'

'Ninety-five per cent.'

'So you're gone?'

There was no pause or thinking music. Mitch said, 'Pretty much.'

He went on to explain how Clarko had approached the conversation, saying it would go no further if he wanted to stay at Hawthorn. Mitch had said he'd have to talk to his family, with Clarko replying, 'Let me know to either park or explore it.'

After talking to Lyndall, my teammate of the past 15 years gave the coach the green light to explore. A deal was then nutted out very quickly. Mitch was currently in New Zealand on holiday and said he was about to go on Melbourne radio to confirm everything.

As I tried to compute what was happening, I sent Lehmo a text. 'I'm off to the Gold Coast as well.'

He saw the funny side of it but I was starting to have trouble seeing any humour when, a few days later, I started getting text messages about Jordan Lewis. We were heading back home on Friday, and before we left I rang him.

It was a similar discussion to the one I'd had with Mitch. Clarko had come around to Lewy's house and had a chat about where he was at, where the club was at and if he thought he could get a longer contract than the one-year he had to go at Hawthorn. He'd again given the 'park or explore' option, adding that if Lewy stayed at Hawthorn and played good enough footy, he'd get a year-to-year contract like all the other players aged over 30.

Understandably, Lewy was a bit shocked at how the meeting had turned out. After some discussions with people close to him, including his best mate Roughy, it looked like he was heading to Melbourne. The link there was Todd Viney, the Demons list manager who'd been an assistant coach at the Hawks in the early days. Initially Melbourne were offering a new two-year deal with the option of a third year.

I thought I'd send a message to my fellow veteran, No. 9. 'A fair bit is going on.'

Shaun Burgoyne quickly came back to me. 'I didn't see any of this coming. How do you feel about the club's dealings?'

I then called him to discuss further. Shaun has always hated change, especially unexpected change. Our conversation pretty much went like this: 'We only signed on because we thought we were going to win another flag.' We were both concerned about the direction this was heading. If the club wasn't looking at winning the flag in 2017, what was the point of Shaun and me hanging around? If it was going to be a re-build, that would take at least three years. We weren't going to be around in 2019 or 2020 and probably not even 2018.

When I got home I rang Clarko. My first words were, 'Mate, have I got any bloody teammates left?'

He laughed, but soon realised I was only semi-joking and gave me his version of events. He said he was concerned with the reliance we had on our senior players. The 2016 best-and-fairest had sounded alarm bells for him. Mitch, at the age of 33, had won it from Lewy, who was 30; then 33-year-old Shaun Burgoyne was third and Birch, who was 29, came fourth. The past eight best-and-fairests had been won by the older generation – Buddy's victory in 2008 was the last time a young player had prevailed.

Clarko felt that the middle group of players had to grow if the team was to prosper. Mitch and Lewy were very big personalities, and the younger players were either too shy or maybe too fearful of repercussions if they spoke up. They needed room to grow, not just as players but as leaders, if the club was to create another successful generation.

The coach's mindset was always that he wanted to be open and honest with his players. He didn't want it to get to Round 19 next year and then have to have a hard conversation with someone like Lewy. Clarko thought he was doing the right thing by talking about options now and giving the players and their families a chance to plan for the future.

As always, he painted a clear picture of the club's direction and our roles as senior players.

I went to the club on Saturday and Roughy was there. We spoke about what had been happening. While there had been reports in the media that Hawthorn were backing away from letting Lewy go, his best mate confirmed otherwise. 'It's very likely,' he said.

By Monday, Jordan Lewis was a Melbourne player.

The next night Roughy, Lewy, Birch, Gunners and I caught up at the old Geebung Polo Club, which had been a popular haunt back in the day, for a few beers. While it felt a bit weird, Lewy was still hanging shit on us as usual and there were already rumours about the draw, with Round 7 slotted in as the Hawks' showdown with Melbourne.

It had been a bizarre couple of weeks, and the next 48 hours followed the same path.

Hawthorn were targeting Gold Coast young gun Jaeger O'Meara, Sydney ball magnet Tom Mitchell and Richmond's tall forward Tyrone Vickery to replace Mitch, Lewy and Brad Hill, who had requested a trade back home to Fremantle to play with his older brother, Stephen. The O'Meara deal was dragging on and seemed in danger of not going through.

I was chatting to Lauren about all the changes and put a hypothetical to her about moving to somewhere like the Gold Coast to play the last couple of years of my career. We agreed a change of scenery wouldn't be a bad thing for the kids in the short-term. The weather would obviously be better, and we were always going to end up living back in Melbourne anyway because of media commitments. The Hawthorn landscape was changing fast and there were names getting thrown up all over the place. Maybe it was in my best interests to step aside and let them rebuild. What if I could help them land O'Meara? After all the dealings in trade week, they had to get him.

I sent my manager, Paul Connors, a message, more joking around than anything. 'Apparently the Gold Coast wants an experienced person going up there? Happy to move.' At the end of it I put a number of laughing emojis.

He quickly replied, 'Are you serious?' This was getting interesting.

I sent back: 'If they need someone to go to Gold Coast to get the O'Meara deal over the line, then I'd consider it.' It could be the perfect challenge in the twilight of my career, particularly if my current club was going in a different direction.

Paul said he wasn't sure that Clarko would survive 'if they shot Bambi', given that the Hawthorn faithful were still trying to come to grips with no Mitchell and Lewis.

'It would be a good challenge to go up there and help develop their young list,' I wrote.

Then Paul said, 'If you're interested, let's chat tomorrow.' Suddenly I was nervous. What was I doing? Things had just become serious very quickly, but I figured it couldn't hurt to hear what they had to say.

Paul rang the next day and told me to meet him at his office. It turned out he'd been in a meeting about the Gold Coast at the AFL with chief executive Gillon McLachlan. The league was looking at how it could help the Suns get their house in order, and my name had been brought up. It had been made clear that the Suns would definitely be interested.

At Paul's office we got the pen and paper out, old-school style, and wrote down pros and cons for my going to Queensland. The main pro was the challenge aspect: go up there for three years and help turn the place around, fix the culture and instil values into the Suns in a similar way to what had happened at Hawthorn.

Then we looked at the cons. 'What about your place in the game when you retire?' Paul asked. 'Can that get any higher if you're up there when you do it? Probably not. Can it drop down if you go up there and things don't work out? It probably can.'

He had a good point.

We went through all the media opportunities that were on the horizon but would be off the table if I went to the Gold Coast. The final con was also a valid one. 'You'd be playing your 300th in Round 16 next year in front of 5000 people on the Gold Coast,' Paul said.

We decided to park it for the moment, but the discussion had certainly been worth having. At that point the chance of me going was maybe 2 per cent unless a ridiculous offer was put on the table.

As the week progressed, the O'Meara deal continued to stall. The Suns were keen on a player as part of the swap, and names thrown up included Jack Gunston, Isaac Smith and Liam Shiels. They'd also flagged interest in Lewy prior to him going to Melbourne.

Paul and I then agreed to end the matter. Staying a one-club player was what I wanted. The only reason I'd even started contemplating other options was because I thought I might be helping the club I loved. That wasn't a reason to leave. The bottom line was that I had brown and gold in my veins.

Ironically, Hawthorn recruitment manager Graham Wright rang and said he wanted me to speak to Jaeger to help ease his mind.

'Mate, stay calm,' I told the young player. 'They're trying to get it done, and if not, then we've got pick ten in the draft and we'll take you at that one.'

Jaeger was concerned about the perception that Hawthorn had cut two legends in Lewy and Mitch to get him in, and that the supporters would hate him as a result. 'That's got nothing to do with you,' I said. 'That is Clarko being honest to his players.

It's him saying, "If you can get a longer contract somewhere else instead of just one here, do you want to consider it?"'

I think Jaeger appreciated the call, and by the end of the week we were all laughing. The deal was done on the final day of the trade period. Jaeger was a Hawk – and, thankfully, so was I.

I had one job, and I stuffed it up.

The previous evening I'd received one of the best phone calls ever, with news that Roughy had got the all-clear. It was the start of December, which meant that it had been nearly seven months since his cancer diagnosis. He was going to tell the boys in a team meeting, and his wife, Sarah, had given me a special job: she wanted me to video the moment as he addressed the group.

I was one of a privileged few who knew what was about to happen, so I positioned myself up the front with my phone at the ready. As Roughy walked in, I pressed record. With a big smile on his face, he stood up the front and delivered the news. The eruption of noise from his teammates was unbelievable – I was actually caught off guard at how loud it was. Then there was mayhem as all the boys tried to get to Rough.

It was a wonderful moment, and . . . I'd missed it.

When I checked to see if everything had worked, I realised I must have bumped the screen and accidentally turned off the recording. All I had was him walking in! I was shattered that I'd let Sarah down. I texted Sarah to reveal the bad news, but in the scheme of bad news they'd received, it didn't come close.

Roughy being cleared to play was great news and I was about to make a decision that was going to affect him in a big way. Given the way the club was going, it was definitely time for me to step back.

I'd spoken to Clarko and chief executive Stuart Fox about it again, and it was decided that we'd proceed as normal and have a players' vote at our pre-season camp in Mooloolaba.

When the votes were counted I was on top from Roughy and then Isaac Smith. Most of the older guys knew about my decision to step down and, after the vote, everyone who polled a leadership vote stayed behind. I addressed the group. 'Boys, I'm not going to be captain any more. It's time for a change,' I said. 'But we have to keep it quiet until the club are ready to make an announcement.'

The club then took their time to evaluate each candidate, going over every detail as they searched for the best person. Others looked at included Liam Shiels and Jack Gunston, and there was also consultation with Roughy and the doctors to make sure his health wouldn't be affected if he took on the job.

When he got the big tick, it was pretty obvious that his incredible couple of months were going to get even better. In January the decision was made: Roughy was captain, with Isaac and Liam his vice-captains.

The second-happiest person about this was me – although Lauren might have challenged for that spot. While captaining the team had been an honour and something I would cherish forever, the workload and time it took up had become a weight on my shoulders. I was going to be a different man, although I agreed to stay in the leadership group to help with the transition. I remembered how tough my first year had been and wanted to be there to help in any way I could.

What I didn't expect was to be in the middle of the new regime's first big decision.

My little brother Dylan had moved in with us midway through 2016 and it was great having him around, particularly to help out with the boys, who adored their uncle. He was now playing district cricket in Melbourne, so we decided to host his 21st birthday party at our house. It was still a couple of weeks until the season started so it was perfect timing.

It was a big event, with lots of family and other relations, a few of my teammates who knew Dylan well, and obviously a bunch of his friends. It was a Sunday-afternoon show and we even hired a couple of security guards to make sure everyone behaved. It went off without a hitch, and all were out the door by around 9 p.m. But there's something about 21st-birthday celebrations and me that don't go well together. This time alcohol wasn't involved, but it still ended up with the same result.

I had to deal with a few private matters the following morning but made the mistake of not communicating to the right people at the club that I'd be missing a training session. As a senior player you do get some flexibility, but given we'd had four days off, this Monday session was compulsory. I knew that, and sent a text message explaining that at best I'd be running late. The mistake I made was that I didn't follow up the text message.

The whole thing was a communication breakdown but I still didn't think it was a major issue when I arrived at the club the next day. I was wrong.

Roughy and his new leadership team had decided they needed to make a statement, and what better way to do that than by punishing the former captain? I had no problem putting my hand up saying I'd done the wrong thing, but I was shocked when they informed me that I'd be missing the opening game of the 2017 season.

Clarko was overseas so he hadn't been involved in the decision, but was quickly on the phone when he got back. 'Sometimes things are more important than football and I would do exactly the same thing again,' I told him. He could see where I was coming from, but the communication breakdown was the issue and I had to cop it. Part of that was getting taken out of the AFL team's final pre-season practice match and instead running around with Box Hill in the VFL.

In the end I understood why the new leadership group had gone with the suspension and, if anything, the saga strengthened my relationship with Roughy as I could see how tough the decision had been for him to make. I spent the opening round in the coach's box watching as an emotional Essendon side, who'd welcomed back a number of players from their 12-month suspension as a result of the drugs scandal, rallied in their return game to beat us by 25 points.

When I came back in, it was quickly obvious that the team had a different feel about it without Mitch and Lewy. And for the next three weeks we definitely had a different look about us – we were getting flogged. A four-goal loss to Adelaide in Round 2 was followed by back-to-back 86-point losses to the Gold Coast and Geelong, which meant after the first month of the 2017 season we were on the bottom of the ladder.

Clarko had been adamant at a number of meetings with the older players and in numerous phone calls to me over the pre-season that we were still chasing the premiership despite the changes. It was now pretty clear that this was unlikely to happen. There was going to be a shift now: it had to be all about pushing up the young players and getting games into them as quickly as possible to kick-start the next era.

A win against West Coast stopped the rot, and over the next month we started to see some good signs, the highlight being a six-point win over Sydney at the SCG in Round 10. Tom Mitchell had slotted in easily and was the definition of a ball magnet, but unfortunately Jaeger had struck problems with his knee and had been sighted only briefly.

Personally, I was surprised at how good I was feeling physically and mentally. There was the odd flicker of thought that I could easily go around in 2018, and that if I pushed that idea I might be able to convince enough people. A couple of clubs had even been in contact, with offers of playing on for another season and then moving into coaching.

But my world at Hawthorn was changing – just little things that were telling me it was time. For example, I was no longer taking the kick-outs or going through the midfield. I'd handed over the responsibility for the defence to Jack Gunston, who'd shifted down from the forward line. I was still assisting the younger guys in the post-game review, watching edits of kick-outs and helping them to understand where they had to stand and how our system worked. But my role had changed and I understood why – it was now all about the development of the younger players.

The backline was certainly getting an overhaul, with the likes of Ryan Burton, Blake Hardwick, Kaiden Brand, Daniel Howe, Conor Glass and James Sicily the future. Watching these guys improve dramatically through the middle of the season had sealed the deal for me. If I played on in 2018, I would potentially be keeping one of them out of a spot, and there was no way I was going to do that.

My back had flared up again midway through the season and I sat out the Round 12 loss to the Gold Coast at the MCG. That turned out to be a stroke of genius as it meant that if I played the next three weeks, then my 300th game would fall in Round 17 against my old nemesis, Geelong. There couldn't be a better stage or a more appropriate game to celebrate the milestone.

And I had another plan.

The thought of doing two press conferences – one for my 300th and then another to announce my retirement a month later – didn't make sense to me. I knew I wasn't playing on and the key people at the club knew, and I didn't want to have to keep lying about my future. The question was already getting asked every time I did an interview.

Clarko didn't like the idea. He thought it could become a circus and the focus for the remaining six weeks of the year would be on me. 'It will be "This is the last time you play here, this is the last time you play against this team",' he said.

I understood what he meant, but I thought the better option was to be open and honest. He spoke to Jason Burt (the club's general manager of football operations) and Andrew Russell, who I'd lobbied, and eventually the club agreed to do both the announcements together.

On the Monday morning leading into the Geelong game, I told the playing group that this was my last hurrah. I was nervous about it because I didn't know if I'd get emotional and, even though I'd spoken in front of these guys a thousand times, I still didn't like public speaking – particularly when I was talking about myself.

'Boys, it's no surprise I'm not going on next year,' I said. 'I just wanted to let you know as I'm doing a press conference at 2 p.m. about pulling the pin and I wanted to give you all a heads-up.'

I lasted just a couple of minutes and managed to keep it together. I'd cut it off because I could feel my emotions building. If I had my time again, I would have spent more time on it.

The floor was then Clarko's. Everyone was keen to hear what he'd say about his former skipper.

Nothing. Meeting over.

He was saving his nice comments for the press conference.

*

Lauren and the three boys were there and it seemed like every camera and journalist in town had crammed into the room. My teammates were also assembled at the back.

Clarko and I took our seats. The flashes of cameras were going off like machine-gun fire. Chase quickly decided it wasn't for him so he decided to keep playing in the gym.

I had some notes – I knew I'd need them. If I didn't have them, I would struggle in this environment.

'Thanks, everyone, for coming. I thought we might as well do this now rather than doing it towards the end of the year,' was my opening line. 'I hate talking in front of media and people anyway, so thought we might as well knock it over in one go.

'After the end of the season I will be hanging up the boots. It's probably a decision we have been pretty clear on for a while in discussions with Clarko and the footy club and, more importantly, the family. I think it is the best thing for the footy club and myself.

'It's weird because mentally I thought that I would have been the first to go, but I'm still loving footy. I'm still really enjoying it, but probably not so much the meetings all the time. Actually playing out there, I still love doing it and my body actually feels good, but what I've realised over the last month is the development of our younger guys. They have really taken steps, and personally if I play on next year I would be taking a spot of a younger guy, and as a senior bloke I would never want to do that.'

I then went through my thank-you list, which included my management team, the medical staff (in particular Mark McGrath), my personal sponsors and my family. 'I better thank my wife, considering I forgot her on our wedding day,' I said. 'To Loz and the boys: football is a rollercoaster, and you have been through some massive highs and some massive lows. Thank you very much for everything.'

I finished with, 'So that's it for me. I don't like talking too much – I probably talked longer than I thought I would. To everyone else I might not have mentioned, thank you.'

I'd managed to get through, but I was suddenly very dry. I gulped down half a glass of water as Clarko started to speak.

'It's been a fascinating journey Hodgey has had at our footy club,' he said. 'He's a once-in-a-generation-type player. I don't think there is a position he didn't play – he even fancied himself as a ruck when the rules allowed it. Without a doubt the most significant thing he has contributed to this footy club and its success is the sacrificial manner in which he has gone about it. He has always put his teammates and his footy club ahead of himself. And that's rare in a game where there is so much adulation placed upon players who have success in this game. They quite often try to portray it as being about the individual when our game is all about the team and your teammates. He has been able to demonstrate that better than any other player I have ever come across, in any form of footy.'

The next ten minutes were spent answering questions from the media. There were a few laughs, particularly when I was asked what might have happened to me if I hadn't played AFL. 'Colac garbo,' was Clarko's suggestion, which got a few too many laughs.

The Chris Judd–Luke Ball super-draft got another run around, and I recalled a conversation I'd had with my uncle. 'My uncle summed it up when Bally and Juddy retired. He said, "Who would have guessed the fat slow one is still going?"'

I signed off by saying, 'Walking in here as a 17-year-old and playing 16 years, you learn a lot. You make a lot of mistakes, but I think the main thing is that you learn from them.'

And then the media circus started. I didn't have a free hour in my diary, with radio and TV interviews all week. It wasn't until

I got home from appearing on the *The Footy Show* on the Thursday night that I was able to draw breath.

The response to my announcement had been overwhelming. I'd tried to stay off social media, but my attention had been drawn to a couple of specific things – in particular a video the club had organised through former tennis champion Pat Cash, who was a mad Hawthorn fan. He'd filmed some of the game's greats at Wimbledon and asked them all whether my goal from the boundary line in the 2015 Grand Final was a fluke or a deliberate shot.

It was bizarre to hear Novak Djokovic, Ivan Lendl, Andy Murray, Lleyton Hewitt, Martina Navratilova and Andre Agassi talking about me. The ending was the best bit, with John McEnroe asking, 'Who the fuck is Hodgey?'

By the time Friday night came around I was exhausted and was in bed by 7.30 p.m. I slept for ten hours.

Playing at the MCG on a Saturday afternoon was what I'd dreamed about as a kid, so it seemed fitting that this was where I celebrated 300 games, particularly as I got to walk onto the ground with my kids.

It was no surprise to anyone that the game was a typical Hawthorn–Geelong nail biter. It was tight all day and the star of the show was Patrick Dangerfield. He appeared to injure his ankle in the first quarter, which should have meant a good result for us but instead of going off the ground he went to full-forward, where he limped around and dominated. At one stage I had to stand him. That didn't go well so I was quick to orchestrate a change. The Cats star kicked five goals and six behinds and was the main reason that, with a minute to go, we were ten points down.

What happened next you couldn't have imagined in your wildest dreams.

My first kick in AFL football had been with my right foot, and the last kick of my 300th game was with my right foot. But instead of going out on the full like my first kick had, the last one somehow sailed through from 40 metres out to give us a chance of stealing the win.

With 20 seconds on the clock, Tom Mitchell got the centre clearance. It was marked by Jack Gunston, who quickly passed it to Isaac Smith. You couldn't make this stuff up. The previous year in the qualifying final, Isaac had missed a goal after the siren that would have given us victory over Geelong. This time, he marked it and played on immediately. I'm not sure if he was worried about the time or he felt better kicking for goal on the run, but unfortunately for him, he again sprayed the shot wide. There was to be no fairytale, and it summed up how my final season was playing out.

The Geelong players and my teammates formed a guard of honour, which was humbling, and then Birch, who hadn't played but had volunteered to carry me off, and Roughy lifted me onto their shoulders as I waved to the fans who had waited behind to pay their respects. It was a nice touch to see the Cats fans there. I'd received a lot of messages saying things like, 'While we don't like Hawthorn, we respect the way you've gone about it.'

There were plenty more messages to follow in the lead-up to Round 23 and the final time I pulled on the boots against the Western Bulldogs. It was a full-on week and an emotional time, particularly when I cleaned out my locker on the Thursday before the game. I tried to keep things as normal as possible but there was no escaping the enormity of the night, which thankfully I got to share with two retiring Bulldogs champions, Bob Murphy and Matthew Boyd.

The game was the easy part and the boys certainly ensured I finished with a smile on my face. What happened after the siren sounded was a magical 30 minutes. The reaction of the crowd was overwhelming, and the reception that Bob, Boydy and I received as we were chaired off by our teammates was simply extraordinary.

There were so many meaningful things said in the lead-up to my final game, but it was something that my teammates told me before my 300th game that resonated with me the most. I'd never been more proud than to hear my teammates say I was selfless – that I'd do anything to look after them and to make them and the club better, including sacrificing my role for them. Those were the words that meant the most, and Roughy repeated a few of them as he presented me with three gifts that the players had chipped in to pay for.

They summed me up perfectly: a bottle of wine, a Flight Centre voucher and . . . a Cabcharge.

ACKNOWLEDGEMENTS

None of this would be possible without the support of my family. I appreciate everything Mum and Dad did, and teaching me right from wrong even though I might have taken a bit longer than others to catch on. My big sister, Bianca, and little brother, Dylan, have been there every step of the way and being able to share everything with them is one of the best things about this crazy journey we've all been on. To my extended family and friends – and there are plenty of them down in Colac – thank you for everything.

A special thanks to the Hawthorn Football Club and everyone associated with it. I feel very fortunate to have been a part of this great club and thank you to a couple of special men in particular, Alastair Clarkson and Andrew Russell, who helped shape my career and life. Thank you to the many others behind the scenes who've played a role – teammates, trainers, physios, doctors, sponsors, supporters – I'd need another book to list you all.

I'd like to thank my management team, Paul Connors and Melissa Oberhofer, who have helped my family and me from day one. To those who contributed to making this book happen, a big thank-you. Ali Watts and Amanda Martin at Penguin Random House and, of course, Scott Gullan, who weaved his magic and made deadline (well, one of them at least).

The biggest thank you of all goes to Lauren and our boys, Cooper, Chase and Leo. My team.

PICTURE CREDITS

Telstra Dome on July 1, 2006 in Melbourne (GSP Images); Lance Franklin of the Swans and Luke Hodge push and shove during the round 19 AFL match between the Hawthorn Hawks and the Sydney Swans at the MCG on July 28, 2017 (Quinn Rooney/ Getty Images).

Page 14: Luke Hodge in action during the Hawthorn Hawks' final training session before the 2008 Grand Final at Waverley Park, Melbourne (Michael Willson).

Page 15: Hawthorn players Brent Guerra, Luke Hodge and Brad Sewell make their way back to the near-empty arena to celebrate their win, long after the 2008 Toyota AFL Grand Final between the Geelong Cats and the Hawthorn Hawks at the MCG (Lachlan Cunningham); Luke Hodge speaks to the crowd after the Hawthorn Hawks win the 2008 Toyota AFL Grand FInal (Sean Garnsworthy).

Pages 16–17: The Hawthorn team celebrates after the 2008 Toyota AFL Grand Final between the Geelong Cats and the Hawthorn Hawks at the MCG (Michael Willson).

Page 18: Luke Hodge displays his Norm Smith and Premiership medallions after the 2008 Toyota AFL Grand Final between the Geelong Cats and the Hawthorn Hawks at the MCG (Michael Willson); Luke Hodge is congratulated by his teammates after the 2008 Toyota AFL Grand Final at the MCG (David Callow).

Page 19: Luke Hodge in action during the AFL Round 15 match between the Geelong Cats and the Hawthorn Hawks at the MCG (Sean Garnsworthy).

Page 20: Luke Hodge runs in pouring rain during a Hawthorn Hawks training session at Pakenham's Toomuc Recreation Reserve, Melbourne (Michael Willson); Luke Hodge is chaired from the field after a win in his 200th game, the AFL Round 20 match between the Hawthorn Hawks and Port Adelaide Power at Aurora Stadium, Launceston (Lachlan Cunningham).

Page 21: Luke Hodge and Brad Sewell look on during the 2012 Toyota Grand Final match between the Hawthorn Hawks and the Sydney Swans at the MCG (Andrew White); Jack Gunston and Luke Hodge celebrate a goal during the 2013 first preliminary final match between the Hawthorn Hawks and the Geelong Cats at the MCG on September 20, 2013 (Lachlan Cunningham).

Page 22: Luke Hodge celebrates winning the 2013 Toyota Grand Final match between the Hawthorn Hawks and the Fremantle Dockers at the MCG on September 28, 2013 (Sean Garnsworthy); Luke Hodge and coach Alastair Clarkson chat during the official 2013 Hawthorn Hawks team photo day at the Ricoh Centre, Melbourne (Justine Walker).

Page 23: The Hawthorn Hawks celebrate winning the 2013 Toyota Grand Final match between the Hawthorn Hawks and the Fremantle Dockers at the MCG, Melbourne on September 28, 2013 (Lachlan Cunningham).

Page 24: Luke Hodge celebrates winning the 2014 Toyota AFL Grand Final match between the Sydney Swans and the Hawthorn Hawks at the MCG on September 27, 2014 (Robert Prezioso).

Page 25: Norm Smith medal winner Luke Hodge holds up his medals after the 2014 Toyota AFL Grand Final match between the Sydney Swans and the Hawthorn Hawks at the MCG on September 27, 2014 (Darrian Traynor); Luke Hodge and Grant Birchall celebrate during the 2014 Toyota AFL Grand Final match at the MCG on September 27, 2014 (Michael Willson).

Pages 26–27: Luke Hodge and Auskick kids celebrate winning the 2014 Toyota AFL Grand Final match between the Sydney Swans and the Hawthorn Hawks at the MCG on September 27, 2014 (Sean Garnsworthy).

Page 28: Luke Hodge leads his team onto the field during the 2015 Toyota AFL Grand Final match between the Hawthorn Hawks and the West Coast Eagles at the MCG on October 3, 2015 (Michael Willson); Luke Hodge celebrates a goal during the 2015 Toyota AFL Grand Final match at the MCG on October 3, 2015 (Justine Walker).

Page 29: Sam Mitchell and Luke Hodge hold the cup with teammates during the 2015 Toyota AFL Grand Final match between the Hawthorn Hawks and the West Coast Eagles at the MCG on October 3, 2015 (Michael Dodge); Luke Hodge holds the notes for his speech during the 2015 Toyota AFL Grand Final match at the MCG on October 3, 2015 (Michael Willson); Luke Hodge celebrates the win with his kids on the fence during the 2015 Toyota AFL Grand Final match at the MCG on October 3, 2015 (Michael Dodge).

Page 30: Luke Hodge comes onto the field with his kids for his 300th game during the 2017 AFL round 17 match between the Geelong Cats and the Hawthorn Hawks at the MCG on July 15, 2017 (Adam Trafford); Luke Hodge's special boots for his 300th game are seen during the 2017 AFL round 17 match at the MCG on July 15, 2017 (Adam Trafford); Luke Hodge is carried off in his 300th game during the round 17 AFL match at the MCG on July 15, 2017 (Quinn Rooney/Getty Images).

Page 31: Luke Hodge poses for a photograph with his family during the Hawthorn Hawks press conference at the Ricoh Centre announcing his retirement on July 10, 2017 in Melbourne (Michael Willson).

Page 32: Luke Hodge and Robert Murphy and Matthew Boyd of the Bulldogs are chaired from the field after their last matches during the 2017 AFL round 23 match between the Hawthorn Hawks and the Western Bulldogs at Etihad Stadium on August 25, 2017 in Melbourne (Michael Willson); Luke Hodge celebrates during the 2017 AFL round 23 match at Etihad Stadium on August 25, 2017 (Michael Willson); Luke Hodge with management team Paul Connors and Melissa Oberhofer in 2017 (Michael Willson).

All photos listed below are courtesy of Newspix.

Page 5: Chris Judd, Luke Hodge and Luke Ball pose during a photo shoot ahead of the AFL draft, in Melbourne (George Salpigtidis).

Page 10: Hawthorn Hawks players Ben Dixon, Richie Vandenberg and Luke Hodge during a recovery session in a cold stream during a team trip to New Zealand (Michael Dodge).

Page 25: Luke Hodge gives his former teammate Lance Franklin a kiss during the Hawthorn Hawks v Sydney Swans AFL Grand Final match at the MCG (Tim Carrafa).

All other photos are from private collections.